Space from Zeno to Einstein

Space from Zeno to Einstein

Classic Readings with a Contemporary Commentary

edited and with a commentary by Nick Huggett

A Bradford Book
The MIT Press
Cambridge, Massachusetts
London, England

This book was set in Times New Roman on the Monotype "Prism Plus" PostScript Imagesetter by Asco Trade Typesetting Ltd., Hong Kong.

Printed and bound in the United States of America.

Library of Congress Cataloging-in-Publication Data

Space from Zeno to Einstein : classic readings with a contemporary
  commentary / edited and with a commentary by Nick Huggett.
     p.   cm.
  A Bradford book.
  Includes bibliographical references and index.
  ISBN 0-262-08271-3 (hc.: alk. paper). — ISBN 0-262-58169-8 (pbk.: alk. paper)
  1. Physics—Philosophy. 2. Physics—History. 3. Space and time.
I. Huggett, Nick.
QC6.S6625   1997
530—dc21   98-36127
                                                   CIP

First then we must understand that place would not have been inquired into, if there had not been motion with respect to place.
—Aristotle, *Physics* IV.4

To Leon and Daniel Weingard, in memory of their father; and to Joanna, my partner in everything

Contents

Preface

This book grew out of readings and lecture notes from a course entitled "Philosophy and Classical Physics," which I taught at the University of Kentucky during the year that I was a visitor there (1994–1995). The idea was to expose the students, most of whom were science and engineering majors, to the history of physics through the original writings of major figures, starting with ancient thinkers. But true to my interests, I also wanted to examine some foundational issues, to convince those taking the course to think about the presuppositions of the science that they used so familiarly. Thus, while we read the historical texts we used them to illustrate basic issues in the philosophy of physics.

In order for our enquiries to be as accurate as possible, I based my classes on a contemporary understanding of the philosophy and physics of space and mechanics: the development of the calculus, analytic geometry, and space-time theory in physics, and in philosophy some of the key work of the past thirty years. The commentaries and their bibliographies bear witness to those who have influenced me the most in this regard, but in particular, this volume follows the lead of John Earman, Michael Friedman, Lawrence Sklar, and Howard Stein in giving a more sympathetic hearing to various "absolutisms" than they received during the heyday of logical empiricism.

After my year at Kentucky, I taught similar courses at Brown and the University of Illinois at Chicago, where the students' backgrounds became more diverse, so that I taught in a way that did not presume extensive familiarity with the sciences. It was my goal that someone coming to the material from either a scientific or a humanistic background would find it both accessible and engaging. Doing so meant explaining key physical ideas in a way that would be helpful to someone for whom they were new, while simultaneously revealing the foundational issues. The commentaries of this book are the results of my efforts to achieve this aim. My hope is that the collection will thus be of use not only to students in philosophy of science courses, but to anyone who wishes to understand more about either the physics, history, or philosophy of space, and their connections, be they scientists, philosophers, historians, or simply readers with an interest in how our physical concepts have evolved.

There is one caveat to my pluralist approach: at certain points in even elementary philosophy of physics, it seems to me that things are just better said formally, if the audience understands the formalism. For this reason I wanted to express some of the ideas of this book mathematically, on the assumption that part of my readership would be able to follow what was going on. To avoid losing other readers without a prior knowledge of the calculus or mechanics, I decided to express my point verbally at such points, and then give a formal restatement in a box separate from the main text. The upshot of this decision is that when you come to a box of math during a discussion, if you can understand it then you should read it, but if you cannot then you can pass over it assured that it is reiterating the last point made.

The book is in the first place an anthology, and so choices had to be made concerning which texts should be included, which excluded, and which passages were most important. My aim has been to provide the key essays by the key thinkers on the topic of space, according to current scholarship in philosophy and physics. I have chosen those articles that are taken as basic in the recent debates over the nature of space, and those which most clearly carry premonitions of contemporary physics. In this way, someone reading the book will come away well prepared to engage in philosophical discussions concerning space, and to go on to learn about and understand relativity theory.

Since my goal is ultimately to explain modern physics and philosophy, the book in some places gives priority to a certain logic rather than to history. For instance, since the idea of space as a geometric object is so important for my discussions, we discuss Euclid in the second chapter, before the historically prior Zeno and Aristotle. In general, while indicating the overall historical narrative of the development of the concept of space—and avoiding being misleading—I stress the logic of the positions over their detailed historical context. For more careful history I have suggested further readings.

The commentaries are in no way intended to be comprehensive discussions of the texts, but rather to focus on key ideas, and to use contemporary understanding to clarify them. My hope is that once they have read the sources and the commentaries once, readers will go back and reread the original texts in light of what they have learned. I believe that they will find a great many points remain to be discussed, and to help them along I have included a few questions for further thought at the end of each section. The suggested readings and the bibliography are clearly not intended to be complete, but simply list the few books that I have either found most helpful or feel would most help a reader who wanted to go further. The suggestions themselves will point towards the more general literature.

This book has benefited from the time and advice of a number of people whom I should mention here. First, I am grateful to Dan Frank and Don Howard at the University of Kentucky (and now Notre Dame in the latter case), for their support then and since, and for their help with the work from the very earliest stages. (I should also mention Roger Jones of the University of Kentucky, who taught me ways to teach this material effectively.) Next, Johnathan Cohen and Maggie Wyckoff of the University of Maine at Farmington and Ciaran Cronin and Mitzi Lee of the University of Illinois at Chicago read drafts of chapters and gave me very useful comments. Jay Hullett was extremely generous with his time and advice. I also received many helpful comments—and much appreciated support—from anonymous referees. My thanks too to my editors at the MIT Press: Betty Stanton for her support, and Judy Feldmann for copyediting above and beyond.

Most of all I would like to thank my wife, Joanna Gardner-Huggett, for her patience and for reading drafts, and also all the students to whom I have taught this material, who have taught me so much about it. Of them I should single out Jason Wellner, who as my research assistant has put a considerable amount of time into the project and given me much to think about. Finally, I would like to thank those who taught me about space-time: Harvey Brown, Rom Harré, David Malament, Tim Maudlin, Christopher Ray, and Robert Weingard.

Of course, I would like to be able to blame the above for all the faults in this book, but unfortunately (for me) it would be more accurate to praise them for its best points. Thank you.

1 Plato

READING

Timaeus

[*50b*] ... Now the same account, in fact, holds also for that nature which receives all
the bodies. We must always refer to it by the same term, for it does not depart from
its own character in any way. Not only does it always receive all things, it has never
in any way whatever taken on any characteristic [*c*] similar to any of the things that
enter it. Its nature is to be available for anything to make its impression upon, and it
is modified, shaped and reshaped by the things that enter it. These are the things that
make it appear different at different times. The things that enter and leave it are
imitations of those things that always are, imprinted after their likeness in a marvellous way that is hard to describe. This is something we shall pursue at another time.
For the moment, we need to keep in mind three types of things: (i) *that which comes
to be*, (ii) *that in which it comes to be*, [*d*] and (iii) *that after which the thing coming to
be is modeled, and which is its source*. It is in fact appropriate to compare (ii) the
receiving thing to a mother, (iii) the source to a father, and (i) the nature between
them to their offspring. We also must understand that if the imprints are to be
varied, with all the varieties there to see, this thing upon which the imprints are to be
formed could not be well prepared for that role if it were not itself devoid of any of
those characters that it is to receive from elsewhere. For if [*e*] it resembled any of the
things that enter it, it could not successfully copy their opposites or things of a
totally different nature whenever it were to receive them. It would be showing its
own face as well. This is why the thing that is to receive in itself all the [elemental]
kinds must be totally devoid of any characteristics. Think of people who make fra-
grant ointments. They expend skill and ingenuity to come up with something just
like this [i.e., a neutral base], to have on hand to start with. The liquids that are to
receive the fragrances they make as odorless as possible. Or think of people who
work at impressing shapes upon soft materials. They emphatically refuse to allow
any such material to already have some definite shape. Instead, they'll even it out
and make it as smooth as it can be. In the [*51*] same way, then, if the thing that is to
receive repeatedly throughout its whole self the likenesses of the intelligible objects,
the things which always are—if it is to do so successfully, then it ought to be devoid
of any inherent characteristics of its own. This, of course, is the reason why we
shouldn't call the mother or receptacle of what has come to be, of what is visible

Excerpts from Plato, "Timaeus," translated by M. L. Gill and P. Ryan, in *Readings in Ancient Greek
Philosophy* (pp. 463–466), edited by S. Marc Cohen, Patricia Curd and C. D. C. Reeve. © 1995 by
Hackett Publishing Co. All rights reserved. Reprinted by permission of Hackett Publishing Company.

or perceivable in every other way, either earth or air, fire or water, or any of their compounds or their constituents. But if we speak of it as an invisible and character-less sort of thing, one that receives all things and shares in a [b] most perplexing way in what is intelligible, a thing extremely difficult to comprehend, we shall not be misled. And insofar as it is possible to arrive at its nature on the basis of what we've said so far, the most correct way to speak of it may well be this: the part of it that gets ignited appears on each occasion as fire, the dampened part as water, and parts as earth or air insofar as it receives the imitations of these....

And the third type is space, [52b] which exists always and cannot be destroyed. It provides a location for all things that come into being. It is itself apprehended by a kind of bastard reasoning that does not involve sense perception, and it is hardly even an object of conviction [pistis]. We look at it as in a dream when we say that everything that exists must of necessity be somewhere, in some place and occupying some space, and that that which doesn't exist somewhere, whether on earth or in heaven, doesn't exist at all....

Now as the wetnurse of becoming turns watery and fiery and receives the character of earth and air, and as it acquires all the properties that [e] come with these charac-ters, it takes on a variety of visible aspects, but because it is filled with powers that are neither similar nor evenly balanced, no part of it is in balance. It sways irregu-larly in every direction as it is shaken by those things, and being set in motion it in turn shakes them. And as they are moved, they drift continually, some in one direc-tion and others in others, separating from one another. They are winnowed out, as it were, like grain that is sifted by winnowing sieves or other such implements. They are carried off and settle down, the dense and heavy ones in [53] one direction, and the rare and light ones to another place.

That is how at that time the four kinds were being shaken by the receiver, which was itself agitating like a shaking machine, separating the kinds most unlike each other furthest apart and pushing those most like each other closest together into the same region. This, of course, explains how these different kinds came to occupy dif-ferent regions of space, even before their constitution rendered the universe orderly at its coming into being....

COMMENTARY AND INTRODUCTION

1.1   Plato and an Overview of the Book

People who know nothing else about philosophy often know that Plato, who lived from 427 to 347 BC, is the source of many of the themes that constitute the subject. He drew on works of both earlier and contemporary philosophers—Socrates in particular—but, like Euclid and Newton, he brought their ideas together in a single coherent body of work. Plato is often popular with newcomers to philosophy because he expressed his thought in the form of dialogues, in which some point is argued back and forth so that the reader can see all sides of a topic. Our reading comes from the dialogue known as the *Timaeus*, in which Timaeus outlines to Socrates and Critias his "cosmogony": his theory of the creation of all aspects of the world, from basic physical elements to the physiology of humans. (The *Timaeus* is, as a matter of interest, the first recorded occurrence of the myth of Atlantis, told by Critias to illustrate his idea of a perfect society.)

The selection reprinted here is typical of the style of the work: Timaeus dominates the discussion, much of which is mystical if not contradictory. As we shall soon see, developing a clear understanding of space is a demanding task, which has tried the greatest philosophical and scientific minds over the last 2,500 years (and even prior to that). Even today, when we understand a great deal about space, many of the same problems that were raised by Plato are constantly reappearing in new guises in contemporary physics. The idea of this book is that we can best understand the modern conception of space by understanding the (inspired) fumblings and debates of the thinkers who led us to that conception. So while Plato does not offer final solutions, we will read him as an introduction to the various problems that arise when we try to understand the nature of space.

The first thing that we need to understand about the *Timaeus* is Plato's threefold distinction between "(i) *that which comes to be*, (ii) *that in which it comes to be*, and (iii) *that after which the thing coming to be is modeled, and which is its source.*" (50c–d*). At the root of Plato's philosophy is the idea that (i), the created world which we inhabit, is a copy of (iii), an ideal world of "forms." In the present context, the world of forms is a world of perfect geometric shapes: ideal pyramids and cubes, for example. The elements of the physical world are created ("come to be") in the image of

---

*All references are to the *Timaeus*, and are according to the numbers in the text. These derive from the page numbers of a standard edition of Plato by Stephanus, in 1578.

such forms, for instance, earth in the shape of the ideal cube, and fire in the shape of the ideal pyramid. It follows on this account that true knowledge requires learning about the forms, not physical bodies; but how is such knowledge to be obtained? Experience can only teach us about the physical world, so that won't help. To learn about the ideal world of forms, Plato believes, we must rely on pure reason. Plato's famous allegory of the cave (in the *Republic*, bk. VII) illustrates this view: prisoners in a dark cave can only watch shadows on the wall and try to imagine which actual objects produce them. Analagously, we are prisoners in the physical world, and we must attempt to discover the forms of which physical objects are only shadows.

Into the dichotomy of the world of physics and the world of forms Plato introduces a third entity, numbered (ii) above: space "provides a location for all things that come into being" (52b), or is "that nature which receives all the bodies" (50b). When the copies of forms were created, they were created in space. Now, we use the word "space" in a variety of ways: "personal space," "outer space," "living space," "empty space," and mathematical "vector spaces." But Plato has none of these uses in mind, and neither do we in this book. Instead, space is, to a first approximation, that in which all physical things are found. We think that everything, large or small, has a location or place, and space, in our sense, is the collection of all such places. For example: atoms have places, so they occupy parts of space; tables and chairs have locations, so they occupy parts of space; similarly for the planet Earth, and the whole solar system; even our galaxy and local cluster of galaxies have locations, and so occupy parts of space. The intuition driving this picture is that everything physical that exists, exists somewhere; space is the collection of all the "somewheres." It is a "container" of all physical things; "everything that exists must of necessity be somewhere, in some place and occupying some space" (52b). We are particularly concerned with this conception because it is presupposed by physical science: for instance, mechanics—the science of motion—assumes that things change their places in space.

Such an entity immediately raises a host of complications for us and for Plato; these are the puzzles that will occupy us throughout the book. First of all, space so conceived is a very strange kind of thing. It seems to be part of the physical world, since it is not mental or spiritual, and since it is presupposed by physics. However, all objects treated by physics are, it seems, material: atoms, baseballs, planets, and galaxies, for instance. But if space is something separate, "in which" such objects exist, then it appears that space itself cannot be a material object; if it were, then it could not be the container of all matter, for what would contain it? The first problem is thus that space seems to be a physical object, but unlike all other physical objects, it seems not to be material. (We have a similar difficulty with the mind: it has physical aspects, such as the ability to affect your body, yet it doesn't seem to be material.) To put the problem more generally: what kind of thing is space if it is both physical and immaterial?

When we inquire into the nature of something at such a basic level, we are pursuing the branch of philosophy known as "metaphysics" (meaning "beyond physics"—metaphysics "goes beyond" ordinary physics, to the most basic nature of reality). Such a question requires considering the very foundations of physics and, as we shall see, cannot be answered without some understanding of the relevant science (though in a nontechnical way). One of the general lessons of this book is that physics and metaphysics are intertwined: metaphysics responds to physics, but physics can often only progress when the metaphysical foundations of a theory are investigated. It is for this reason that most of the authors in this anthology are both philosophers and physicists: there is ultimately no clear distinction between the two.

So how does Plato answer the metaphysical problem concerning space of how it can be physical but not material? Given such a puzzling situation, it may be no surprise that Plato—and many others following him (Aristotle, Descartes, Leibniz, Berkeley, and Mach, in this collection)—denies that space is something separate from matter at all. According to this view, we get into metaphysical trouble concerning space precisely because we try to imagine the physical world as comprised of an immaterial container plus matter located within it. The alternative, which comes in many guises, is to claim that there is only matter, and then to explain how the features that we think belong to space belong to matter instead. For instance, we have accepted that all things are "in space." How could this feature belong to matter?

Plato explains that space is the matter of which material objects—copies of forms—are composed: "Its nature is to be available for [any element] to make its impression upon, and it is modified, shaped, and reshaped by the things that enter it" (50c). The idea is that space is like a block of clay into which the shapes of the elements are "impressed": just as we might press a circle into clay, space might be pressed into a cube, creating a piece of earth. That is, we should not think of pieces of matter existing in a separate space, but rather of material objects as being regions of "space/matter" of a particular shape. In this case, when we talk of an object being "in space," what we mean is that shapes of the elements that make up the object are impressed on space/matter.

But the analogy with clay breaks down: once a circle is impressed on a block of clay, the clay is circle-shaped, but space "has never in any way whatever taken on any characteristic similar to any of the things that enter it" (50b). Instead, space is "pure matter," somehow capable of carrying copies of forms but without taking a particular form itself. If this were not the case, and space took on the characteristics of earth, say, then it would not be able to contain pure water, but rather a water-earth hybrid. Plato thinks that space is like a piece of clay on which shapes can be stamped, but which also always remains smooth: it should be thought of "as an invisible and characterless sort of thing, one that receives all things and shares in a most perplexing way in what is intelligible, a thing extremely difficult to comprehend...." (51a–b). As we read through the essays in this book, we will see attempts to make the nature of space more comprehensible.

Other questions now suggest themselves: space is indeed "perplexing," so how can we hope to find out about it? If we develop a theory concerning space, how could we hope to decide whether it is true? Space is invisible (though it seems to be all around—and throughout—us), so how can we tell what it is like? We can measure how material objects behave under various circumstances, but how can we do anything comparable with space?

Questions like these concerning the justification of beliefs are part of "epistemology": the philosophy of knowledge and belief. Because it is so hard to come to know anything substantial about space, theories of space highlight dramatically many of the central problems of explaining the nature of knowledge. In the readings, we will see a variety of accounts of how knowledge is possible and hence how knowledge of space is possible. Some, for instance, Descartes and Kant, believe that our knowledge of space is grounded on reason and not on experience, whereas others, such as Aristotle, Newton, Berkeley, Mach, and Poincaré, believe that we can learn about space from experience, though they are deeply divided about what it is that experience teaches. Plato seems stuck between the two camps: space is not part of the world of forms, to be understood by pure reason; but neither is space a physical object—a "shadow on the wall"—to be experienced. Instead, space is "apprehended by a kind of bastard reasoning that does not involve sense perception,... as in a dream" (52b). The essays in this volume attempt to awaken us and to apply to space the methods of science and reason that teach us about the rest of the world.

The third kind of question we will deal with is physical: what role does space play in science, and in particular what interaction (if any) is there between space and material bodies? In a sense, the readings constitute the history of this question; as different answers have been developed, they have pointed towards new philosophical understandings of space. Most of the writers in the collection are responding directly to advances in our understanding of the role of space in physics.

For instance, according to Plato, as space has the elements impressed upon it, it is disturbed and in turn agitates the elements: "It sways irregularly in every direction as it is shaken by those things, and being set in motion it in turn shakes them" (52d–e). In this way, space shook the elements so that they were sorted from one another: so that all the earth moved to one place, forming our planet, for instance. There is, then, a symmetry to Plato's account, for matter acts on space and space reacts on matter.

In the rest of the book, we will read from some of the greatest physicists as they try to understand the role of space within mechanics: the role that space plays in determining the motions of objects. Aristotle, for example, believed that space has a privileged center, which determines the motions of objects: intrinsically heavy things fall toward it, light things rise away from it, and the matter of the stars rotates around it. Newton (following Galileo and Descartes) realized that a true theory of motion needs a law of inertia: objects will maintain their motions unless acted on by a force. He believed that space is required to understand this law: that space induces matter to move in straight paths at constant speeds unless constrained to do otherwise. However, in his theory, space is absolutely unchanging, so although space acts on matter there is no back-reaction from matter.

In the last chapter of this book we will read an article by Einstein that brings us essentially up-to-date on the role of space in science. In his theory of general relativity, space plays an inertia-determining role, acting on matter, but space is itself curved by material objects, so matter has an effect on space. The action-reaction symmetry of Plato's theory is restored.

A study of the theory of relativity falls outside of the scope of this book, which (with the exception of Einstein) covers figures from antiquity to the nineteenth century. But one of the goals of this book is to introduce in an informal way some of the key concepts of the theory, and to explain how their origins can be seen in historical works. Thus we will study Euclid for the idea that geometry is a science of space; we will discuss Zeno's paradoxes for the influence they had on our understanding of the nature of infinity; we will read Newton to understand the nature of inertia; Leibniz, Berkeley, Mach, and Poincaré will be seen to emphasize that it is the behavior of material bodies that shows the properties of space; and when we consider Kant, we will see what it might mean for space to be curved.

As you can see from this introduction, and as we will discover further, there are many threads to the story which has just begun, so it will be useful to have a fixed center around which to organize the ideas. For us that center will be the three problems that Plato raised: the metaphysical question, what kind of thing is space; the epistemological question, how can we come to know anything about space; and the physical question, in what way do space and matter interact?

Before we consider these questions further, we will need to establish some common ground by explaining some basic philosophical ideas.

1.2   Logic

As we discuss the texts in this book, it will be helpful to use basic logical concepts without having to explain them throughout. These concepts will be familiar to some readers, but everyone should make sure that they are comfortable with the material in the next two sections.

Reflect on the scope and power of human communication and you may well marvel at how effectively we can exchange ideas. It is important in this exchange that we are *consistent* in what we say. That is, if we say one thing—for instance, "Snow is white"—we mustn't immediately contradict ourselves—by adding, "Snow is not white." If someone made both claims then he really would not have told us anything at all, since they cancel each other out. Information is given and then immediately taken away, leaving nothing communicated. Or imagine trying to learn the language of a people who were constantly contradicting themselves. For example, suppose you wanted to find out whether "urgle" was their name for a xylophone. You might point to a xylophone and say "urgle?" The contradictors would completely confuse you by agreeing, but then immediately disagreeing. In these conditions, how could you ever discover their word for xylophones?

Avoiding inconsistency is thus of the greatest importance, and one way to understand logic is as a formal study of inconsistency and how it can be avoided. The first step is to say in general what it is to be inconsistent. The reason the speakers in our examples fail to be informative is that they describe situations that cannot possibly be the case. It cannot be that snow is both white and not white (simultaneously) and it cannot be the case that a xylophone is both an "urgle" and not an "urgle." And the problem is not just that physical or human limitations prevent these things from being true, but rather that the very words used show that the situations are impossible. Even if we had no idea what snow was, we would know that the situation described could not occur. Thus we shall say that a collection of sentences is *inconsistent* if, simply because of the words used, there is no way in which they could all be true at once. Notice that collections of false sentences can be consistent: for example, "the moon is made of cheese" and "the cow jumped over the moon" could both be true, if only things were different.

Sometimes inconsistency occurs because a person says one thing—such as "I am the president of the United States"—and then denies it—"I am not the president of the United States"—but other inconsistencies occur because of what follows from what a person says. For instance, imagine someone telling you, "I'm British, and no British citizens are president." It follows that they are not the president, and so they would be inconsistent if they went on to say "and I am the president." That is, there is an argument from what they first tell you to their nonpresidency, which can be displayed as follows:

1. *X* is British.
2. No British citizens are president.
∴ C. *X* is not president.

Lines 1–2 are the *premises* of the argument, and they are what is assumed in it. The final line, C, is the *conclusion* that the premises seek to establish. This particular argument is an example of a *valid* argument. In logic, to say some argument is valid means specifically that if its premises are true, so must be its conclusion, simply because of the words used. It follows then that if an argument is valid, anyone who accepts its premises must accept its conclusion, or else be inconsistent; simply because of the meanings of the words used, there is no way for the premises and the denial of the conclusion all to be true. Thus no one can consistently assert premises 1 and 2, and yet claim that *X* was president. If we can get someone to agree to the premises of a valid argument, then they must agree with the conclusion, or be inconsistent.

Consider some examples:

1. All triangles have internal angles summing to 180°.
2. Figure 3 is a triangle.
∴ C. Figure 3 has internal angles summing to 180°.

Valid: The "all" in premise 1 means that figure 3 must have angles summing to 180°.

1. Some people become nuns.
2. I'm a person.
∴ C. I'll become a nun.

Invalid: I certainly believe 1 and 2, but I am in no way inconsistent by also believing that I will never be a nun! The "some" in premise 1 means that we cannot assume that *any* person will become a nun. (Note that this argument remains invalid regardless of who the person is in premise 2.)

1. 99.99% of flights end safely.
2. I'm flying to Newark.
∴ C. My flight to Newark will end safely.

Invalid: Of course, the conclusion is overwhelmingly probable, but unfortunately it is not absolutely certain, and so it would not be inconsistent to believe the premises and still think that the plane will crash.

1. All humans are immortal.
2. Socrates is human.
∴ C. Socrates is immortal.

Valid: In this example, a valid argument leads to a false conclusion—but one that would have to be true if the premises were themselves true. This example thus shows that we can consistently deny the conclusion of a valid argument, by denying at least one premise: in this example, premise 1.

An analogy between valid arguments and mathematical reasoning may be helpful (in fact, mathematical reasoning is logical reasoning, so there is more than an analogy). If you are given a math problem and you work it through correctly, then you cannot get a wrong answer. If, for example, you follow the correct method for finding 987×234 then you will get the right answer (230,958). The same applies to valid arguments: the premises are like a problem posed, reasoning through the argument is like performing mathematical steps, and if the argument is valid then the conclusion must be the "right answer"—that is, the answer that most be true if the premises are.

Thinking in terms of this analogy, what should we say if we get the "wrong answer"? In mathematics, if your answer disagrees with that of the answer book, then something has to give. Either you were asked the wrong problem, or you followed the steps incorrectly, or the book has the wrong answer. Analogously we might start with some premises that we believe to be true and deduce (using valid reasoning) something that we believe to be false. For instance, suppose we could infer from the premise "100m is infinitely divisible" that "it takes an infinite time to traverse 100m"? If our argument were valid, then it would be inconsistent to believe the premise but deny the conclusion. In parallel to the mathematical example, we have three choices; either the premise is untrue (so for all we know the conclusion that follows is false too), or our reasoning was flawed and the conclusion doesn't follow, or we must indeed accept the conclusion.

This observation gives us another way to argue for a given conclusion. Suppose that someone holds a belief with which you disagree—perhaps that we have free will. And further suppose that you can show that this belief entails (i.e., has as a valid consequence) a conclusion that is absolutely unacceptable—perhaps that our actions are random. If the argument is valid and the conclusion false, it must be that some premise is false, and so in this case we must deny that we have free will. To do otherwise would be inconsistent (since we would deny the premises' logical consequences), and that must be avoided at all costs. This mode of argument is known as *indirect proof* or *reductio ad absurdum*. It has the sometimes confusing feature that it requires first assuming, "for argument's sake," the claim that is to be rejected. But the assumption is only in order to show that the claim has unacceptable consequences. This mode of reasoning plays a prominent role in the essays we will read; you can find it summarized in a glossary of logical concepts at the end of this chapter.

1.3 Scientific Theories

Why are we interested in validity? Not only does it help us analyze the arguments in the readings, but it also enables us to take a logical view of scientific theories.

Our understanding will be that a theory is a set of basic principles (such as laws and definitions) from which further truths can be derived as valid consequences, typically by employing mathematical reasoning. For instance, we can derive from the laws and definitions of classical Newtonian mechanics that momentum is always conserved in a collision. Or we could add to the laws some specific information about the mass, position, velocity of, and forces on some object and derive its trajectory. Assuming that our derivations are logically valid, if the laws are true then so are all their consequences. Hence the concept of validity allows us to go from a small set of laws to a whole world of consequences.

Now what makes a theory "good"? We need to distinguish two answers. On the one hand there is a factual answer; we want our theories to describe the world accurately, so a theory is good if what it says "matches the facts." Newtonian mechanics is true if momentum really is conserved, and objects actually do move as the theory says they do, and so on. So the major question is "how can we tell whether some proposed theory does describe the world accurately?" The modern scientific "empirical" method is to perform experimental tests of the logical consequences— the predictions—of the laws. If the phenomena we observe in our experiments agree with the predictions of the laws then we obtain empirical justification for the theory. Note that such an inference is not a logically valid one, for it is quite possible for some predictions of a theory to be correct while the theory itself is false; perhaps we just haven't yet investigated a false consequence. Adopting a particular philosophical position, we will say that the inference from experiment to the truth of a theory is "abductive." That is, if the consequences of a theory are correct then we accept the theory because it explains the phenomena predicted.

Among the issues ahead of us is to see how much can be learned of space using an experimental method, and whether other methods might give more information. The use of abductive inference is far from being universally accepted by the authors of the texts in this book, or by contemporary philosophers of science. Since these questions concern the justification of our beliefs—in this case our beliefs about science—they fall within the field of epistemology, described in the first section.

The second sense in which a theory may be "good" is purely logical. Consider our discussion of validity. Validity does not depend on the actual truth or falsity of premises, just on what would follow if the premises were true. We imagine an abstract situation (or possible way the world might have been) in which the premises are true (whether or not they in fact are) and determine whether the conclusion must also be true in that situation. We can extend this idea to theories: we imagine an abstract situation or world in which the basic principles (for instance, the laws) are true. If the laws are true in the abstract world, so are all their logical consequences. In this way, then, we can specify an entire abstract world by specifying a few basic laws; everything that can be validly inferred from the laws must also be true, which "fills out" that entire world.

Is there a possible abstract world for every possible set of laws? No, for a set of laws might be inconsistent, so that there was no possible situation in which all were true at once. To say that a set of claims is inconsistent is just to say there is no possible world, real or abstract, in which they are all true. Hence one way to refute a theory is to show that it is inconsistent, for if it is true of no possible world then it is certainly untrue of the actual world. To show that a theory is inconsistent it is sufficient to show that it has inconsistent logical consequences. This is just an indirect refutation of the laws, showing that if they were true an unacceptable, inconsistent consequence would be true. In the next two chapters we will first propose that Euclidean geometry can be understood as a theory of space, and then consider how Zeno attempted to prove that it was inconsistent.

Consider now a consistent set of laws, with a possible abstract world in which they hold true. Plato took the existence of such worlds seriously, and (though he called them "worlds of forms") we might call them "Plato's paradises," a term which indicates their ideality. We need neither accept nor deny their literal reality here, but we do need to acknowledge their distinctness from our world. In modern logic one refers to such abstract situations (possible worlds) as "models": like scale models, they can be used as replicas of the real world. For instance, we can work out the consequences of Newtonian mechanics for quite imaginary objects.

The part of science concerned with mapping out abstract models using logical and mathematical reasoning we call "pure." However, there is more to science than pure science, for we are interested not just in consistent theories, but in theories that match the facts of our world. Thus, pure science becomes "applied" (to the world) when we hypothesize that our theory describes not only an abstract realm but also the actual world. We start doing applied science when, for instance, we hypothesize (as Laplace did) that the universe is a Newtonian world.

So we have the following picture of scientific theories: A theory is stated by a set of basic principles that define an abstract Platonic paradise of pure science. A critic of the theory may question the consistency of the laws by attempting to show that they entail a contradiction, or she may question that the laws in fact hold in the actual world. The proponents of the theory will hypothesize that the theory is a true description of the actual world. They are then faced with the challenge of justifying this claim; most likely they will perform experiments to check its predictions. If the predicted phenomena occur, they will infer, not deductively but abductively, that the laws are justified because they explain the results.

The job of the next chapter will be to construct the theory of space that is, either implicitly or explicitly, the topic of discussion in all the readings of this book.

Glossary of Logical Terms

Inconsistency: A set of claims is inconsistent (or contradictory) if, because of the words alone, it is impossible for them all to be true at once.
Validity: An argument is valid if, if the premises were true, they would guarantee the truth of the conclusion. Equivalently, an argument is valid if it is inconsistent to accept the premises but deny the conclusion. We also say that the premises entail the conclusion, or that the conclusion can be deduced from the premises.
Indirect proof (or *reductio*): To refute some claim, first assume that it is true, then deduce some unacceptable conclusion—something either known to be false, or self-contradictory, or inconsistent with the claim. Since the conclusion must be rejected, so must the premise.

Problems

1. Which of the following are valid? Explain what makes the others invalid.

(a)   1. All electrons have spin 1/2.
      2. The particle in the detector is an electron.
      ∴ C. The particle in the detector has spin 1/2.

(b) 1. If the moon is made of cheese then the sky is green.
     2. The moon is made of cheese.
     ∴ C. The sky is green.

(c) 1. If the moon is made of cheese then the sky is green.
     2. The sky is green.
     ∴ C. The moon is made of cheese.

(d) 1. Virtually every μ-particle decays within 10ms.
     2. A μ-particle has just been produced.
     ∴ C. The μ-particle will decay within 10ms.

2. One might argue that if God were an all good all powerful being, then there would be no evil. In logical terms, why might this be an indirect proof that God does not exist? (How might it be overcome?)

3. Give an example of an abductive justification of a scientific theory. What are the laws? What consequence is tested? Explain why the inference from experimental outcome to theory is not (logically) valid. Is the inference reasonable? Why or why not?

Further Readings and Bibliography

Giere, R. N. 1997. *Understanding Scientific Reasoning*, fourth edition. Fort Worth, TX: Harcourt Brace College Publishers. √*

Salmon, W. C. 1984. *Logic*, third edition. Englewood Cliffs, NJ: Prentice-Hall. √*

Vlastos, G. 1975. *Plato's Universe*. Seattle, WA: University of Washington Press.

*Throughout this book, the symbol "√" next to a reference indicates its particular suitability for readers encountering this material for the first time.

2 Euclid

READING

The Elements

Book I

Definitions

1. A *point* is that which has no part.

2. A *line* is breadthless length.

3. The extremities of a line are points.

4. A *straight line* is a line which lies evenly with the points on itself.

5. A *surface* is that which has length and breadth only.

6. The extremities of a surface are lines.

7. A *plane surface* is a surface which lies evenly with the straight lines on itself.

8. A *plane angle* is the inclination to one another of two lines in a plane which meet one another and do not lie in a straight line.

9. And when the lines containing the angle are straight, the angle is called *rectilineal*.

10. When a straight line set up on a straight line makes the adjacent angles equal to one another, each of the equal angles is *right*, and the straight line standing on the other is called a *perpendicular* to that on which it stands.

11. An *obtuse angle* is an angle greater than a right angle.

12. An *acute angle* is an angle less than a right angle.

13. A *boundary* is that which is an extremity of anything.

14. A *figure* is that which is contained by any boundary or boundaries.

15. A *circle* is a plane figure contained by one line such that all the straight lines falling upon it from one point among those lying within the figure are equal to one another;

16. And the point is called the *centre* of the circle.

17. A *diameter* of the circle is any straight line drawn through the centre and terminated in both directions by the circumference of the circle, and such a straight line also bisects the circle.

Excerpts from Euclid, *The Thirteen Books of Euclid's Elements* (vol. 1, pp. 153–317), translated and edited by T. L. Heath. Reprinted by permission of Cambridge University Press.

18. A *semicircle* is the figure contained by the diameter and the circumference cut off by it. And the centre of the semicircle is the same as that of the circle.

19. *Rectilineal figures* are those which are contained by straight lines, *trilateral* figures being those contained by three, *quadrilateral* those contained by four, and *multilateral* those contained by more than four straight lines.

20. Of trilateral figures, an *equilateral triangle* is that which has its three sides equal, an *isosceles triangle* that which has two of its sides alone equal, and a *scalene triangle* that which has its three sides unequal.

21. Further, of trilateral figures, a *right-angled triangle* is that which has a right angle, an *obtuse-angled triangle* that which has an obtuse angle, and an *acute-angled triangle* that which has its three angles acute.

22. Of quadrilateral figures, a *square* is that which is both equilateral and right-angled; an *oblong* that which is right-angled but not equilateral; a *rhombus* that which is equilateral but not right-angled; and a *rhomboid* that which has its opposite sides and angles equal to one another but is neither equilateral nor right-angled. And let quadrilaterals other than these be called *trapezia*.

23. *Parallel* straight lines are straight lines which, being in the same plane and being produced indefinitely in both directions, do not meet one another in either direction.

Postulates

Let the following be postulated:

1. To draw a straight line from any point to any point.
2. To produce a finite straight line continuously in a straight line.
3. To describe a circle with any centre and distance.
4. That all right angles are equal to one another.
5. That, if a straight line falling on two straight lines make the interior angles on the same side less than two right angles, the two straight lines, if produced indefinitely, meet on that side on which are the angles less than the two right angles.

Common Notions

1. Things which are equal to the same thing are also equal to one another.
2. If equals be added to equals, the wholes are equal.
3. If equals be subtracted from equals, the remainders are equal.
4. Things which coincide with one another are equal to one another.
5. The whole is greater than the part.

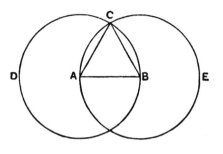

Figure 2.1

Propositions

PROPOSITION 1 *On a given finite straight line to construct an equilateral triangle.* [Fig. 2.1]

Let *AB* be the given finite straight line.*

Thus it is required to construct an equilateral triangle on the straight line *AB*.

With centre *A* and distance *AB* let the circle *BCD* be described [Post. 3]; again, with centre *B* and distance *BA* let the circle *ACE* be described [Post. 3]; and from the point *C*, in which the circles cut one another, to the points *A*, *B* let the straight lines *CA*, *CB* be joined [Post. 1].

Now, since the point *A* is the centre of the circle *CDB*, *AC* is equal to *AB* [Def. 15].

Again, since the point *B* is the centre of the circle *CAE*, *BC* is equal to *BA* [Def. 15].

But *CA* was also proved equal to *AB*; therefore each of the straight lines *CA*, *CB* is equal to *AB*.

And things which are equal to the same thing are also equal to one another [*C.N.* 1]; therefore *CA* is also equal to *CB*.

Therefore the three straight lines *CA*, *AB*, *BC* are equal to one another.

Therefore the triangle *ABC* is equilateral; and it has been constructed on the given finite straight line *AB*. (Being) what it was required to do. . . .

PROPOSITION 29 *A straight line falling on parallel straight lines makes the alternate angles equal to one another, the exterior angle equal to the interior and opposite angle, and the interior angles on the same side equal to two right angles.* [Fig. 2.2]

---

*Note that in this book, unlike many texts, "*AB*," not "$\overline{AB}$," refers to the line segment defined by points *A* and *B*.

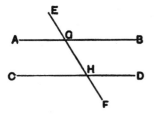

Figure 2.2

For let the straight line *EF* fall on the parallel straight lines *AB*, *CD*; I say that it makes the alternate angles *AGH*, *GHD* equal, the exterior angle *EGB* equal to the interior and opposite angle *GHD*, and the interior angles on the same side, namely *BGH*, *GHD*, equal to two right angles.

For, if the angle *AGH* is unequal to the angle *GHD*, one of them is greater.

Let the angle *AGH* be greater.

Let the angle *BGH* be added to each; therefore the angles *AGH*, *BGH* are greater than the angles *BGH*, *GHD*.

But the angles *AGH*, *BGH* are equal to two right angles [1. 13]; therefore the angles *BGH*, *GHD* are less than two right angles.

But straight lines produced indefinitely from angles less than two right angles meet [Post. 5]; therefore *AB*, *CD*, if produced indefinitely, will meet; but they do not meet, because they are by hypothesis parallel.

Therefore the angle *AGH* is not unequal to the angle *GHD*, and is therefore equal to it.

Again, the angle *AGH* is equal to the angle *EGB* [1. 15]; therefore the angle *EGB* is also equal to the angle *GHD* [*C.N.* 1].

Let the angle *BGH* be added to each; therefore the angles *EGB*, *BGH* are equal to the angles *BGH*, *GHD* [*C.N.* 2].

But the angles *EGB*, *BGH* are equal to two right angles [1. 13]; therefore the angles *BGH*, *GHD* are also equal to two right angles.

Therefore etc.   Q.E.D.

PROPOSITION 30   *Straight lines parallel to the same straight line are also parallel to one another.* [Fig. 2.3]

Let each of the straight lines *AB*, *CD* be parallel to *EF*; I say that *AB* is also parallel to *CD*.

For let the straight line *GK* fall upon them.

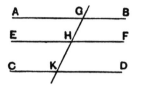

Figure 2.3

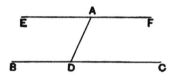

Figure 2.4

Then, since the straight line *GK* has fallen on the parallel straight lines *AB, EF,* the angle *AGK* is equal to the angle *GHF* [1. 29].

Again, since the straight line *GK* has fallen on the parallel straight lines *EF, CD,* the angle *GHF* is equal to the angle *GKD* [1. 29].

But the angle *AGK* was also proved equal to the angle *GHF*; therefore the angle *AGK* is also equal to the angle, *GKD* [*C.N.* 1]; and they are alternate.

Therefore *AB* is parallel to *CD*.   Q.E.D.

PROPOSITION 31   *Through a given point to draw a straight line parallel to a given straight line.* [Fig. 2.4]

Let *A* be the given point, and *BC* the given straight line; thus it is required to draw through the point *A* a straight line parallel to the straight line *BC*.

Let a point *D* be taken at random on *BC*, and let *AD* be joined; on the straight line *DA*, and at the point *A* on it, let the angle *DAE* be constructed equal to the angle *ADC* [1. 23]; and let the straight line *AF* be produced in a straight line with *EA*.

Then, since the straight line *AD* falling on the two straight lines *BC, EF* has made the alternate angles *EAD, ADC* equal to one another, therefore *EAF* is parallel to *BC* [1. 27].

Therefore through the given point *A* the straight line *EAF* has been drawn parallel to the given straight line *BC*.   Q.E.F.

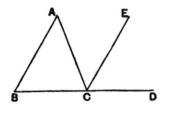

Figure 2.5

PROPOSITION 32   *In any triangle, if one of the sides be produced, the exterior angle is equal to the two interior and opposite angles, and the three interior angles of the triangle are equal to two right angles.* [Fig. 2.5]

Let *ABC* be a triangle, and let one side of it *BC* be produced to *D*.

I say that the exterior angle *ACD* is equal to the two interior and opposite angles *CAB*, *ABC*, and the three interior angles of the triangle *ABC*, *BCA*, *CAB* are equal to two right angles.

For let *CE* be drawn through the point *C* parallel to the straight line *AB* [1. 31].

Then, since *AB* is parallel to *CE*, and *AC* has fallen upon them, the alternate angles *BAC*, *ACE* are equal to one another [1. 29].

Again, since *AB* is parallel to *CE*, and the straight line *BD* has fallen upon them, the exterior angle *ECD* is equal to the interior and opposite angle *ABC* [1. 29].

But the angle *ACE* was also proved equal to the angle *BAC*; therefore the whole angle *ACD* is equal to the two interior and opposite angles *BAC*, *ABC*.

Let the angle *ACB* be added to each; therefore the angles *ACD*, *ACB* are equal to the three angles *ABC*, *BCA*, *CAB*.

But the angles *ACD*, *ACB* are equal to two right angles [1. 13]; therefore the angles *ABC*, *BCA*, *CAB* are also equal to two right angles.

Therefore etc.   Q.E.D.

COMMENTARY

2.1 Introduction

It is probably impossible to overestimate the influence of Euclid's system of geometry since around 300 BC, when it was presented in his book *The Elements*. Aside from its practical applications in surveying and architecture, Euclidean geometry has influenced aesthetic values, stood as a model of the nature of reasoning, and provided a paradigm of knowledge. In this chapter, however, we are interested in the system because it can be taken as a theory of space; indeed, both Newtonian mechanics and special relativity assume space to be Euclidean. This approach is historically misleading for it is not how Euclid intended his theory to be understood; but we are adopting it because it will help us understand later work in the clearest light. The goals of this chapter, then, are to understand what it means to treat Euclidean geometry as a theory of space, and precisely what the theory thus understood tells us about space.

2.2 Axiomatic Geometry

Reading through the definitions and postulates of the theory for the first time, one might wonder what the point of stating them is—"Isn't it simply obvious that a straight line can be drawn between any two points? Why do we need to say that?" But to take this view is to miss the achievement of Euclid, and to appreciate that achievement requires some appreciation of the development of geometry. Before *The Elements*, geometry was not a fully systematic science: for instance, the Egyptians knew many geometrical truths and how to apply them in surveying, but they had no account of the logical relations between those truths. More significantly, their knowledge was primarily derived not from valid inference, as in *The Elements*, but from experience.

Egyptian knowledge was adopted and advanced by the Greeks (exactly what was taken from northern Africa and what was discovered by the Greeks is a contentious issue). Thales brought Egyptian learning about geometry to Greece in around the seventh century BC, and he and others (including Eudoxus and Theaetetus) developed proofs of certain geometric truths in terms of simple assumptions. In this way the logical connections between the known geometric truths were discovered; it started to become clear that all of them followed from basic principles. Euclid perfected this trend by organizing the known proofs of his day, clarifying some and adding his own. His *Elements* demonstrates that all geometric knowledge (or at least all of the hundreds of "propositions" contained in the fifteen volumes) is a deductive consequence of five basic "postulates" and definitions (starting with those of Book I); the purpose of stating these seemingly obvious postulates is thus to systematize a vast body of truths into a compact system. Once we assume the five postulates, then the rest of geometry is a matter of deduction, so in a real sense all of geometry is "contained" in the *axioms*, waiting to be unpacked as *theorems*. (In modern terminology we call the postulates—and, strictly speaking, the "common notions"—"axioms" of the system, and the propositions the "theorems.")

Thus Euclid's genius does not lie in discovering that the postulates are true, for they seem rather trivial. His contribution lay rather in finding which five axioms lead you to the rest of geometry. Later we will see that Newton compared the logic and scope of his system of mechanics to Euclid's geometry, but we can also compare the two historically. Both were men of brilliance at the right time in history, both "stood on the shoulders of giants" to see how to perfect a systematization that others had begun. Both understood exactly what had to be captured by a theory, and both had the insight to do know how to do it.

In fact, strictly, it is not possible to derive all the truths of geometry from just the given axioms; others are needed. This is clear in the derivation of the very first proposition: even the earliest commentators pointed out that Euclid assumes that there will be a point C at which the circles intersect, an assumption that does not appear in the postulates (or follow from them). Of course, that they intersect should be true in geometry, but that is not the issue. We want all the necessary assumptions stated in advance, so that we can then prove all geometric knowledge from them—this is the idea of an axiomatic system. Fortunately, as David Hilbert showed at the end of the nineteenth century, Euclidean geometry can be captured in twenty axioms (though Hilbert added a further questionable "axiom of completeness"). However, even in modern formulations, the five postulates listed do a lot of the work, and for simplicity we will continue for the most part as if they were indeed adequate.

Euclid's definitions, axioms, and theorems still speak eloquently for themselves, so there is no need to comment on them in detail. However, for later work, it is worthwhile clarifying a few points and introducing some standard modern terminology for the basic elements of the system, *points* and *lines*. Euclid defines a point to be "that which has no part," and we will thus take it that points have neither magnitude nor dimensions. Next, he defines lines to be "breadthless length," meaning that lines have only length, and so are one-dimensional. He doesn't add explicitly that lines are collections of points, but they are, in geometry. Euclid also fails to state explicitly that on any straight line connecting two points is a third point dividing the line in two; this property is known as "denseness," and it is a consequence of Hilbert's axiomatization.

In the translation used here, "line" refers to any continuous set of points, whether straight or not, but following modern terminology we will generally use "curve" instead, and take it as understood that all "lines" are straight curves. We will also need an alternative to Euclid's intuitive definition of "straight." For our purposes, the key feature of (straight) lines in space is that they are the shortest paths between two points: stray slightly off the straightest route and your trip will be longer. Also instead of using Euclid's term "finite line" to describe the part of a line between two points, we shall use the more modern term "segment." Note also that implicit in the common notions is the assumption that it makes sense to compare the lengths of segments. Further, it is clearly intended that one can take two segments and construct a third whose length is equal to the sum of the lengths of the first two. Finally, it is also the case that if a given segment is completely divided into two (or more) smaller segments such that none overlap, then the length of the segment equals the sum of the lengths of the parts.

2.3   The Theory of Space

Now that we understand the significance of Euclid's work, we can see that it fits the picture of a scientific theory that we developed earlier. In *The Elements*, the basic principles of the theory are presented as definitions and postulates, which determine an abstract world—"Euclid's paradise" (or "the plane," in two dimensions)—of pure geometry. In deriving the theorems, Euclid discovers which other truths must hold in this geometric world: the derivations are logically valid, so if the axioms are true then the theorems are too. For instance, since all the postulates hold in the plane, so does Proposition 1, and hence any finite line in the plane is one side of an equilateral triangle.

Now, as a point of logic, if *P* entails *Q* and *Q* entails *R*, then it follows that *P* entails *R*. This is of enormous help in an axiomatic system. It means that once a theorem has been proven, it can be assumed in the proof of further theorems. We can be sure that everything so proven is a deductive consequence of the axioms without having to fill in every step explicitly from axioms to theorem. For example, having proven Proposition 1, we can now use it in the proof of other theorems directly, without having to write out its proof again. The utility of this is clear in the proof of Proposition 32, which makes use of Propositions 13, 29, and 31, which in turn rely on Propositions 11, 13, 15, 23, and 27, and so on back to the axioms. This method of building on previous proofs is repeated throughout *The Elements* until

Euclid has presented us with a comprehensive map of the abstract world defined by his axioms.

If Euclidean geometry is a theory in the sense introduced earlier, then we should ask whether it is any good. As we saw, there are two senses in which this question can be taken: First, is Euclidean geometry logically consistent? Second, does it accurately describe the physical world? We shall discuss the issue of consistency in the next chapter; here we will consider whether Euclidean geometry is an accurate theory of the actual world. This topic will reappear later in the book (starting with Kant's *Critique*) but first we need to clarify what aspect of the physical world it is supposed to describe.

Of course, many material things, such as blackboards, fields, and race tracks, are described by Euclidean geometry (away from their edges that is). But we are interested in space, and hence in the "Euclidean hypothesis": *Euclidean geometry correctly describes physical space*. (Remember our earlier caution: Euclid himself did not propose this hypothesis, but it is implicit in various ways in the debates that we will be studying.) Here we should think of space in the way we discussed in the introduction, as an admittedly peculiar physical object, distinct from matter but comprised of all possible locations of material objects. As we noted earlier, many philosophers have found this notion unacceptable, and many of the later readings concern their attempts to prove that matter-independent space does not exist. However, if we temporarily accept that space is a genuine entity, then we can understand the Euclidean hypothesis to state that it has the geometric properties described by Euclid. Later we will see how the truth of Euclid's postulates might also be maintained by someone who denies the independent existence of space.

Ultimately, the "possible locations" of which space is comprised are points, and so space is just the kind of thing of which Euclid's axioms might be true. For instance, some collections of these points form lines, and those lines can be the boundaries of certain figures, such as squares and triangles; so the objects mentioned in the definitions are parts of space. Further, it does seem that there is a line between any two points in space, as between the points occupied by the tip of your nose and the top of the Eiffel tower, and so the axioms potentially are true of space. That is, space is a fundamentally geometric object, and a set of axioms like Euclid's are needed to describe it. (It is worth mentioning that throughout the book we will talk as if space has only two dimensions, and so discuss plane geometry. This is purely for simplification, and any conclusions that we draw about two dimensions also carry over to three.)

It is one thing to realize that space is amenable to a geometric treatment, but it is another to tell whether the proposed treatment is true. How can we tell whether

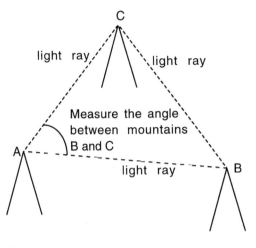

Figure 2.6
Gauss's experiment.

Euclid correctly describes the properties of space? The question may appear absurd, for the axioms seem to be so trivial that it is incomprehensible how they could be false: How could a geometric line have an end? How could it be that two lines crossed at right angles by a third were not parallel? Many mathematicians and philosophers have thought that such situations were indeed impossible, and hence that we could be sure that Euclidean geometry is a correct description of space. (This claim of course raises the important question of how we came to know such a thing.) But if we are going to view Euclidean geometry as a theory in a modern scientific sense, then we ought to consider what experimental evidence can be gathered for it. As we discussed in the introduction, we need to construct experiments to test the predictions of the theory.

What are the particular consequences of Euclidean geometry that we might test? The theorems, of course. For instance, the "internal angles theorem" (Proposition 32) seems ideal for an empirical test. It is easily converted into an experimental prediction, and it requires all five axioms for its derivation. Hence if this theorem is true of particular triangles in space, then we have evidence for the whole set of axioms (and were it to be found false, we would have an indirect proof that not all the postulates were true). The one remaining problem is to find a triangle in space, measure its internal angles, and see whether their sum is two right angles as the theorem states. There is however a block to this experiment: space may be everywhere as a background, but its immateriality makes it impossible to measure directly. In the important sense we can't even see it: it is before our eyes in every direction, but no image of space is present in our field of vision. The situation seems like that we find with subatomic particles that are too small to see. In that case we construct experiments whose results can be directly observed, and infer what is happening to the atoms. The same strategy must be adopted with space.

In the early nineteenth century, the mathematician Carl Friedrich Gauss carried out just the kind of experiment that we are envisaging. (Why did no one perform a test earlier? Because, as we shall learn, until then no one seriously considered the possibility that space might not be Euclidean.) He made the natural assumption that light rays travel along straight lines in space, and so he measured the internal angles of a spatial triangle by measuring the internal angles of a triangle whose sides were light rays. He accomplished this by setting up surveying equipment on three mountain tops—the three corners of a triangle—and from each he measured the angle between the other two, sighting them through his equipment.

On the assumption that light travels along straight lines from the mountain tops to the sighting apparatus, he inferred that the angles that he measured were the internal angles of the triangle in space between the mountain tops. Gauss found that the internal angles of his triangle summed to two rights (within experimental error), apparently confirming the Euclidean hypothesis.

Now that we better understand the idea that space is a geometric object, we are ready to embark on a trip through the history of thought about space. We will see those who question the consistency of the geometric description. We will see the problems that arise when one tries to understand what kind of thing space is. We will see the ways in which space might be connected with the theory of motion. And we will return to the question of how one might determine whether the Euclidean hypothesis is true.

Problems

1. Repeat Gauss's experiment on as large a scale as possible, using a cord pulled tight between three points. What is assumed about the cord to make this a test of Euclid? What do you find?

2. Suppose it weren't true that light travels along straight lines in space, but perhaps along outward bulging curves between the mountain tops. What might Gauss have observed then in his experiment? So if Gauss had found that the angles of his triangle

did not sum to two rights, would he then have had to infer that Euclid's axioms were untrue?

3. While the plane is a model of the Euclidean axioms, it is not the only one. Consider a "lattice" of points lined up in regular rows and columns, each 1 cm away from the next. If we consider "lines" to be composed of these lattice points only, and that the points are their normal distances apart, show that the Euclidean axioms also hold in the lattice. Why does Proposition 1 now fail?

Further Readings and Bibliography

Abbott, E. A. 1992. *Flatland: A Romance in Many Dimensions*. New York: Dover. √

Greenberg, M. J. 1980. *Euclidean and Non-Euclidean Geometries: Development and History*, second edition (see chaps. 1–3). San Francisco: W. H. Freeman and Co.

3 Zeno

READING

Plato's Parmenides

[*127*] Antiphon said that Pythodorus said that Zeno and Parmenides once [*b*] came to the Great Panathenaia. Parmenides was already quite venerable, very gray but of distinguished appearance, about sixty-five years old. Zeno was at that time near forty, a tall, handsome man, who had been, as rumor had it, the object of Parmenides' affections when he was a boy. Antiphon [*c*] said that the two of them were staying with Pythodorus, outside the wall in the Potters' Quarter, and that Socrates had come there, along with quite a few others, because they were eager to hear Zeno read his book, which he and Parmenides had just brought to Athens for the first time. Socrates was then quite young.

Zeno himself was reading to them; Parmenides happened to be out. Very [*d*] little remained to be read when Pythodorus, as he related it, came in, and with him Parmenides and Aristotle (the one who later became one of the Thirty). They listened to a little of the book at the very end. But Pythodorus had himself heard Zeno read it before.

Then Socrates, after he had heard it, asked Zeno to read the first hypothesis of the first argument again; and when he had read it, asked, "Zeno, [*e*] what do you mean by this: if things are many, they must then be both like and unlike, but that is impossible, because unlike things can't be like or like things unlike? That's what you say, isn't it?"

"It is," Zeno said.

"So if it's impossible for unlike things to be like and like things unlike, it follows that it's also impossible for them to be many? Because, if they were many, they would have incompatible properties. Is this the point of your arguments—simply to maintain, in opposition to everything that is commonly said, that things are not many? And so you suppose that each of your arguments is proof for this position, so that you think you give as many proofs that things are not many as your book has arguments? Is that what you're saying—or do I misunderstand?" [*128*]

Excerpts from Plato, "Parmenides," translated by D. J. Zeyl, in *Readings in Ancient Greek Philosophy* (pp. 432–433), edited by S. Marc Cohen, Patricia Curd, and C. D. C. Reeve. © 1995 by Hackett Publishing Co. All rights reserved. Reprinted by permission of Hackett Publishing Co.

"No," Zeno replied. "On the contrary, you grasp the general point of the book splendidly."

"Parmenides," Socrates said, "I understand that Zeno wants to be on intimate terms with you not only in friendship but also in his book. He has, in a way, written the same thing as you, but by changing it round he tries to fool us into thinking he is saying something different. You say in your poem that the all is one, and you give splendid and excellent proofs for [b] that; he, for his part, says that it is not many and gives a vast array of very grand proofs of his own. So, with one of you saying 'one,' and the other 'not many,' and with each of you speaking in a way that suggests that you've said not at all the same thing—although you mean practically the same thing—what you've said you appear to have said over the heads of the rest of us."

"Yes, Socrates," Zeno said. "Still, you haven't completely discerned the truth about my book, even though you chase down its arguments and follow their spoor as well as a young Spartan hound. First of all, you have [c] missed this point: the book doesn't at all preen itself on having been written with the intent you described, while disguising it from people, as if that were some great accomplishment. You have mentioned something that happened accidentally. The truth is that the book comes to the defense of Parmenides' argument against those who try to make fun of it by claiming that, if it is one, many absurdities and self-contradictions result from his [d] argument. Accordingly, this book argues against those who assert the many and pays them back in kind with something for good measure, since it aims to make clear that their hypothesis, if it is many, would, if someone examined the matter thoroughly, suffer consequences even more absurd than those suffered by the hypothesis of its being one. I wrote a book, then, in that competitive spirit when I was a young man. Someone made an unauthorized copy, so I didn't even have a chance to decide for myself whether or not it should see the light. So this eluded you, Socrates: you [e] think it was written not out of a young man's competitiveness, but out of a mature man's vainglory. Still, as I said, your portrayal was not bad." . . .

READING

Aristotle and Simplicius on Zeno's Paradoxes

Fragment 1: Aristotle 239b10

Zeno's arguments about motion, which cause so much trouble to those who try to answer them, are four in number.

Fragment 2: Simplicius 1012,22–1013,2

[Aristotle] says that Zeno's arguments concerning motion are four, by means of which he exercised his audience and seemed to deny the most self-evident thing among the things that are, [namely] motion, so that even Diogenes the Cynic, having heard these puzzles once, said nothing in reply to them, but stood up and walked and by means of self-evidence itself resolved the paradoxes in the arguments. He says that the arguments that provide difficulties to those attempting to solve [them] are four, either because all the arguments concerning motion were four, all of them happening to be difficult to confront, or because, although there were more, the most serious were four. It was fitting for one who was writing a treatise concerning motion to resolve the arguments that attempted to deny it, and above all those which were attempted on the basis of physical principles, such as Zeno's arguments also were, since they exploited the cutting of magnitudes to infinity, and the fact that everything moves or is at rest, and so many such things.

Excerpts from Aristotle, "The Physics," translated by R. P. Hardie and R. K. Gaye, in *The Oxford Revised Aristotle* (vol. 1, pp. 393–439), edited by J. Barnes. © 1984 by The Jowett Trustees. Reprinted by permission of Princeton University Press.

Excerpts from Simplicius, *On Aristotle's "Physics 6"* (pp. 114–116), translated and edited by D. Konstan. © 1989 by David Konstan. Reprinted by permission of the American Publisher, Cornell University Press, and Gerald Duckworth & Co Ltd.

Excerpts from Simplicius, "On Aristotle's Physics," in *The Presocratic Philosophers: A Critical History with a Selection of Texts* (p. 267), translated and edited by G. S. Kirk, J. E. Raven and M. Schofield. © 1957, 1983 by Cambridge University Press. Reprinted by permission of Cambridge University Press.

Fragment 3: Aristotle 239b11–13

The first asserts the non-existence of motion on the ground that that which is in locomotion must arrive at the half-way stage before it arrives at the goal. This we have discussed above.

Fragment 4: Simplicius 1013,3–14

The first of the four arguments proving that certain impossible things follow upon the fact that motion exists is as follows: if there is motion, it is necessary that a moving thing will entirely traverse an infinite number of things in a finite time; but this is impossible: consequently, there is no motion. He used to prove the conditional premise on the basis of the fact that a moving thing moves [over] a certain interval. Given that every interval is divisible to infinity, it is necessary that the moving thing first traverse half of the interval [over] which it is moving, and then the whole: but, even before [it traverses] half of the whole, [it must traverse] half of that, and again half of this. If, accordingly, the halves are infinite because it is possible to take a half of everything that is taken, and it is impossible to traverse an infinite number of things in a finite time—this Zeno used to take as self-evident.

Fragment 5: Aristotle 233a14–31

Moreover, the current arguments make it plain that, if time is continuous, magnitude is continuous also, inasmuch as a thing passes over half a given magnitude in half the time, and in general over a less magnitude in less time; for the divisions of time and of magnitude will be the same. And if either is infinite, so is the other, and the one is so in the same way as the other; i.e. if time is infinite in respect of its extremities, length is also infinite in respect of its extremities; if time is infinite in respect of divisibility, length is also infinite in respect of divisibility; and if time is infinite in both respects, magnitude is also infinite in both respects.

   Hence Zeno's argument makes a false assumption in asserting that it is impossible for a thing to pass over or severally to come in contact with infinite things in a finite time. For there are two ways in which length and time and generally anything continuous are called infinite: they are called so either in respect of divisibility or in respect of their extremities. So while a thing in a finite time cannot come in contact with things quantitatively infinite, it can come in contact with things infinite in respect of divisibility; for in this sense the time itself is also infinite: and so we find that the time occupied by the passage over the infinite is not a finite but an infinite time, and the contact with the infinites is made by means of moments not finite but infinite in number.

Fragment 6: Aristotle 263a15–22

But, although this solution is adequate as a reply to the questioner (the question asked being whether it is impossible in a finite time to traverse or count an infinite number of units), nevertheless as an account of the fact and the truth it is inadequate. For suppose the distance to be left out of account and the question asked to be no longer whether it is possible in a finite time to traverse an infinite number of distances, and suppose that the inquiry is made to refer to the time itself (for the time contains an infinite number of divisions): then this solution will no longer be adequate, and we must apply the truth that we enunciated in our recent discussion.

Fragment 7: Simplicius 1013,14–30

Aristotle had this argument in mind earlier when he said that it is impossible to traverse an infinite number of things and to touch an infinite number of things in a finite [time]; but in fact every magnitude has infinite divisions; consequently, it is impossible to traverse any magnitude in a finite time. [Aristotle] resolved it by saying that there is not an infinite number of things in the interval actually, but rather potentially, and that nothing can entirely traverse in a finite time halves insofar as they are actually infinite, but [insofar as they are] potentially [so] nothing prevents [this]. For neither will the moving thing traverse the interval by dividing it into infinite halves, but rather as a single and continuous thing. Therefore it is not prevented from entirely traversing things infinite in this way, for if it should divide [the interval] into halves, it will no longer move as though on a single and continuous thing, nor will the motion be continuous. Thus, accordingly, he resolved the argument according to a distinction [in the kinds] of infinity, and further also on the basis of the fact that the puzzle is alike both in the time and in the interval, so that [the moving thing] will traverse an infinite [interval] not in a finite time, but rather in a similarly infinite [time]. For in fact the time too is divisible to infinity. But the infinity is potential and not actual. Accordingly, it will traverse a potentially infinite number of [bits] of the magnitude in a potentially infinite number of [bits] of the time.

Fragment 8: Aristotle 239b14–29

The second is the so-called Achilles, and it amounts to this, that in a race the quickest runner can never overtake the slowest, since the pursuer must first reach the point whence the pursued started, so that the slower must always hold a lead. This argument is the same in principle as that which depends on bisection, though it differs from it in that the spaces with which we have successively to deal are not divided into halves. The result of the argument is that the slower is not overtaken; but it proceeds along the same lines as the bisection-argument (for in both a division of the space in a certain way leads to the result that the goal is not reached, though the Achilles goes further in that it affirms that even the runner most famed for his speed must fail in his pursuit of the slowest), so that the solution too must be the same. And the claim that that which holds a lead is never overtaken is false: it is not overtaken while it holds a lead; but it is overtaken nevertheless if it is granted that it traverses the finite distance. These then are two of his arguments.

Fragment 9: Simplicius 1013,35–1015,2

This argument too has been attempted on the basis of division to infinity in another version. It would be as follows: if there is motion, the slowest will never be overtaken by the fastest. But in fact this is impossible. Consequently, there is no motion. The conditional premise is self-evident, and he establishes the additional premise which says that it is impossible for the slowest to be overtaken by the fastest, by taking a tortoise as the slowest, which the story too took as slow by nature in the contest with the horse, and Achilles as the fastest, who seemed so much the swiftest of foot that "help-foot" [*podarkês*] seems to be his personal epithet in Homer because the speed of his feet helped [*arkein*] both himself and his allies. The argument was called "Achilles," accordingly, from the fact that Achilles was taken [as a character] in it, and the argument says it is impossible for him to overtake the tortoise when pursuing it. For in fact it is necessary that what is to overtake [something], before overtaking [it], first reach the limit from which what is fleeing set forth. In [the time in] which what is pursuing arrives at this, what is fleeing will advance a certain interval, even if it is less than that which what is pursuing advanced, by virtue of the fact that it is slower. Nevertheless, it will advance: for it is not, indeed, at rest. And in the time again in which what is pursuing will traverse this [interval] which what is fleeing advanced, in this time again what is fleeing will traverse some amount by so much less than that which it moved earlier as it itself is slower than what is pursuing. And thus in every time in which what is pursuing will traverse the [interval] which what is fleeing, being slower, has [already] advanced, what is fleeing will also advance some amount. For even if it is always less, nevertheless it will itself too traverse some amount if it is moving at all. By taking one interval less than another to infinity by the cutting of the magnitudes to infinity, not only will Hector not be overtaken by Achilles, but not even the tortoise [will be]. For, let it be hypothesized that the pre-scribed [interval] is a stade, and that the tortoise is ahead [by] half a stade, and that Achilles moves [a distance] ten times greater than the tortoise in the same time. Once Achilles, then, has begun to pursue the tortoise from the beginning of the stade, in however much [time] he will advance the half-stade, so as to reach the half from which the tortoise set forth, the tortoise too will be traversing a tenth of the remain-ing half-stade. Again, in however much [time] Achilles will traverse a tenth of this half-stade, the tortoise traverses a tenth of a tenth of a half-stade, and if upon every tenth that is taken of any interval it too has a tenth, the tortoise will forever be somewhat ahead of Achilles and never will either of them entirely traverse the stade.

Fragment 10: Aristotle 239b30–32

The third is that already given above, to the effect that the flying arrow is at rest, which result follows from the assumption that time is composed of moments: if this assumption is not granted, the conclusion will not follow.

Fragment 11: Aristotle 239b5–9

Zeno's reasoning, however, is fallacious, when he says that if everything when it occupies an equal space is at rest, and if that which is in locomotion is always in a now, the flying arrow is therefore motionless. This is false; for time is not composed of indivisible nows any more than any other magnitude is composed of indivisibles.

Fragment 12: Aristotle 239b33–240a16

The fourth argument is that concerning equal bodies which move alongside equal bodies in the stadium from opposite directions—the ones from the end of the stadium, the others from the middle—at equal speeds, in which he thinks it follows that half the time is equal to its double. The fallacy consists in requiring that a body travelling at an equal speed travels for an equal time past a moving body and a body of the same size at rest. That is false. E.g. let the stationary equal bodies be AA; let BB be those starting from the middle of the A's (equal in number and in magnitude to them); and let CC be those starting from the end (equal in number and magnitude to them, and equal in speed to the B's). Now it follows that the first B and the first C are at the end at the same time, as they are moving past one another. And it follows that the C has passed all the A's and the B half; so that the time is half, for each of the two is alongside each for an equal time. And at the same time it follows that the first B has passed all the C's. For at the same time the first B and the first C will be at opposite ends, being an equal time alongside each of the B's as alongside each of the A's, as he says, because both are an equal time alongside the A's. That is the argument, and it rests on the stated falsity.

Fragment 13: Simplicius (Kirk et al.)

In this argument [*sc.* that proving the many both large and small] he proves that what has neither magnitude nor solidity nor bulk would not even exist. "For," he says, "if it were added to something else that is, it would make it no larger; for if it were of no magnitude, but were added, it [*sc.* what it was added to] could not increase in magnitude. And thus what was added would in fact be nothing. If when it is taken away the other thing is no smaller, and again when it is added will not increase, it is clear that what was added was nothing nor again what was taken away." And Zeno says this, not by way of abolishing the One, but because each of the many infinite things has magnitude, since there is always something in front of what is taken, because of infinite division; and this he proves having first proved that it has no magnitude since each of the many is the same as itself and one.

Unlimitedness in magnitude he proved earlier by the same method of argument. For having first proved that if what is had no magnitude, it would not even exist, he goes on: "But if it is, it is necessary for each to have some magnitude and thickness, and for the one part of it to be away from the other. And the same argument holds about the part out in front; for that too will have magnitude and a part of it will be out in front. Indeed it is the same thing to say this once and to go on saying it always; for no such part of it will be last, nor will there not be one part related to another.—Thus if there are many things, it is necessary that they are both small and large; so small as not to have magnitude, so large as to be unlimited."

COMMENTARY

3.1   Introduction

We will discuss Zeno's work as a challenge to the Euclidean hypothesis, so I should note explicitly that Zeno lived in the fifth century BC and that his arguments thus predate Euclid's systematization of geometry by around 150 years. These readings are not chronological, but rather follow the logical development sketched in the introduction: first we developed a theory of space and now we see what problems it raises. Remember too that many of the theorems and concepts gathered together in the *Elements* were known previously, so Zeno would have known a significant portion of Euclidean geometry and the view that space (and time) are geometric. Thus the ordering of the texts does not give too misleading a version of history.

Zeno's book, to which Plato refers in his dialogue *Parmenides*, did not survive to modern times, so our knowledge of him comes instead from Plato, Aristotle's *Physics*, and Simplicius's *Commentary on Aristotle's* Physics. Though Simplicius apparently quotes Zeno directly in places, he was writing in the sixth century AD, over a millennium later, so in most cases scholars cannot be sure that his quotations are accurate. For this reason we have to rely on works of Plato, Aristotle, and Simplicius as interpretations of Zeno's arguments.

A common response to Zeno is to wonder what the point of the paradoxes is supposed to be. After all, as Diogenes demonstrated according to Fr. 2*, things do move, so why try to show that they cannot? Of course the answer is that we have to worry about arguments with premises that we believe, but which appear to entail unwanted conclusions. Since it is inconsistent to both accept the premises of a valid argument and deny its conclusion, we have to take Zeno's paradoxes seriously, and figure out whether they reveal a contradiction in our beliefs. In particular, the paradoxes question whether the Euclidean hypothesis is consistent, for ostensibly they are arguments of the following form:

Space is described by Euclidean geometry

∴ Motion is impossible.

Recall that there are only three consistent responses to an argument with an undesirable conclusion and apparently true premises. First, we could accept that the argument is valid and that the premises true, in which case we would have to accept the truth of the unwanted conclusion. Second, we could accept that the argument is

---

* The references in this chapter are to the "fragment" numbers used in the selections.

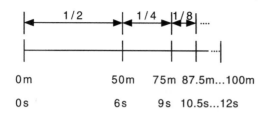

Figure 3.1
The Dichotomy Paradox: the remaining track and the time are ever divided into halves.

valid but deny the conclusion, thereby refuting at least one of the premises by the method of indirect proof. Finally, we could try to show that the argument is invalid, which would allow us to maintain (consistently) the truth of its premises and the falsity of its conclusion. Our task is to analyze Zeno's paradoxes and see under which of these three categories they fall. Since we are proposing the view that space is as described by Euclid, we aim to show that the paradoxes are not indirect refutations of the Euclidean hypothesis. As we do so, we will see how these ancient arguments helped spur development of the modern understanding of the infinite.

First, let us pause briefly to consider Zeno's intentions, which are a matter of debate. In the *Parmenides*, Plato sees all the paradoxes as attempts to establish that there cannot be more than one thing: as attempts to prove that "things are not many." On this interpretation, Zeno is replying to the opponents of his mentor, Parmenides, who argued that reality is a single object, unchanging throughout time and space. Other philosophers ridiculed this idea, and, according to Plato, Zeno sought to "pay them back in their own kind, with something for good measure," by showing that the alternative itself is paradoxical. Alternatively, it could be argued that Zeno was attempting to prove directly the absurdity of the standard view of space, that the paradoxes of motion attempt to show that space can be neither indefinitely divisible (Fr. 3–9) nor atomic (Fr. 10–12).

Whatever Zeno's original intentions, if his arguments are correct then there is something terribly wrong with our view of space, and so we will focus on the problems that they raise for geometric theories. We will find that the arguments are more involved than the simple model above, but even so the basic concern is the same: the paradoxes could well be indirect refutations of the Euclidean hypothesis.

3.2   The Dichotomy

Zeno's first argument claims that motion is impossible because "that which is in locomotion must first arrive at the halfway stage before it arrives at its goal" (Fr. 3).

It gets its name from the fact that it involves the division of a line into two. Traditionally, two arguments are extracted from this brief statement. The *Progressive* argument asserts that a runner cannot get to the end of a track, because she must eternally go half the remaining distance before the end. The *Regressive* asserts that the runner cannot even get started, because an infinite number of "halfways" must be crossed to get anywhere at all (Fr. 4). I will discuss the Progressive argument here, leaving the Regressive as an exercise.

Imagine our runner—her name is Atalanta—bursting over the starting line and hurtling toward the finish at top speed. First she must travel half the distance, namely 50m, leaving 50m to go. Then half the remaining distance, 50m ÷ 2 = 25m. Then 25m ÷ 2 = 12.5m. Then 6.25m. And so on. There is no end to the number of times we can halve the remaining distance; hence Atalanta must cover an infinite number of finite distances to get to the finish. But if, as Zeno assumes, "it is impossible to traverse an infinite number of [finite] things in a finite time" (Fr. 4), then the end of the track cannot be reached in a finite time. Generally, to move anywhere one must first travel halfway, then half of the remaining way = 1/4 of the way, then half the remaining way = 1/8 of the way, and so on. And so, if Zeno is correct, traveling any distance is impossible.

Consider Aristotle's reply to this paradox (Fr. 5); unfortunately, it doesn't defeat Zeno, but it will point us in the right direction. Aristotle claims that there is a difference between having an infinite number of parts and being infinitely big. Although one cannot travel an infinite distance in a finite time, one can traverse the infinite number of parts of a finite distance. This is because time is divisible in just the same way as space: if it takes 12 seconds (12s) to run the track, then Atalanta can spend the first 6s running the first 50m, the next 3s running the next 25m, the following 1.5s running the following 12.5m, and so on. For every length she must cover, there is a corresponding time period within the 12s in which to do it. Hence there is enough time to get to the end, and the runner can finish the race.

Aristotle thus questions Zeno's premise that it requires an infinite time to traverse an infinite number of finite lengths. Without this assumption the unwanted conclusion does not follow, thereby saving Euclid from absurdity. However, as Aristotle points out (Fr. 6), this reply is not a complete answer to the problems raised by the paradox, for he has to assume that the infinite number of intervals into which the 12 seconds are divided themselves add up to a finite time. That is, Aristotle assumes that $6s + 3s + 1.5s + \cdots$ adds up to 12s, but Zeno could reasonably dispute this; after all, shouldn't an infinite number of finite quantities add up to infinity?

Aristotle invokes a distinction between "potential infinities," such as the endless division of an interval, and "actual infinities," such as an infinitely long line (Fr. 7).

The idea is that whereas it is impossible to travel an actually infinite distance in a finite time, it is possible to travel a finite distance that is only potentially divided into an infinity of parts. We won't pursue this position, for the actual/potential distinction is not applicable to contemporary mathematics. For instance, one might imagine endlessly cutting up a segment with (ideal) scissors, a process which one could only "potentially" complete. But our inability to complete this process is irrelevant to the composition of a segment: the infinity of half segments that make it up are there all the time, whether we think about them or not.

Aristotle describes this new difficulty as a problem for periods of time, but it is equally a problem for intervals of space. Both finite periods and finite intervals are divisible into endless halves, so we can ask in either case how it is possible for an infinity of distinct finite parts to add up to a finite length. Now, the reason periods and intervals are endlessly divisible is that the Euclidean hypothesis says that they are finite lengths—segments—of time or space, and according to Euclid all segments are divisible. So at the root of the paradox is a challenge to the supposition of Euclidean geometry that the finite line segment is a consistent notion. We can analyze Zeno's argument into three steps, showing how our Euclidean claims (apparently) lead to contradiction:

1. All segments can be divided into two segments.
∴ C1. All segments can be divided into segments without limit.
∴ C1'. All segments are composed of an infinity of segments.

C1'. All segments are composed of an infinity of segments.
2. All segments have finite length.
3. The length of any segment = sum of lengths of segments of which it is composed.
∴ C2. The length of any segment = an infinite sum of finite lengths.

C2. The length of any segment = an infinite sum of finite lengths.
4. All infinite sums of finite quantities are infinite.
∴ C3. All segments are infinitely long.

Again, taking the argument to be valid, we apparently have only two choices; (i) accept the premises and hence the conclusion too, or (ii) deny at least one premise, in which case we can consistently deny the conclusion. Let us consider these options.

(i) On the face of it, each premise seems to be correct. Premises 1–3 are part of the Euclidean theory that we developed in the last chapter: (1) because of the "denseness" of points on a line; (2) because a segment is a finite line; (3) because the common notions imply that when we add segments together we get a segment whose length is the sum of the lengths of its parts. Without a knowledge of modern calculus, we would view (4) as very plausibly a mathematical truth. The intuitive idea is that whenever two (positive) numbers are added, their sum is greater than either. So if (positive) numbers are added together without end, then the total must grow endlessly, and surely that means that their total is infinite. As we shall see, this intuition is in fact flawed, ultimately saving us from the paradox.

But the premises cannot all be true, for the conclusion contradicts premise (2) (given that a segment only has one length), and hence the argument shows that the premises are inconsistent. If all four were true, then since the argument is valid it would have to be the case that segments were both finite and infinite in length. Thus the premises cannot all be true, and (i) is simply not an option.

(ii) So one of the premises must be false. It is plausible to suppose (for now) that premise (4) is a mathematical truth, which cannot be false. In which case it follows that premises (1)–(3) cannot all be true. But premises (1)–(3) are just part of our theory of space, and if they are inconsistent then the whole theory must be too: the paradox appears to be an indirect refutation of the Euclidean hypothesis. Remember the rhetorical force of such arguments: take someone's beliefs and derive from them a conclusion that they cannot accept. They must either reject some of their beliefs or else be committed to inconsistency. Zeno is offering the argument here, and the beliefs he draws on are premises (1)–(3). Whose beliefs are they? Obviously not his, because he is using an indirect argument to attack them. The beliefs belong to us, as subscribers to the Euclidean hypothesis. Unless we can find a flaw in his reasoning, we will have to accept that Euclid's geometry is inconsistent and hence unfit as a theory of space.

Fortunately, we can keep premises (1)–(3) and the Euclidean view, by giving up the supposed mathematical truth, premise (4). Aristotle attempted do so with his distinction between potential and actual infinities, but it required centuries of thought, culminating in the nineteenth-century work of Augustin-Louis Cauchy on the calculus, to resolve this paradox satisfactorily. We need to see from the modern perspective just how an infinite sum of finite quantities could be finite, and hence just what is wrong with premise (4).

Consider finite positive addition, the math of adding pairs of positive numbers. Any such sum is greater than either of its parts; so it seems reasonable to infer that the sum of any infinite collection of numbers must itself be equal to infinity. But this inference is fallacious, for the very concept of the "sum of an infinite collection of numbers" is not defined within finite arithmetic. Finite arithmetic only involves adding pairs of numbers together, and that operation will only ever yield finite sums. For instance, we can sum $a + b$, and hence $(a + b) + c$, and hence $((a + b) + c) + d$, and so on, but all we get from this is a growing sum of a finite number of terms, not a final total of an infinity of terms.

Thus it is no surprise that premise (4) led us into trouble, for it concerns infinite sums, but the reasoning behind it is based on finite mathematics. Until we clearly state what it means to add an infinite series of numbers, we cannot infer, from the fact that finite sums always grow, that "all infinite sums of finite quantities are infinite." It was Cauchy who completed a theory of the calculus that gave us the required clear statement of what infinite addition is.

Consider a sum of an infinite series of terms, $s_1 + s_2 + s_3 + \cdots + s_n + \cdots$, for example, the series $1/2 + 1/4 + 1/8 + \cdots + 1/2^n + \cdots$. Using finite addition, we can start to add these numbers together, obtaining the sequence of totals $s_1, s_1 + s_2$, $(s_1 + s_2) + s_3, \ldots$, in our case the sequence $1/2$, $1/2 + 1/4 = 3/4, (1/2 + 1/4) + 1/8 = 7/8, \ldots$. As we add more and more terms the total keeps growing, as expected, but it won't necessarily grow indefinitely large: however many terms of the series $1/2 + 1/4 + \cdots$ that we add together, for instance, the total will never equal or exceed 1. This observation gives us a way to extend finite addition to infinite addition such that infinite sums can have finite totals after all.

Let me make the following definitions: If an infinite sequence of increasing positive numbers eventually gets arbitrarily close to some number, L, without ever exceeding it, then L is the *limit* of that sequence. Thus 1 is the limit of the sequence $1/2, 3/4, 7/8, \ldots$. On the other hand, the sequence $1, 2, 3 \ldots$ has no limit, for every number is eventually exceeded. Next, the *sum of an infinite series $s_1 + s_2 + s_3 + \cdots$* is equal to the limit of the sequence $s_1, s_1 + s_2, (s_1 + s_2) + s_3, \ldots$ (as long as the limit exists). According to this definition, the sum of $1/2 + 1/4 + 1/8 + \cdots$ is the limit of the sequence $1/2, 3/4, 7/8, \ldots$, which is 1. However, the series $1 + 1 + 1 + \cdots$ has no finite sum, for the sequence $1, 1 + 1 = 2, 1 + 1 + 1 = 3, \ldots$ has no limit.*

---

*This book is written for a readership with mixed backgrounds in science and humanities, and in particular without presupposing great familiarity with mechanics and calculus. However, it is important for those who have a solid grounding in those topics to see how the points raised relate to what they have learned of math and physics. Hence, at various places more formal material will be introduced in "boxes" separated from the main text. This material always states in more mathematical terms what has just been explained, and is intended for those with an appropriate background. Since the boxes recapitulate what is said in the text, readers who are not comfortable with the math can "read around" the boxes without losing the sense of the arguments.

DEFINITION: An infinite sequence of increasing positive numbers $\{n_1, n_2, \ldots\}$ *converges* to a finite *limit L* if and only if, for all numbers $\varepsilon > 0$, there is some number d such that for all (integers) $c \geq d, |L - n_c| < \varepsilon$.

DEFINITION: The *sum of an infinite series* $s_1 + s_2 + \cdots$ is the limit of the sequence of sums $\{s_1, s_1 + s_2, s_1 + s_2 + s_3, \ldots\}$, if a limit exists.

We have already said enough to see that according to this definition $1/2 \times 100\text{m} + 1/4 \times 100\text{m} + 1/8 \times 100\text{m} + \cdots = 1 \times 100\text{m}$. But this is just the sum of the lengths of the intervals that Atalanta must run, which is now shown to be 100m, not infinitely long. If we adopt this definition then we can accept premises (1)–(3) of Zeno's argument and deny the conclusion, by denying the supposed "mathematical truth," premise (4). In fact it is not a mathematical truth at all, but rather, according to our definition, fails in exactly the kind of case that Zeno considers in his paradoxes. It is not the Euclidean hypothesis that led to the unwanted conclusion but Zeno's further assumption, and so the consistency of our theory is saved.

Before we let euphoria overwhelm us, let's review what we've done. We began with finite arithmetic and defined the new notion of an infinite sum. It is tempting to think that we have "proven" that the sum of an infinite series is the limit, as if we now know that were we to sit down for eternity adding up $1/2 + 1/4 + 1/8 + \cdots$, we would get 1 as the final answer. But this picture is badly askew, for what do we mean by "getting a final answer"? There is no final moment in an eternity! We are making the same mistake as before, namely, supposing that finite arithmetic by itself can take us to infinite sums. No, the definition is really just a new stipulation of what it means to add such a series, not a proof of what the sum is.

So one might question whether we, in our use of Cauchy's work, have done any more than Aristotle. He claimed that infinite extent and infinite divisibility were distinct, and our definition makes the same point. His claim was unsatisfactory because it was made without proof, but we have also seen that our definition doesn't "prove" within finite arithmetic that infinite sums have finite totals. So why accept Cauchy's reply when we wouldn't accept Aristotle's? The answer is that Cauchy *has* done much more than Aristotle, for he specified a precise, consistent definition of infinite sums, thereby showing that infinite sums can consistently be ascribed finite totals; Aristotle merely asserted that they could.

Insofar as we have treated the paradox as an issue of consistency, we have not dealt with other important questions that it raises. For instance, it is one thing to present a consistent theory of space, and it is another to show that it is correct. In particular, is Cauchy's definition of an infinite sum appropriate for physical lengths and times? (If this question seems odd, note that regular addition is inapplicable to volumes of mutually soluble liquids: 1 liter of water $+1$ liter of alcohol < 2 liters of liquid.) Such questions can be explored through the readings listed in the bibliography. We will add our notion of an infinite sum to the Euclidean hypothesis and claim that it is correct for the addition of real spatial (and temporal) intervals. The empirical success of the hypothesis helps to confirm this claim.

3.3   The Paradox of Plurality

The next argument is reconstructed from two rather confusing passages in Simplicius (Fr. 13). We will read it as an attempted refutation of the Euclidean view that a line is composed of smallest elements—points—and hence as a Parmenidean argument against plurality. Part of the problem is to understand how anything with no magnitude can exist: How can a point be smaller than any length and still itself be something? To follow Zeno's reasoning, however, we should at first put to one side the fact that we have decided that points will be dimensionless.

Consider a finite interval. The points along it are its smallest parts, there are an infinity of them, and they are all identical. Either the points have finite size, in which case an infinity of them has infinite length, and the interval of all of them is infinitely long; or, the points have zero length, so the sum of their lengths is zero, and the interval has zero length. (Points could logically be infinitely long, but that would be of no help here; or they could be "infinitesimally" big, but without an account of infinitesimals we must put that idea aside too.) Whether the points have zero or finite length, Zeno thinks that it follows in Euclidean geometry that the interval cannot be finite. He is attempting to show that our theory has absurd (actually, contradictory) consequences and so must be rejected. More precisely, the argument takes the following form:

1. All finite segments are composed of an infinity of identical points.

2. The points have either zero length or finite length.

∴ C1. The total length of the   ∴ C2. The total length of the
    segment is zero.   segment is infinite.

The argument notation indicates that we find ourselves on the horns of a dilemma. According to the second premise we have to pick between two alternatives: if we claim that points have no size, then we conclude that no number of them can have any length either; but if we take the second horn, we conclude that the line that is the sum of them is infinite. Neither of these positions is tenable given our view of space, according to which segments are finite. But if we deny the conclusion then the burden is on us to show either that the argument is invalid, or reject one of the premises.

The latter option is unattractive: premise (1) is true on the Euclidean view, and premise (2) exhausts all the available possibilities. However, it is not clear that the argument is valid given our earlier work. The inferences to (C1) and (C2) are pieces of mathematical reasoning about the addition of an infinity of point lengths, and the conclusions only follow if the math is correct. At first glance the inferences seem dubious, for we have recently seen that infinite sums can have finite totals, so we might try to question whether (C2) follows. But the idea that resolved the Dichotomy will not help here. The earlier series summed to a finite total because its terms decreased, so that however many were added together the total never reached 1. In this case, if all the points have the same finite length, l, then their infinite sum is $l + l + l + \cdots$. But this sum has no limit: pick any number, N, and however small l is, enough added together will exceed N. Intuitively, if an infinity of finite intervals are lined up, they will be infinitely long. Thus (C2) cannot be avoided if points are finite, and we must take the first horn of the dilemma, accepting, as expected, that points have no magnitude.

At first sight, we are led straight to the unacceptable (C1), because Cauchy's account of infinite addition agrees with intuition that $0 + 0 + 0 + \cdots = 0$. Adding up the lengths of dimensionless points, according to our definition, can only result in a segment that has zero length. So has Zeno firmly impaled us, then, by showing the impossibility of finite segments, and hence the inconsistency of the Euclidean hypothesis? No. The Dichotomy arose because we tried to apply finite addition to infinite sums; the Plurality has arisen because we've tried to apply Cauchy's infinite summation to points when there are *more* of them in a line than there are terms in an infinite sum, as we shall now see.

First let me clarify what it means for two (possibly infinite) collections to have the same number of elements. If you have some martinis and some olives, then you can check that you have the same number by counting both of them up. But with infinite collections, "counting up" is impossible, and so is not the way to compare sizes: we need a different understanding of equal infinite quantities. Another property the olives and martinis have is that they can be paired off one-to-one without remainder. There are exactly the same number if we can put just one olive in every glass, and have no olives left over. This property is applicable to infinite collections, and so we say that any two collections, finite or otherwise, have the same number of elements exactly if their elements can be paired off one-to-one without remainder (or, can be "put in one-to-one correspondence").

Consider the infinite collection of intervals from the Dichotomy: 50m, 25m, 12.5m, ... We can distinguish the first distance (50m) from the second (25m) and from the third, and so on. Hence every segment can be paired off with a number in the sequence $1, 2, 3, \ldots$, with no numbers left over: according to our definition there are the same number of intervals in the collection as there are numbers in the sequence. The sequence $1, 2, 3, \ldots$ is called the sequence of *natural numbers*, and any collection with the same number of elements is *denumerably infinite* or *countably infinite*.

Natural numbers:	1	2	3	...	n	...
Intervals:	50m	25m	12.5m	...	$1/2^n \times 100m$	...
Infinite series:	s_1	s_2	s_3	...	s_n	...

Cauchy's definition of infinite sums applies only to denumerably infinite series. In calculating the limit (and hence the total), one starts with the first term, then adds the second, then the third, then the fourth, and so on. But this requires that the terms be numbered $1, 2, 3, \ldots$ —that is, that they be countable.

However, as Georg Cantor proved at the end of the nineteenth century, there are more points in a line segment than there are natural numbers: the number of points in a line is *uncountably infinite*. It may seem surprising that there can be infinities of varying sizes, but Cantor's proof (see this chapter's references) proceeds just as our definition of "same size" suggests: it shows that in any pairing of points to natural numbers, there are always points left unpaired. To keep the infinities distinct, one says that there are χ_0 ("aleph null") natural numbers, and c (for "continuum") real numbers; so, while both χ_0 and c are infinite numbers, $\chi_0 < c$.

If Cauchy's definition of infinite addition applies only to denumerably infinite sums and there are uncountably many points in a line, then we cannot conclude anything about what length these points "add up" to. But this does not let us off the hook; all that is established is that our understanding of infinite addition is inapplicable to points, not that an infinity of zeroes can make a finite segment. After all, the idea that it cannot has considerable intuitive appeal. One wants to picture points stacked up to make a line (much as one might stack up a pile of pancakes), but if they have no size, how can stacking them ever get you anywhere? Now we know that there is something wrong with this picture already, for points are dense (see chap. 2) and pancakes are not: it is true only of points that between any two is a third. We need, then, to learn more about the continuum of points in a line. (Note that between any two fractions there is a third, so the "rational" numbers are dense, but

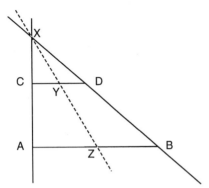

Figure 3.2
Cantor's proof: the lines XYZ pair points on AB with those on CD one-to-one without remainder.

there only countably many of them: it is not the denseness of points alone that means there are c of them.)

In our theory of space we want the following four things to be true: that points have zero length, that segments have finite length, that a segment contains an infinite continuum of points, and that the length of a segment is equal to the sum of the lengths of its parts. We have resisted the paradox so far by pointing out that the addition of the lengths of points is not included in our definition of infinite addition, and so we do not have to conclude that the zeroes amount to zero. But this reply is only any good if we can give a consistent account of how points can comprise a finite interval. The obvious thing to do is try to extend Cauchy's definition of infinite addition to the continuum of points. However, this won't work because, surprisingly, there are the same number of points in any line or segment. Thus any rule based on the number and length of points will entail that all segments are the same length! Let's work through this astonishing result, also due to Cantor.

From parallel lines take any two different length segments, *AB* and *CD*, as in figure 3.2. Extend segments *AC* and *BD*, and label their point of intersection *X*.

For each point *Z* on *AB*, the line through *X* and *Z* will intersect *CD* at a unique point *Y*. Similarly, each point *Y* can be paired to the unique point *Z*, and so the points of the two lines are paired one-to-one without remainder. Therefore *AB* and *CD* have the same number of points, as claimed.

Nothing in this proof depends on the actual length of the lines, so the same conclusion applies to any segments: they all contain the same number of points. The result may seem paradoxical in its own right, since it implies, for instance, that half a line has the same number of points as a whole line (similarly, the even numbers are countable). But really there is no paradox in this; it simply shows that infinite collections have some very counterintuitive properties.

Our way out of Zeno's paradox is thus to deny that the length of a segment is determined by addition of the lengths of its points, so we need not extend Cauchy's definition to uncountable sums. If every segment has the same number of points, it makes no sense to think of length as fixed by a simple compounding of points. There is no way to "add up" c points to find out if they are a 1mm, 1 light-year, or infinitely long line, since all three distances contain the same number of points. On this view, the property of length is not intrinsic to a collection of points, but is defined to be something logically independent and then "pasted on" later. Any such properties having to do with the distances between points are known as *metrical*. What we have discovered is that the same bare collection of points is compatible with a range of different metrical properties. For instance, two points could be 1mm or 1 light-year apart, and nothing about the number of intervening points could determine which.

We have defeated Zeno's challenge and saved the Euclidean hypothesis from the paradox of plurality. We accept that points are dimensionless, but we deny that it follows that segments have zero length, because segments do not get their length from the points of which they are composed; their length is a further independent metrical property. Finally, the length of a segment is equal to the sum of the length of its parts, so long as those parts are segments themselves. Our resolution is again definitional, this time concerning the nature of length, and so once again the success of our theory supports the applicability of the definition.

3.4 The Arrow

The final paradox that we will study calls into question our geometric understanding of motion. The problem arises because we view both space and time as composed of indivisible points, and because motion is the change of position over time. Zeno thus asks us (Fr. 11) to consider an arrow, supposedly in flight, and its motion at any smallest instant of time. We take such instants to be points, and hence without parts according to Euclid's definitions. It follows that no motion can occur during an instant, for if it did, something like what's shown in Figure 3.3 would hold.

The trajectory of the arrow as it moves forward (in the x-direction) is plotted against instants of time, t_1, t_2, and so on. If the arrow moves during any instant, say t_2, from point a to point b through point c, then that instant has parts: the part before c is reached, and the part after. But instants are points and hence have no parts, and thus motion during any instant is impossible. Put succinctly, there is no time during a point-like instant.

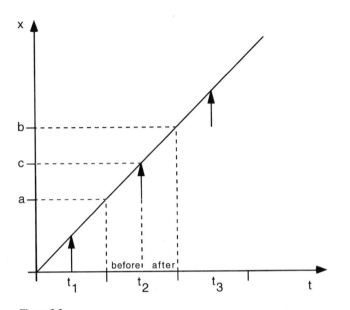

Figure 3.3
The Arrow Paradox: the arrow moves in the x direction as time goes on, but if it moves during t_2 then t_2 has "before" and "after" parts and is not an instant.

Now time, on the Euclidean view (contrary to Aristotle in Fr. 11), is composed of instants just as the line is composed of points, and nothing more. But if the arrow doesn't move during any instant, and time contains nothing but instants, how can it move at all? It appears to have no time to do so. We can analyze the argument as follows:

1. Instants have no parts.
2. If the arrow moves during any instant then that instant has earlier and later parts.

∴ C1. The arrow doesn't move during any instant.

C1. The arrow doesn't move during any instant.
3. If the arrow doesn't move during any instant, then it doesn't move at all.

∴ C2. The arrow doesn't move at all.

By now the logic of Zeno's arguments should be clear. This formulation is valid, premise (1) is part of the Euclidean view of time, and premise (2) has been demonstrated above. If we wish to avoid the paradox, then we must reject premise (3). And this is what part of modern mathematics, due to Cauchy and Karl Weierstrass, allows us to do.

In line with (C1), we deny that there is motion during any instant; instead, motion between points p and q occurs if *at* every instant during the journey the arrow is *at* the appropriate place along the trajectory. One might feel that motion occurs if from one instant to the next the arrow flows from one place to the next, but this would be misleading, because space and time are dense and so there is no "next" point. Instead, objects move simply by being at a continuous series of locations over a continuous interval of instants. To picture this, imagine the trajectory of the tip of the arrow moving through space, and an analog clock marking off the time of the journey: the times marked by the clock can all be paired with positions of the tip in space.

This "at-at theory of motion" requires modern mathematics for it relies on the notion of a *function*. Suppose that the position, x, of an arrow at an arbitrary time, t, is given as a function, $x(t)$. Then $x(0)$ might be the position at the start of the flight, $x(1)$ after one second, and so on. According to the "at-at" theory, the arrow moves when for every time—that is, every value of t—$x(t)$ has a value such that there are no "jumps" in x as t varies. At every t, the arrow is at some x.

Differential calculus exemplifies the at-at theory. An arrow is moving if its instantaneous velocity is nonzero, given by:

$$dx/dt \equiv \lim_{\Delta t \to 0} \frac{x(t + \Delta t) - x(t)}{\Delta t}.$$

Thus the arrow is moving at time t as long as it is at an appropriate series of points at the series of subsequent times $t + \Delta t$.

This theory of motion once again saves us from Zeno, because it denies premise (3): Motion is not something that happens during an instant, but is rather just a matter of being at the right sequence of places at the right sequence of times.

We have studied Zeno in part because his paradoxes represent a serious challenge to the Euclidean hypothesis, which we are investigating throughout this book. We have defeated the challenge and been rewarded with many deep insights into the nature of infinity. We saw how to understand the division of a segment into an infinity of pieces. We saw how to understand the composition of a line in terms of points. Finally, we have seen that we can safely take points to be structureless. These insights are among the most important treasures of mathematics, and all of them were inspired by the paradoxes presented by Zeno.

Problems

1. The regressive form of the Dichotomy argues that to reach any point one must first go halfway, and that to reach halfway one must first go quarter of the way, and so on. In other words, before Atalanta can even get started on her run she must cover an infinity of finite distances; hence, Zeno argues, she cannot start moving. Logically analyze this argument and see whether we have the resources to solve it.

2. The paradoxes have been interpreted in a variety of ways; for instance, we interpreted the Dichotomy as a problem concerning distance (i.e., as a metrical problem), but it could also be treated as a problem concerning order. That is, on her run Atalanta has to reach the series of points, 1/2 the way, 3/4 of the way, 7/8 of the way, ... A problem arises because there is no last place in this sequence that she has to get to before she reaches the end, and if that is the case, how can she finish? (Hint: see Salmon 1970.)

3. Prove that the following collections of numbers are denumerably infinite:

(a) $\{0, 1, 2, 3, \ldots\}$

(b) $\{2, 4, 6, 8, \ldots\}$

(c) $\{0, 10, 100, 1000, \ldots\}$

(d) $\{\ldots -2, -1, 0, 1, 2, \ldots\}$

(e)   The set of all fractions

4. According to the at-at theory of motion, an arrow does not move out of one place and into the next, but is rather in the right place at the right time. But in this case, what justifies our saying that it is the same arrow at every point of a trajectory, rather than saying that some arrow is found at each point?

Further Readings and Bibliography

Boyer, C. B. 1949. *The History of the Calculus and Its Conceptual Development*. New York: Dover.

Eves, H. 1983. *Great Moments in Mathematics: After 1650*. Washington, D.C.: Mathematical Association of America, Lecture 34.

McLaughlin, W. I. "Resolving Zeno's Paradoxes." *Scientific American*, November 1994, pp. 84–89.

Parmenides. Fragments, in *Readings in Ancient Greek Philosophy: From Thales to Aristotle*, edited by S. M. Cohen, P. Curd, and C. D. C. Reeve. 1995. Indianapolis, IN and Cambridge, MA: Hackett Publishing Co., pp. 35–41.

Salmon, W. C. 1980. *Space, Time, and Motion: A Philosophical Introduction*, second edition (see chap. 2). Minneapolis, MN: University of Minnesota Press. √

Salmon, W. C., ed. 1970. *Zeno's Paradoxes*. Indianapolis, IN: Bobbs-Merrill.

4 Aristotle

READING

Physics

Book IV

Chapter 1

[208ª26] The physicist must have a knowledge of place, too, as well as of the infinite—namely, whether there is such a thing or not, and the manner of its existence and what it is—both because all suppose that things which exist are [30] *somewhere* (the non-existent is nowhere—where is the goat-stag or the sphinx?), and because motion in its most general and proper sense is change of place, which we call "locomotion."

The question, what is place? presents many difficulties. An examination of all the relevant facts seems to lead to different conclusions. Moreover, we have inherited nothing from previous thinkers, whether in the way of a statement of difficulties or of a solution.

The existence of place is held to be obvious from the fact of mutual [208ᵇ1] replacement. Where water now is, there in turn, when the water has gone out as from a vessel, air is present; and at another time another body occupies this same place. The place is thought to be different from all the bodies which come to be in it [5] and replace one another. What now contains air formerly contained water, so that clearly the place or space into which and out of which they passed was something different from both.

Further, the locomotions of the elementary natural bodies—namely, fire, earth, and the like—show not only that place is something, but also that it exerts a [10] certain influence. Each is carried to its own place, if it is not hindered, the one up, the other down. Now these are regions or kinds of place—up and down and the rest of the six directions. Nor do such distinctions (up and down and right and left) hold only in relation to us. To *us* they are not always the same but change with the [15] direction in which we are turned: that is why the same thing is often both right *and* left, up *and* down, before *and* behind. But in *nature* each is distinct, taken apart by itself. It is not every chance direction which is up, but where fire and what is light

Excerpts from Aristotle, "The Physics," tr. by R. P. Hardie and R. K. Gaye, in *The Oxford Revised Aristotle* (vol. 1, pp. 354–362), ed. by J. Barnes. © 1984 The Jowett Trustees. Reprinted by permission of Princeton Univ. Press. Excerpts from Aristotle, *On the Heavens* (pp. 49–169), tr. by S. Leggatt. © 1995 Stuart Leggatt. Reprinted by permission of Aris and Phillips Ltd.

are carried; similarly, too, down is not any chance direction but where what has [20] weight and what is made of earth are carried—the implication being that these places do not differ merely in position, but also as possessing distinct powers. This is made plain also by the objects studied by mathematics. Though they have no place, they nevertheless, in respect of their position relatively to us, have a right and left as these are spoken of merely in respect of relative position, not having by nature these various characteristics. Again, the theory that the void exists involves the existence [25] of place; for one would define void as place bereft of body.

These considerations then would lead us to suppose that place is something distinct from bodies, and that every sensible body is in place. Hesiod too might be held to have given a correct account of it when he made chaos first. At least he says: "First of all things came chaos to being, then broadbreasted earth," [30] implying that things need to have space first, because he thought, with most people, that everything is somewhere and in place. If this is its nature, the power of place must be a marvellous thing, and be prior to all other things. For that without which nothing else can exist, while it can exist without the others, must needs be first; for [209^{a}1] place does not pass out of existence when the things in it are annihilated.

True, but even if we suppose its existence settled, the question of what it is presents difficulty—whether it is some sort of "bulk" of body or some entity other than that; for we must first determine its genus.

[5] Now it has three dimensions, length, breadth, depth, the dimensions by which all body is bounded. But the place cannot *be* body; for if it were there would be two bodies in the same place.

Further, if body has a place and space, clearly so too have surface and the other limits of body; for the same argument will apply to them: where the bounding planes [10] of the water were, there in turn will be those of the air. But when we come to a point we cannot make a distinction between it and its place. Hence if the place of a point is not different from the point, no more will that of any of the others be different, and place will not be something different from each of them.

What in the world, then, are we to suppose place to be? If it has the sort of [15] nature described, it cannot be an element or composed of elements, whether these be corporeal or incorporeal; for while it has size, it has not body. But the elements of sensible bodies are bodies, while nothing that has size results from a combination of intelligible elements.

[20] Also we may ask: of what in things is space the cause? None of the four modes of causation can be ascribed to it. It is neither cause in the sense of the matter of existents (for nothing is composed of it), nor as the form and definition of things, nor as end, nor does it move existents.

Further, too, if it is itself an existent, it will be somewhere. Zeno's difficulty demands an explanation; for if everything that exists has a place, place too will have [25] a place, and so on *ad infinitum*.

Again, just as every body is in place, so, too, every place has a body in it. What then shall we say about *growing* things? It follows from these premises that their place must grow with them, if their place is neither less nor greater than they are.

By asking these questions, then, we must raise the whole problem about [30] place—not only as to what it is, but even whether there is such a thing.

Chapter 2

Something can be said of a subject either in virtue of itself or in virtue of something else; and there is place which is common and in which all bodies are, and which is the proper and primary location of each body. I mean, for instance, that you are now in the world because you are in the air and it is in the world; and you are in the air because you are on the earth; and similarly on the earth because you are in this place which contains no more than you.

[209^{b}1] Now if place is what *primarily* contains each body, it would be a limit, so that the place would be the form or shape of each body which the magnitude or the matter of the magnitude is defined; for this is the limit of each body.

[5] If, then, we look at the question in this way the place of a thing is its form. But, if we regard the place as the *extension* of the magnitude, it is the matter. For this is different from the magnitude: it is what is contained and defined by the form, as by a bounding plane. Matter or the indeterminate is of this nature; for when the [10] boundary and attributes of a sphere are taken away, nothing but the matter is left.

This is why Plato in the *Timaeus* says that matter and space are the same; for the "participant" and space are identical. (It is true, indeed, that the account he gives there of the "participant" is different from what he says in his so-called unwritten teaching. Nevertheless, he did identify place and space.) I mention Plato because, [15] while all hold place to be something, he alone tried to say *what* it is.

In view of these facts we should naturally expect to find difficulty in determining what place is, if indeed it *is* one of these two things, matter or form. They demand a very close scrutiny, especially as it is not easy to recognize them [20] apart.

But it is at any rate not difficult to see that place cannot be either of them. The form and the matter are not separate from the thing, whereas the place can be separated. As we pointed out, where air was, water in turn comes to be, the one [25] replacing the other; and similarly with other bodies. Hence the place of a thing is neither a part nor a state of it, but is separable from it. For place is supposed to be something like a vessel—the vessel being a transportable place. But the vessel is no part of the thing.

In so far then as it is separable from the thing, it is not the form; and in so far as [30] it contains it, it is different from the matter.

Also it is held that what is anywhere is both itself something and that there is a different thing outside it. (Plato of course, if we may digress, ought to tell us why the form and the numbers are not in place, if "what participates" is place—whether what participates is the Great and the Small or the matter, as he has written in the [210ª1] *Timaeus*.)

Further, how could a body be carried to its own place, if place was the matter or the form? It is impossible that what has no reference to motion or the distinction of up and down can be place. So place must be looked for among things which have these characteristics.

If the place is in the thing (it must be if it is either shape or matter) place will [5] have a place; for both the form and the indeterminate undergo change and motion along with the thing, and are not always in the same place, but are where the thing is. Hence the place will have a place.

Further, when water is produced from air, the place has been destroyed, for the [10] resulting body is not in the same place. What sort of destruction then is that?

This concludes my statement of the reasons why place must be something, and again of the difficulties that may be raised about its essential nature. . . .

Chapter 4

[210ᵇ32] What then after all is place? The answer to this question may be elucidated as follows.

Let us take for granted about it the various characteristics which are supposed correctly to belong to it essentially. We assume first that place is what contains that of which it is the place, and is no part of the thing; again, that the primary place of a [211ª1] thing is neither less nor greater than the thing; again, that place can be left behind by the thing and is separable; and in addition that all place admits of the distinction of up and down, and each of the bodies is naturally carried to its appropriate place and rests there, and this makes the place either up or down. [5]

Having laid these foundations, we must complete the theory. We ought to try to conduct our inquiry into what place is in such a way as not only to solve the difficulties connected with it, but also to show that the attributes supposed to belong to it do really belong to it, and further to make clear the cause of the trouble and of [10] the difficulties about it. In that way, each point will be proved in the most satisfactory manner.

First then we must understand that place would not have been inquired into, if there had not been motion with respect to place. It is chiefly for this reason that we suppose the heaven also to be in place, because it is in constant movement. Of this kind of motion there are two species—locomotion on the one hand and, on the other, increase and diminution. For these too involve change: what was then in this place [15] has now in turn changed to what is larger or smaller.

Again, things are moved either in themselves, actually, or accidentally. In the latter case it may be either something which by its own nature is capable of being moved, e.g. the parts of the body or the nail in the ship, or something which is not in [20] itself capable of being moved, but is *always* moved accidentally, as whiteness or science. These have changed their place only because the subjects to which they belong do so.

We say that a thing is in the world, in the sense of in place, because it is in the air, and the air is in the world; and when we say it is in the air, we do not mean it is in [25] every part of the air, but that it is in the air because of the surface of the air which surrounds it; for if all the air were its place, the place of a thing would not be equal to the thing—which it is supposed to be, and which the primary place in which a thing is actually is.

When what surrounds, then, is not separate from the thing, but is in continuity with it, the thing is said to be in what surrounds it, not in the sense of in place, but as [30] a part in a whole. But when the thing is separate and in contact, it is primarily in the inner surface of the surrounding body, and this surface is neither a part of what is in it nor yet greater than its extension, but equal to it; for the extremities of things which touch are coincident.

Further, if one body is in continuity with another, it is not moved *in* that but [35] *with* that. On the other hand it is moved *in* that if it is separate. It makes no difference whether what contains is moved or not.

Again, when it is not separate it is described as a part in a whole, as the pupil [211ᵇ1] in the eye or the hand in the body: when it is separate, as the water in the cask or the wine in the jar. For the hand is moved *with* the body and the water *in* the cask.

It will now be plain from these considerations what place is. There are just four [5] things of which place must be one—the shape, or the matter, or some sort of extension between the extremities, or the extremities (if there is no extension over and above the bulk of the body which comes to be in it).

[10] Three of these it obviously cannot be. The shape is supposed to be place because it surrounds, for the extremities of what contains and of what is contained are coincident. Both the shape and the place, it is true, are boundaries. But not the same thing: the form is the boundary of the thing, the place is the boundary of the body which contains it.

The extension between the extremities is thought to be something, because [15] what is contained and separate may often be changed while the container remains the same (as water may be poured from a vessel)—the assumption being that the extension is something over and above the body displaced. But there is no such extension. One of the bodies which change places and are naturally capable of being in contact with the container falls in—whichever it may chance to be.

If there were an extension which were such as to exist independently and be [20] permanent, there would be an infinity of places in the same thing. For when the water and the air change places, all the portions of the two together will play the same part in the whole which was previously played by all the water in the vessel; at the same time the place too will be undergoing change; so that there will be another place which is the place of the place, and many places will be coincident. There is [25] not a different place of the part, in which it is moved, when the whole vessel changes its place: it is always the same; for it is in the place where they are that the air and the water (or the parts of the water) succeed each other, not in that place in which they come to be, which is part of the place which is the place of the whole world.

[30] The matter, too, might seem to be place, at least if we consider it in what is at rest and is not separate but in continuity. For just as in change of quality there is something which was formerly black and is now white, or formerly soft and now hard—this is why we say that the matter exists—so place, because it presents a similar phenomenon, is thought to exist—only in the one case we say so because *what* was air is now water, in the other because *where* air formerly was there is now [212^{a}1] water. But the matter, as we said before, is neither separable from the thing nor contains it, whereas place has both characteristics.

Well, then, if place is none of the three—neither the form nor the matter nor an extension which is always there, different from, and over and above, the [5] extension of the thing which is displaced—place necessarily is the one of the four which is left, namely, the boundary of the containing body at which it is in contact with the contained body. (By the contained body is meant what can be moved by way of locomotion.)

Place is thought to be something important and hard to grasp, both because the matter and the shape present themselves along with it, and because the [10] displacement of the body that is moved takes place in a stationary container, for it seems possible that there should be an interval which is other than the bodies which are moved. The air, too, which is thought to be incorporeal, contributes something to the belief: it is not only the boundaries of the vessel which seem to be place, but also what is between them, regarded as empty. Just, in fact, as the vessel is transportable place, so place is a non-portable vessel. So when what is within a thing [15] which is moved, is moved and changes, as a boat on a river, what contains plays the part of a vessel rather than that of place. Place on the other hand is rather what is motionless: so it is rather the whole river that is place, because as a whole it is motionless.

Hence the place of a thing is the innermost motionless boundary of what [20] contains it.

This explains why the middle of the world and the surface which faces us of the rotating system are held to be up and down in the strict and fullest sense for all men: for the one is always at rest, while the inner side of the rotating body remains always coincident with itself. Hence since the light is what is naturally carried up, and the [25] heavy what is carried down, the boundary which contains in the direction of the middle of the universe, and the middle itself, are down, and that which contains in the direction of the extremity, and the extremity itself, are up.

For this reason place is thought to be a kind of surface, and as it were a vessel, i.e. a container of the thing.

Further, place is coincident with the thing, for boundaries are coincident with [30] the bounded.

Chapter 5

If then a body has another body outside it and containing it, it is in place, and if not, not. That is why, even if there were to be water which had not a container, the parts of it will be moved (for one part is contained in another), while the whole will be moved in one sense, but not in another. For as a whole it does not simultaneously change its place, though it will be moved in a circle; for this place is [212^{b}1] the place of its parts. And some parts are moved, not up and down, but in a circle; others up and down, such things namely as admit of condensation and rarefaction.

As was explained, some things are potentially in place, others actually. So, when you have a homogeneous substance which is continuous, the parts are [5] potentially in place: when the parts are separated, but in contact, like a heap, they are actually in place.

Again, some things are *per se* in place, namely every body which is movable either by way of locomotion or by way of increase is *per se* somewhere, but the world, as has been said, is not anywhere as a whole, nor in any place, if, that is, no body contains it. But the line on which it is moved provides a place for its parts; for [10] each is contiguous to the next.

Other things are in place accidentally, as the soul and the world. The latter is, in a way, in place, for all its parts are; for on the circle one part contains another. That is why the upper part is moved in a circle, while the universe is not anywhere. For what is somewhere is itself something, and there must be alongside it some [15] other thing wherein it is and which contains it. But alongside the universe or the Whole there is nothing outside the universe, and for this reason all things are in the world; for the world, we may say, is the universe. Yet their place is not the same as the world. It is part of it, the innermost part of it, which is in contact with the [20] movable body; and for this reason the earth is in water, and this in the air, and the air in the aether, and the aether in the world, but we cannot go on and say that the world is in anything else.

It is clear, too, from these considerations that all the problems which were raised about place will be solved when it is explained in this way.

There is no necessity that the place should grow with the body in it, nor that a [25] point should have a place; nor that two bodies should be in the same place; nor that place should be a corporeal interval (for what is between the boundaries of the place is any body which may chance to be there, not an interval in body).

Further, place is indeed somewhere, not in the sense of being in a place, but as the limit is in the limited; for not everything that is is in place, but only movable body.

[30] Also, it is reasonable that each kind of body should be carried to its own place. For a body which is next in the series and in contact (not by compulsion) is akin, and bodies which are united do not affect each other, while those which are in contact interact on each other.

Nor is it without reason that each should remain naturally in its proper place. For parts do, and that which is in a place has the same relation to its place as a [213ᵃ1] separable part to its whole, as when one moves a part of water or air: so, too, air is related to water, for the one is like matter, the other form—water is the matter of air, air as it were the actuality of water; for water is potentially air, while air is potentially water, though in another way.

These distinctions will be drawn more carefully later. On the present occasion [5] it was necessary to refer to them: what has now been stated obscurely will then be made more clear. If the matter and the fulfilment are the same thing (for water is both, the one potentially, the other in fulfilment), water will be related to air in a way as part to whole. That is why these have contact: it is organic union when both become actually one.

[10] This concludes my account of place—both of its existence and of its nature. . . .

READING

On the Heavens

Book I

Chapter 1

[268ª1] Knowledge about nature is clearly concerned for the most part with bodies and magnitudes, and their properties and changes, and, further, with all the principles that belong to this kind of substance. For of things formed naturally, some are bodies and [5] magnitudes, others possess bodies and magnitude, and others are the principles of those that possess body and magnitude.

That which is divisible into ever-divisible parts is continuous, and that which is divisible in all ways is body. Of magnitude, that divisible in one way is line, that in two surface, that in three body; and besides these there is no other magnitude, because three [10] is equivalent to all and "in three ways" to "in all." For, as the Pythagoreans say, the whole cosmos and all things are determined by "three"; for end, middle, and beginning possess the number of the whole, and these are the number of the triad. Which is why, having taken it from nature as if it were one of her laws, we also [15] use this number in the service of the gods. We apply predicates also in this way; for we call two objects "both" and two people "both," and do not say "all," but we first use this term in respect of three. We follow these practices as has been said, due to nature herself pointing us in this direction.

[20] And so, since "all things" and "the whole" and "the complete" do not differ from each other according to their form, but, if indeed they do, in their matter and the things of which they are said, then body alone would be complete among magnitudes; for it alone is determined by "three," and this is "all." Being divisible in three ways, it is divisible in all ways; [25] of the other magnitudes, one is divisible in two ways, the other in one; for the manner in which the magnitudes are numbered is also the manner in which they are divisible and continuous. For one is continuous in one way, another in two, and the third is such in every direction. Every magnitude, therefore, that is divisible is also continuous.

But whether everything continous is divisible is not yet clear from the present considerations. This, however, is clear: there [268ᵇ1] cannot be a transition to another kind of magnitude, as from length to surface, and from surface to body; for magnitude of such a kind would no longer be complete. For the change must occur according to the defect, but what is complete cannot be deficient; [5] for it is complete in all directions.

Consequently, each of the bodies in the form of a part of the whole cosmos is such by definition—for it has all the dimensions—but is determined in respect of the next part in contact with it, which is why each of the bodies is, in a way, many. But the whole of which these are parts must be complete, and, as the word signifies, [10] must be so in all directions, and not in one direction but not in another.

Chapter 2

An investigation into the nature of the whole—whether it is unlimited in size or its total bulk is limited—must be made later. For the moment let us consider its specific parts, making this our starting-point.

All physical bodies [15] and magnitudes are in themselves, we say, mobile in respect of place; for we maintain that nature is a principle of movement in them. And all movement in respect of place, which we call locomotion, is either straight, in a circle, or a combination of these; for these two alone are simple. The reason is that these magnitudes alone are simple, [20] the straight line and the circular. Movement about the centre, then, is in a circle, movement upwards and downwards is rectilinear. By "movement upwards" I mean movement away from the centre, by "movement downwards" that towards the centre. So that all simple locomotion must be away from the centre, towards the centre, or about the centre. This seems to follow [25] reasonably what was said at the beginning; for both body and its movement reach completion in "three."

Since some bodies are simple and others compounds of these (I mean by "simple" all those that have a principle of movement according to nature, such as fire, earth, their forms, and their congeners), movements must also be simple or some kind of combination, [269^{a}1] and simple bodies must have simple movements, compound bodies combined movements (moving according to that component which predominates).

Thus, if there is such a thing as simple movement, and movement in a circle is simple, and the movement of a simple body is simple and simple movement belongs to a simple body (for even if [5] simple movement belongs to a compound body, it will belong according to that component which predominates), there must be a simple body that is such as to move in a circle according to its own nature. For although this may undergo the movement of another, different body by force, according to nature it cannot, if the natural movement that belongs to each of the simple bodies is single.

Further, if movement contrary to nature is contrary to [10] that according to nature, and one thing is contrary to one thing, then, since movement in a circle is simple, unless it were according to the nature of the moving body, it must be contrary to its nature. If, then, fire or some other such body is that which moves in a circle, locomotion according to its nature will be contrary to movement in a circle. But one thing is contrary to one thing: movement upwards and that downwards [15] are contrary to one other. If, however, that which moves in a circle contrary to nature is some other body, some other movement will belong to it according to nature. This is impossible: for if movement upwards belongs to it, it will be fire or air, but if movement downwards, water or earth.

Moreover, such locomotion must be primary. For that which is complete is prior [20] by nature to what is incomplete, and the circle is a complete entity, whereas no straight line is so. For an unlimited line cannot be complete (for it would then have an end and a limit), nor can any that are limited (for something is outside of all these, since it is possible to increase any one of them). And so, if primary movement does belong to a body primary by nature, and movement [25] in a circle is prior to rectilinear movement, and movement in a straight line belongs to the simple bodies (for fire moves upwards in a straight line, and earthy bodies downwards towards the centre), movement in a circle must belong to one of the simple bodies; for we said that the locomotion of mixed bodies is according to that component which predominates in the mixture of the simple bodies.

[30] From these arguments it is clear, then, that there is some other bodily substance besides the formations found here, more divine and prior to all these. If, further, one were to accept that all movement is either according to nature or contrary to nature, and that movement contrary to nature for one body is according to nature for another, as is the case with movement upwards and downwards—for movement contrary to nature for fire is according to nature for earth, and *vice versa*—[269[b]1] then movement in a circle, too, since it is contrary to nature for these, must be according to the nature of some other body.

In addition to these considerations, if movement in a circle is locomotion according to nature for some particular body, it is clear that it would be a simple and primary one, such as [5] to move in a circle according to its nature, just as fire moves upwards and earth downwards. If those bodies that move in a circle move around contrary to nature, it would be amazing and completely absurd for this movement alone which is contrary to nature to be continuous and everlasting; for in other cases those bodies that move contrary to nature are observed to perish quickly. [10] And so, if that which moves in a circle *is* fire, as some say, this movement is no less contrary to nature for it than movement downwards; for we see that the movement of fire is that away from the centre in a straight line.

Which is why, if all these arguments are taken together, one may be confident that there is a body different from those [15] found here, separated and apart from those about us, its nature the more noble in proportion to its distance from those here....

Chapter 8

[276ª18] Let us now say why there cannot be many worlds either, for we said this had to be looked at, if it is not considered proved in general [20] of bodies that none can exist outside of this world, but that the argument applies only to those bodies with no definite position.

All bodies both rest and move both naturally and by force, and where they rest without force they move to naturally as well, and where they move to without force, there they rest naturally as well; [25] on the other hand, where they rest by force they move to by force as well, and where they move to by force, there they rest by force as well. Further, if one locomotion is by force, its opposite is natural. If, then, earth moves from another world to the centre of our world by force, it will move from here to there naturally; and if earth from there rests here without force, it will move to here [30] naturally as well. For natural movement is single.

Further, all the worlds must be formed from the same types of body, if, at any rate, they are similar in their nature. Yet each body must possess the same [276ᵇ1] power, I mean, for instance, fire and earth and the bodies between them; for if these are homonyms and the names of bodies in our own and other worlds are not used on the basis of an identity of form, then the universe could only be called a world homonymously as well. It is clear therefore that one of these bodies is such as to move from the centre, [5] another such as to move to the centre, if fire *is* completely like in form to fire and so too for each of the other bodies, just as are the portions of fire in this world.

That things must be so, however, is clear from the assumptions concerning movements: for the movements are limited, and each element is spoken of in terms of [10] each movement. In consequence, if movements *are* the same, the elements must be everywhere the same.

Therefore the parts of earth in another world are such as to move to the centre here and fire there towards the extremity of our world. Yet this is impossible: for if this happens, [15] earth in its own world must move upwards, while fire must move to the centre, and similarly earth from this world must move from the centre naturally in moving to the centre in that world, because of the way in which the worlds are mutually positioned. For either we ought not to lay down that the simple bodies in the many worlds have the same nature, or [20] in saying that they do we must make the centre single, as well as the extremity; yet if this is so, there cannot be more than one world.

To think that the simple bodies have a different nature the more or less distant they are from their own place is unreasonable—for what is the difference in saying that they are distant to this or that extent? They will differ [25] in proportion to their increase in distance, but their form will remain the same.

Yet they must certainly possess some type of movement, for *that* they move is evident. Shall we say, then, that all movements, even contraries, are by force? Yet what is not of a nature to move at all cannot be moved by force. If, therefore, some type of natural movement belongs to them, [30] the movement of individual bodies of the same form must be in relation to a place that is numerically single, that is, in relation to this particular centre and this particular extremity. Now if the movements are in relation to places that are the same in form [277ᵃ1] but many, given that individual bodies are also many but each is undifferentiated in form, then it will not be that this and not that portion of an element has a place of this sort, but each portion alike will have one; for all portions of an element are equally undifferentiated from one another in form, but any one is numerically different from any other. I mean [5] this: if the portions here relate to one another in the same way as they relate to portions in another world, then a given portion from this world will not relate any differently to portions in another world than it does to those in the same world as it, but in the same way; for they do not differ from one another in form. Consequently, either our assumptions must be questioned, or [10] the centre as well as the extremity is single. If this is so there also has to be only one world and not many, by these same proofs and the same necessities.

It is clear from other considerations also that there is some location to which it is natural for earth as well as for fire to move. For in general, what moves changes from something to something, [15] and these—the "from which" and the "to which"—differ in form. Now, all change is limited; for instance, what recovers its health changes from sickness to health, what grows does so from a small to a large size. Therefore what moves does so as well; for this also comes to be from somewhere to somewhere. Therefore the "from which" and the "to which" a thing naturally moves have to differ in form, just as what recovers its health [20] has no random goal nor one that the mover wants.

Therefore fire and earth do not move to an unlimited extent either, but towards opposite points; in terms of place "up" is opposed to "down," so that these will be the limits of locomotion. Since even movement in a circle has in a sense opposite points in respect of the diameter (though nothing is contrary to the whole movement), [25] consequently these too have, in a way, movement towards opposite, limited points. Therefore there has to be some goal and not movement to infinity.

A proof that there is not movement to infinity is the fact that earth, by as much as it is closer to the centre, and fire, by as much as it is closer to the upper place, move more quickly. Now if the movement were unlimited, [30] the speed would also be unlimited, and if the speed were, so too would the weight or lightness be; for just as, if one body were fast by virtue of being lower, another would be as fast by virtue of its weight, so if the increase in weight were unlimited, the increase in speed would be as well.

[277^{b}1] Yet nor is it by the agency of another that one element moves upwards and another downwards; nor is it by force, by "ejection," as some people maintain. For in that case a greater amount of fire would move upwards, and a greater amount of earth downwards, more slowly. As it is, however, the opposite happens: the greater amount of fire and that of earth invariably move more quickly [5] to their places. Nor would they move more quickly as they approach their goal if they moved by force, that is, by "ejection"; for all things move more slowly the further they get from the cause of the enforced movement, and the place from which they move by force they move towards without force. And so by considering these points one may be sufficiently assured of what we are saying.

Further, the matter might also [10] be shown by means of the arguments from first philosophy, as well as on the basis of movement in a circle, which would need to be everlasting here and in the other worlds alike.

It will become clear by considering the matter in this way that the world has to be single. For since there are three bodily elements, the places of the elements will also be three, [15] one about the centre belonging to the body that is situated beneath the others, another, the extremity, belonging to the body that moves in a circle, and the third between these two which belongs to the middle body. For what rises has to be in this place. For unless it is there, it will be outside; but it cannot be outside. For one body is weightless, another has weight, [20] and the lower place belongs to the body with weight, if the place towards the centre *does* belong to what is heavy. Yet nor could it be there counternaturally, for the place will belong to another naturally, but there was no other body. Therefore it has to be in the region between. What the differences in this region are we shall say later.

Concerning the bodily elements, then, of what sort they are [25] and how many, and what the place of each is, and, further, in general the number of places there are, is clear from what we have said. . . .

Book II

Chapter 4

[286^{b}10] The world must have a spherical figure, since this is both most appropriate to its substance and by nature primary.

Let us speak generally, however, about what sort of figure is primary, both among plane surfaces and among solids. Every plane figure, then, is either rectilinear or curvilinear. The rectilinear [15] is bounded by several lines, the curvilinear by a single line. Since in each class the one is prior by nature to the many, and the simple to the compound, the circle will be the primary plane figure.

Further, if the complete is that outside of which none of its parts can be found, as it was defined [20] earlier, and there is always the possibility of adding to a straight line, but never to the circumference of a circle, it is clear that the line bounding the circle will be complete; in consequence, if the complete is prior to the incomplete, the circle will also thereby be the primary figure.

Similarly, the sphere is also the primary solid, since it alone is bounded by a single [25] surface, whereas rectilinear solids are bounded by many; for as the circle is among plane surfaces, so is the sphere among solids.

Further, even those who divide bodies into surfaces and generate them from surfaces apparently are witnesses to this; for alone of the solids they do not divide the sphere, seeing how it does not possess more [30] than one surface; for the division into plane surfaces is not effected in the way that someone who cut a thing up into parts would divide the whole, but by dividing it up into parts that are specifically different.

That, then, the sphere is the primary solid figure is clear. When one orders figures numerically, it is also most reasonable to lay them down in this order, the circle corresponding to the one, the triangle [287^{a}1] to the dyad, since it is equal to two right angles. If, however, the one corresponds to the triangle, the circle will no longer be a figure.

Since the primary figure belongs to the primary body, and the body in the outermost revolution is the first body, then the body which undergoes locomotion in a circle will be spherical. [5] Also, therefore, the body continuous with it; for a body continuous with what is spherical is spherical. So too the bodies towards the centre of these; for bodies bounded by what is spherical and wholly in contact with it must be spherical; and the bodies below the locomotion of the planets are in contact with the sphere above them. In consequence, [10] it will be spheriform as a whole, since everything is in contact and continuous with the spheres.

Further, since the whole is seen, and is being assumed, to rotate in a circle, and it has been shown that outside of the outermost revolution is neither void nor place, it must also thereby be spherical. For if it is rectilinear, [15] there will turn out to be place and body and void outside of it. For the rectilinear, turning in a circle, will never occupy the same space; rather, where previously there was body, now there will not be, and where there is not at present body, again there will be, due to the changing position of the angles.

The same goes even if it were to be some other shape with unequal [20] lines from the centre, e.g. lentil- or egg-shaped; for in all cases there will turn out to be both place and void outside of its locomotion, due to the fact that the entire shape does not occupy the same space.

Further, if the locomotion of the heavens is the measure of movements due to it alone being continuous and regular and everlasting, and if in each class [25] the smallest member is the measure, and if the quickest movement is the shortest, it is clear that the movement of the heavens will be the quickest of all movements. Yet the line of the circle is shortest of those that go from and to the same point, and the quickest movement is that along the shortest line; so that, if the heavens move in a circle and move most quickly, [30] they have to be spherical.

One may also be assured of this on the basis of the bodies situated about the centre. For if water lies about the earth, and air about the water, and fire about the air, and the upper bodies on the same line of reasoning (for these are not continuous, but are in contact with them), [287[b]1] and the surface of water is spherical, and what is continuous with what is spherical or lies about what is spherical must itself be so as well; then it will also thereby be clear that the world is spherical.

Yet that the surface of water [5] is like this is clear, if one takes it as an assumption that water is such as always to flow into what is more hollow, and that what is nearer the centre is more hollow. Let, then, the lines AB and AC be drawn from the centre, and let them be joined by line BC. The line AD drawn to the base, then, is smaller than those from the centre; [10] therefore the place is more hollow. In consequence, the water will flow about it until it is equalised. Now, line AE is equal to those from the centre. Consequently, the water must reach the lines from the centre, since it will rest at that moment. Now, the line in contact with those from the centre is the circumference; therefore the surface BEC of the water is spherical.

That, then, the world is spherical [15] is clear from these points, as well as that it is accurately turned in such a way that nothing made by hand nor anything else that appears before our eyes comes close to it. For none of the things from which its formation has been taken can receive so regular and accurate a finish as the nature of the surrounding body; [20] for it is clear that the bodies at successive distances from the co-ordinate elements are also in proportion, just as water is in proportion to earth. . . .

Chapter 13

[293[a]15] It remains to speak of the earth—where it lies, whether it is something at rest or in motion and about its shape.

Concerning its position, then, not everyone has the same opinion; rather, whereas most people say that it lies at the centre—all those, in fact, who maintain that the entire world is limited—[20] the Italian thinkers called Pythagoreans hold a contrary position: they maintain that at the centre there is fire, whilst the earth, which is one of the stars, in moving about the centre in a circle produces night and day. Further, they make up another earth opposite to this one, which they give the name "anti-earth," [25] not seeking their theories and explanations in relation to the apparent facts, but dragging the apparent facts towards, and endeavouring to co-ordinate them with, certain of their theories and opinions.

Many others might think along with them that one should not assign the region at the centre to the earth; these others consider what is credible not on the basis of the apparent facts, but [30] rather on the basis of their theories. For they deem it proper that the most honourable region belongs to what is most honourable, and that fire is more honourable than earth, the limit than what is between limits, and that the extremity and the centre are limits. In consequence, reckoning from these points, they do not think that earth lies at the centre of the sphere, but rather [293^{b}1] fire.

Further, the Pythagoreans at any rate, because it is especially proper that the most important point in the whole universe is guarded, and because the centre is the most important point, call the fire that occupies this region the "guard of Zeus"—as if "centre" is used in an absolute sense, and the [5] centre of the magnitude is also the centre of the thing or of the nature. Yet just as with animals the centre of the animal and of the body are not the same, so one should suppose it more so in the case of the entire world as well. For this reason, then, there is no need for them to fear for the whole universe, nor to introduce a guard at the [10] centre; instead they should seek the other centre, what sort of thing it is and where it is. For that centre is a principle and is honourable, whereas the local centre is more like an end than a beginning, since the thing that is determined is the centre, but what determines is the limit. It is what surrounds, i.e. the limit, that is more honourable than what is limited: the one is the [15] matter, the other the substance of the formation. . . .

Chapter 14

[296^{a}24] Let us say first whether the earth has a movement or rests, since, [25] as we said, some people make it one of the stars, whereas others put it at the centre and say that it winds i.e. moves about the central axis. That this is impossible becomes clear by taking as a starting-point the following: if it moves, whether it is outside of the centre or at the centre, then it has to undergo this movement by force; [30] for the movement does not belong to the earth itself, since each of its parts would in that case have this locomotion; as it is, however, they all move in a straight line towards the centre. Which is why the movement cannot be everlasting, given that it is enforced and counter-natural; the order of the cosmos, however, is everlasting.

Further, all the bodies that undergo the circular locomotion are observed to be left behind and to move with more [296^{b}1] than a single locomotion, except for the primary locomotion, so that the earth must also, whether it moves about the centre or lying at the centre, undergo two locomotions. If this happens, however, there has to occur passing and turnings of the fixed stars. [5] Yet this is not observed to occur, and instead the same stars always rise and set at the same regions of the earth.

Further, the natural locomotion of the parts and of the whole earth is towards the centre of the whole universe; indeed, it is because of this that it now lies at the centre. One might be puzzled, however, since the centre of both is the same, [10] as to toward which of them bodies with weight and the parts of earth move naturally: is it because it is the centre of the whole universe, or because it is the centre of the earth? It must, then, be towards the centre of the whole universe, since light bodies and fire, in moving in the direction opposite to heavy bodies, move towards the extremity of the region that surrounds [15] the centre. It so happens, however, that the earth and the whole universe have the same centre; for heavy bodies also move towards the centre of the earth, but incidentally, in so far as it has its centre in the centre of the whole universe. A sign that they move towards the centre of the earth as well is the fact that weights moving toward it move not in parallel trajectories, [20] but at equal angles, so that they are moving towards a single centre, which is also that of the earth.

It is evident, therefore, that the earth must be at the centre and motionless, both for the reasons given, and because weights thrown straight upward by force return to the same point, even if the force flings them an unlimited distance.

[25] That, then, the earth neither moves nor lies outside the centre, is evident from these points; in addition to them, the reason for its rest is clear from what has been said. For if it is such as to move by nature from anywhere toward the centre, as it is observed to do, and fire such as to move from the centre to the extremity, it is impossible [30] for any part of it to move from the centre unless by being forced; for a single body has a single locomotion and a simple body has a simple locomotion, but not contrary locomotions, and locomotion from the centre is contrary to that to the centre. If, therefore, it is impossible for any part to move from the centre, it is evident that it is in fact still more impossible for the earth as a whole; for the place to which the part is such as to move is also the place to which the whole is such as to move; consequently, [297^{a}1] if it cannot move without a stronger force, it would have to stay at the centre.

What the mathematicians say in astronomy also testifies to this, since the apparent facts—that is, [5] the changing of the configurations in terms of which the arrangement of the stars is determined—result from the supposition that the earth lies at the centre.

Concerning, then, the earth's place, and the manner of its rest or movement, enough has been said....

[297^b23] Further support also derives from perceptual evidence, since lunar eclipses would not [25] have such demarcating lines; for, as it is, in its monthly configurations the moon takes on all manner of distinguishing line (indeed, it becomes straight and gibbous and crescent), but during eclipses it always has a convex dividing line, and so, if it is eclipsed because of the interposition of the earth, the circumference of the earth, [30] being spherical, will be responsible for the shape.

Further, from the appearance of the stars not only is it clear that it is round, but also not great in size; for if we make a slight change of position southward or northward, the horizon visibly changes, so that the [298^a1] stars above our head change greatly, and the same stars do not appear when we travel northward or southward; for some stars are observed in Egypt and about Cyprus, but are not observed in the regions towards the north, [5] and those stars seen continuously in the northern regions set in these regions. In consequence, not only is it clear from this that the earth's shape is round, but also that it has the shape of a sphere of no great size, since it would not make it obvious so quickly when we change our position by so little.

Which is why those who suppose that [10] the area about the Pillars of Heracles adjoins that about India, and that in this way the sea is single, do not seem to suppose anything too incredible. Using elephants as their evidence, they say that their kind occurs in both of these outlying regions, supposing that it is due to the connection between these outlying areas [15] that they are like this.

As well as this, all the mathematicians who attempt to reckon up the size of the circumference say that it approaches four hundred thousand stades. Judging from this evidence, not only must the bulk of the earth be spherical, but also not great in relation to the size of the other [20] stars.

COMMENTARY

4.1 Introduction

Aristotle lived during the fourth century BC, after Zeno and overlapping with Plato (his teacher) and just before Euclid. His influence was enormous, first in Greece, then in the Arab world, and finally in medieval Europe after the thirteenth century AD, during which Aristotelian thought formed the basis for much of what was counted as knowledge. His work spanned the now separate fields of philosophy (e.g., ethics and epistemology), science (especially in biology and physics), and aesthetics. The early modern period (around the mid-1600s, starting with Descartes in this collection) saw the final replacement of Aristotelian science with the theories that we recognize today. We will read Aristotle for the important questions he poses about space, but we will also bear in mind that the picture he gave dominated Europe for nearly five hundred years, either directly or through his interpreters.

To best understand Aristotle, it is important to know something about the texts. Compared with the dialogues of Plato, they are typically far less polished and are more like drafts toward more complete manuscripts (such works are mentioned by early commentators but sadly no longer exist). Indeed, many scholars believe that the surviving texts are notes Aristotle used when giving lectures, to be expanded upon by further discussion in class. (One can also imagine them being reworked over time—and "edited" by transcribers—which would explain their repetitions and tensions.) Thus, although the works are a challenge to read, they are also exciting to study because they offer an unedited insight into how Aristotle thought and worked.

It will also be helpful to appreciate the method that Aristotle proposed, particularly for science. He argued (in his *Posterior Analytics*) that scientific explanations should take the form of logical deductions from first principles, as Euclid would later deduce geometric theorems from his axioms. But if all the subject matter of some science is to be explained in terms of basic principles, how are we to understand the principles themselves? In the absence of yet more basic postulates, they can have no scientific explanation, and instead they must be developed and grasped from experience, through an innate power of comprehension of the thinking subject's mind. While this account of scientific method is in a sense "empirical," it differs from that developed in the introduction, for it does not involve justifying the basic principles by testing their consequences. According to our interpretation, Aristotle believed that our comprehension of the basic principles behind our experience was sufficient justification alone.

Ordinarily, a modern scientist arguing for a new idea must not only produce new tests, but must also persuade her colleagues that it accords with their basic scientific beliefs and generally accepted experimental data. Something similar holds for Aristotle: in practice, to establish first principles he first lists reputable basic opinions on a topic, and then evaluates proposed theories against them. Book IV, chapter 4 of the *Physics* is an example of this methodology at work. To find out what "place" is, Aristotle first lists "the various characteristics which are supposed correctly to belong to it" (210^b34*), and then rejects theories that disagree with those characteristics. Only a theory compatible with these suppositions is acceptable. This methodology Aristotle calls "dialectic" as it is like the discussion of a proposal back and forth between people with common assumptions.

We have just stressed a similarity between the Aristotelian and the modern scientific method, but Aristotle does not read like a modern text, so what are the differences? We cannot possibly do full justice to this question here, but the following remarks might be useful. In general, for both Aristotle and in modern science, if a principle is to be accepted it must be compatible with the fundamental beliefs of experts whose knowledge is rooted in experience. In modern science, these experts are highly trained scientists. Their knowledge is grounded in delicate experiments that allow the study of a "hidden" nature that can be very different from that of everyday experience. For instance, consider the care with which a chemical must be prepared to determine its unique properties, and contrast the hidden atomic structure of some element with its appearance as a liquid in a test tube.

But in Aristotle's world there was far less specialization, and hence the range of "reputable" opinions was much broader. Anyone educated or with relevant experiences was potentially an "expert" and a source of common assumptions to be satisfied by scientific theories. Furthermore, although Aristotle thought that discovering basic principles required careful reason and investigation, he did not think that the principles would be of a radically different kind from our everyday concepts. That is, he held that there is no fundamentally different hidden structure underlying reality. Thus he thought that ordinary observations and everyday concepts should be sufficient to understand nature, and that one could reliably comprehend scientific first principles without sophisticated, abductive testing. Of course, modern science teaches that Aristotle was wrong in this expectation; and even his work does not always seem to fit "everyday understanding."

---

*All references are to the *Physics* or *On the Heavens* and are according to the bracketed numbers in the text. These derive from the page and line numbers of a standard edition of Aristotle by Bekker, in 1831.

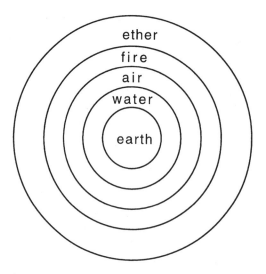

Figure 4.1
Aristotle's universe in its natural state.

Finally, before our more detailed reading, we should overview the account of space that he developed. In Aristotle's cosmology the universe is a finite sphere. At rest at the center is the (spherical) planet Earth (*On the Heavens,* Bk. II, chaps. 4 and 13–14). It is composed of the element earth and is surrounded sequentially by the elements water, air, and fire. Containing it is the region of the stars and planets, composed of the fifth element, "ether." In an ideal state, the earth would be a perfect sphere at rest at the center, surrounded by static shells of water, air, and fire, about which shells of ether would rotate. The outer shell, referred to as the "heavens" (though this term can mean other things for Aristotle too), extends from the moon's orbit to the edge of the universe. In the less than ideal actual world, any object not in the appropriate place will, as a principle of nature, move toward it. Thus water poured from a bucket falls, and air released under water rises, in agreement with ordinary experience. Of course, it is possible to force objects into unnatural motions, say, by lifting up water in a bucket or trapping an air pocket under water, but the force must be continually applied to maintain the unnatural state.

Two things are crucial to this account: first, the elements move to their appropriate places, so Aristotle requires a scientific notion of place. The readings from the *Physics* deal with this topic. Second, objects move in order to reach their proper places—to achieve certain goals. So Aristotle's theory is *teleological*: it assumes that natural phenomena occur for some purpose. One of the key innovations of modern science is the realization that such factors have no place in the explanations of (at least physical) science. For instance, gravitational force is not now thought to exist "for the purpose" of bringing rocks to the ground.

With these points in mind, we will now study Aristotle's theory of space in more detail.

4.2 Place

In Book IV of the *Physics*, Aristotle enumerates common beliefs about place, propounds puzzles surrounding it, and tests theories against them: he applies the method of dialectic. The lists of beliefs and puzzles raise many important questions about space, but in order to understand Aristotle's view of place and its role in motion, we shall focus on just a few items.

First, there are the common beliefs. (1) A place can be separated from the objects it contains: "What now contains air formerly contained water, so clearly the place ... was something different from both" (208^b6). (2) Places don't have places. This view is implicit in Zeno's paradox of place: "if everything that exists has a place, place too will have a place, and so on *ad infinitum*" (209^a24). If every place has a place, then we begin a regress which concludes that there is a real, not potential, infinity of places—an impossibility for Aristotle. (3) The difference between up and down (and left and right) is not just relative to us but absolute: "in nature each is distinct, taken apart by itself" (208^b17). It would be interesting to consider to what extent we accept these propositions, but we will be more concerned to see where they lead Aristotle.

Second, there are the puzzles. We will focus on just a pair of these. They correspond to two of the central interests of this book: "What kind of thing is space?" and "How does it interact with matter?" First, place is extended in three dimensions as are material objects, and yet it is not itself material: "Now it has ... length, breadth, and depth.... But the place cannot be body" (209^a5). And second, how does space affect physical objects, for if it doesn't then it appears to be irrelevant to physics: "Of what in things is space the cause?" (209^a20).

Aristotle considers four theories about place: place is either "[a] the shape, or [b] the matter, or [c] some sort of extension between the extremities, or [d] the extremities" (211^b7). Our job is to see what these proposals mean, and how Aristotle is led to reject the first three by measuring them against the common notions and puzzles.

(a) By "shape," Aristotle means the outer surface of an object. But place cannot be shape because the surface of an object cannot be separated from it, and so this theory is incompatible with notion (1) (211^b10–14). (Of course, a particular shape will be "separated" from an object if it changes shape; perhaps what Aristotle should say is that sometimes objects move, changing place, without changing shape.)

(b) When Aristotle refutes the idea that place is matter, he is explicitly attacking Plato's view (209^a11–16), which we discussed in the introduction. This theory is rejected on the same grounds as the last proposal: the matter of an object cannot be separated from it, and so the view conflicts with (1) (211^b30–212^a2).

(c) The third possible theory suggests that place may be some sort of "extension between the extremities." By "extremity," Aristotle does not mean an object's outer surface, but the inner surface of whatever contains the object: the inside surface of a bottle containing water, for instance. The "extension between" this surface is the volume enclosed; however, this "volume" is not the matter enclosed, but something independent of the object. This proposal is like that which we used to understand the Euclidean hypothesis, in which space is a separate container of matter, and place is a region of space. The difference is that Aristotle sees the region as attached to the material container, and so not as independent of all matter. His argument against this view (211^b19–29) is not terribly clear, but we can take it as showing an incompatibility with common belief (2). Consider a bucket of water; according to the current proposal, the place of the water is the space bounded by the sides of the bucket and the air on top. As the water pours out, the surface drops, and the place of the remaining water changes continuously. In fact, at each instant the water is in a "different place" because it has a different boundary with the air, and the "extremities" define the "extension." But each such place will be stacked within the previous places like the layers of a Russian doll: "there will be another place which is the place of the place, and many places will be coincident" (211^b23). This consequence is inconsistent with (2). If we think of space as a matter-independent Euclidean plane, we can put the issue this way: Any finite region of space is contained by other finite regions, therefore every place has a place, which begins the infinite regress that (2) insists we avoid. But in modern mathematics we are comfortable with infinities, and so we would not accept Aristotle's argument.

(d) As Sherlock Holmes says, "once you have eliminated the impossible, whatever remains, however improbable, must be the case." In this way, Aristotle adopts the fourth view concerning place. The place of an object is "the boundary of the containing body at which it is in contact with the contained body" (212^a6). Since Aristotle rejects the existence of vacuums, this will be no distance at all from the surface of the contained body: the shape and extremities coincide. As Aristotle emphasizes, this is a commonsense view, for it is common sense to think of place as similar to some kind of vessel, as it is on this view. It is also worth noting that this basic spatial notion is, for Aristotle, defined by observable material objects, not by pure Euclidean space itself. The issue of whether space is independent of matter or must be understood in terms of material objects will feature prominently in later readings from Descartes to Kant. Let me stress, however, that Aristotle does not avoid Zeno's challenge to the Euclidean hypothesis by asserting that space is to be understood in terms of material objects and not as something independent of matter. He believes that material objects are geometric, and so his conception of matter will also fall if Euclidean geometry is inconsistent. For example, Aristotle accepted that material objects, such as running tracks, were (potentially) divisible into endless halves, and so he had to respond to the Dichotomy.

In Aristotle's dialectical method one has to show that a theory is compatible with common views and that it resolves the puzzles. Although Aristotle doesn't say so explicitly, if place is a containing surface then an object is separable from its place, as demonstrated by pouring water from a jug. Hence his theory is consistent with (1). Places as inner surfaces don't themselves have places, though they are in the containing body as parts, "as the limit is in the limited" (212^b29), avoiding Zeno's paradox of place and satisfying (2). The first puzzle is resolved because place itself—a two-dimensional surface, with no thickness—is only three-dimensional in the sense of bounding a volume (212^b25). To show that Aristotle's view of space is compatible with (3), so that up and down are absolute and it answers the question of the physical role of space, we need to move on to his theory of motion: mechanics.

4.3 Motion

"Of what in things is space the cause" for Aristotle? The answer sketched previously is that the elements, or "simple bodies," naturally move to certain places in the universe. (*On the Heavens*, Bk. I, chap. 2 lays out the theory.) Since places are parts of space, space, roughly speaking, is the cause of natural motions: it makes heavy things fall and light things rise. However, Aristotle's view is subtler than this reply allows. (Aristotle never fully explains the role of natural places in his mechanics, so the following is a plausible account of what he intended, extrapolated from his explicit views on causation and motion; the story for ether is rather more complex.)

First of all, the answer makes it sound as if the natural places attract the elements by somehow reaching out and pulling them in. But this is not the case; instead it is the internal nature of the elements to seek out their proper places. Aristotle puts it this way: Everything has a certain natural "form" that in the ideal course of events it would manifest. For instance, the form of a plant might include being a certain height and shape and producing a certain kind of fruit. Not everything will actually realize its form at a given time, as seen in the example of a seed: though it takes time for it to grow, it always contains the form of the plant. The form is something internal, and so the appropriate form of the plant does not depend on the external environment: interference can only prevent the plant from obtaining its form. Analogously, part of the ideal form of an element is its occupying its proper place, and thus its nature causes it to move to that place. For instance, part of the ideal form of the element earth is location at the center of the univese, so any earth not at the center moves there. In the case of fire, the ideal form is to be just below the heavens, and so fire rises. An analogy might help: if place "caused" motion then it would be as if one person grabbed another and pulled him toward her. On Aristotle's view it is as if he had instead walked over of his own volition—the form of an element is akin to the desire inside him. This analogy also captures the teleological aspect of Aristotle's philosophy: one person walks over in order to stand next to the second, and earth moves to achieve its goal of being centrally located. (On the other hand, this analogy downplays Aristotle's claim [*Physics*, Bk. VIII, chap. 4] that in some lesser sense there must be an external source of motion up or down.)

Thus space plays a physical role for Aristotle in that the forms of the elements naturally make them move "away from the centre or towards the centre or about the centre" (268^b23), into their appropriate places. In other words, his account of place does resolve the problem of the causal role of space. We can also see that it is compatible with view (3), that up and down are absolute.

What Aristotle has in mind is that, for instance, if one climbed a ladder, then a high shelf might no longer be positioned up, relatively, but down: "the same thing is often both ... up and down" (208^b16). But there is an absolute sense of up and of down which is independent of the position of any person: at the top or foot of the ladder, one will always point in the same direction when asked to indicate "up." Aristotle's discussion of this phenomenon (212^a14–28) unfortunately does not find him at his most eloquent. However, his argument seems to run as follows. First, place is taken to be some kind of vessel or container, of which there are two sorts: those that move and those that do not. In a sense, the truer places are those of the latter kind (the original Greek supports our understanding Aristotle as saying that "ideally," places are motionless). For instance, to talk about something moving, we have to identify some motionless places through which it moves. It would be no use if its place were moving with it, as the water surrounding a boat drifting downstream does: if this were the case the moving boat would not change place, which is a contradiction. Instead, Aristotle claims, place is "the innermost motionless boundary of what contains..." (212[a]20): that is, presumably, the river banks in our example. (As commentators have pointed out, this view seems problematic: particularly, it clashes with the common opinion that objects and their places are the same size [211[a]1].)

Since the earth sits at the center of the universe and the spherical shell of stars and planets just rotates, two such motionless places do exist: the inner boundary of the air and water surrounding the earth and the inner boundary of the heavens. These places—and by extrapolation the middle and the entirety of the heavens—are the absolute up and down demanded by common opinion (3) (212[a]25–28). Here we have the suggestion (developed far further by Mach) that the specific natural motion of an object depends on the arrangement of the matter of the universe. For instance, the specific motion of a piece of fire depends on the direction of "up," which in turn depends on the position of the heavens. (Whether Aristotle consistently held to this view is contentious.)

Many of the key features of Aristotle's mechanics will be central in the later readings, so it is valuable to emphasize certain points and their relation to later theories of motion. A useful distinction here is the modern one between *kinematics* and *dynamics*: the former refers to the study of natural motions, and the second to the study of constrained motions. Kinematics is the theory of what would happen in the absence of forces, and dynamics of what happens when forces act. One of the pillars of Aristotelian mechanics is the implicit recognition that such a distinction should be drawn, and that if one first isolates how objects would move naturally, one can then describe how deviant motions are produced by forces. This is a basic idea that underlies modern mechanics, whether Newton's, Einstein's, or quantum mechanics, and Aristotle was the first to articulate it clearly—albeit not explicitly, and not in modern terms.

Aristotle took nature to be much as it appears to common perception, and so his view of what is natural turned out to be quite wrong. He took motion to certain places to be natural, and forces to be required to prevent heavy things from falling or light things from rising. On the view we inherited from Newton, the natural motion of an object is constant speed in a straight line, from which forces cause deflections. On this view, final position plays no role at all: the straight path does not depend on distant places, and though an object might end up in a certain place, it certainly doesn't make sense to think of it as its natural "goal." Indeed, when an object does move toward a certain place, it is typically because there is another body there exerting a force. For instance, for Newton, heavy things fall because they are attracted to the Earth (just how the Earth can "reach out and grab" an object is another fascinating story), but for Aristotle, they fall because that is their nature. In other words, motion to a final place is kinematical for Aristotle, but dynamical for Newton. A strong case can be made that Aristotle's view comes close to a literal reading of common experience, for it does seem to take special work to stop heavy things falling, and so on. It took two millennia to discover that a precise, quantitative account of motion must differ from such literalism.

This said, Aristotle is partially vindicated in modern relativity theory (see the concluding essay by Einstein). According to that theory, matter causes space to curve, so that the straightest, natural, "Newtonian" path for an object is itself curved. Such curving explains the action of gravity, so the fall of heavy objects is today indeed considered natural, and unforced. But we are running ahead of ourselves. In the rest of this chapter we will consider two Aristotelian views about cosmology: that space has three dimensions, and that it is unique.

4.4 The Universe

That space is three-dimensional is of course uncontroversial (we have treated space as a plane only for convenience), but explaining why is difficult. On a sympathetic reading of Book I, chapter 1 of *On the Heavens*, Aristotle expresses the idea that there can be no more than three dimensions because there is no further direction in which to point. (He thinks that the world cannot have fewer than three dimensions because then some dimensions wouldn't be filled, which would be a "defect.") Simply stated, this begs the question, for if there were a fourth dimension, then by definition, there would be a fourth direction. Aristotle offers the argument that in Greek (as in English) one speaks of "both things" when there are two, but "all things" when there are three. Hence the three dimensions are "all," and there are no more. Now leaving aside the point that on this reasoning four dimensions would also be "all," the argument rests too heavily on the assumption that a particular (and "everyday") language correctly captures the features of nature. Indeed, in French the expression "all two" (*tous les deux*) is used instead of "both", so in French one can say "two" is "all." Perhaps one could instead argue that a fourth dimension is impossible because it is inconceivable in some way; you will find arguments for and against such a claim later, in Kant and Poincaré.

Aristotle argues at length that our world—the totality of the Earth and the heavens—is unique, or, meaning by "universe" all that physically exists, that "the world, we may say, is the universe" (212^b18). The arguments of chapter 8 of Book I of *On the Heavens* are particularly interesting as they show Aristotle's theory of motion at work (they are an example of the use of first principles in science). What is at stake is the question of whether there could be other worlds like ours, composed of the same elements.

The first step in understanding Aristotle's answer is to understand that he took the form of something to be definitional of what it is. Thus, for instance, part of what it is to be earth is to move naturally toward the center, and similarly for the other elements. Given its nature, it is impossible for earth to move some other way, for then it would have to have a different form, which is to say, it would no longer be earth. (This is not so different from modern practice, which, for instance, distinguishes atomic particles by their motions in electromagnetic fields.) Next, if supposed other worlds are truly worlds and not just called "worlds," then they must be formed from the same elements as ours, not other elements with the same names. Thus their elements must have the same forms as ours: If the names of the elements in another "universe" "are not used on the basis of an identity of form, then the universe can only be called a world homonymously" (276^b2). This principle is akin to the modern assumption that all regions of the universe, however distant, obey the same laws of physics: it says that elements of other worlds must have the same natural behaviors as ours. But this seems impossible, for earth in another world must fall toward two contrary centers—ours and its own. If it moves naturally to the center of our world then it goes naturally up in its world, and so wouldn't have the correct form of earth. Conversely, if it moves to the center of its own world then it doesn't fall to our center, and again doesn't have the correct form of earth. The problem is this: earth must fall to the center, but if there are two genuine worlds, then there are two centers.

An obvious response (276^b22) is to suggest that the natural motion in the two worlds depends on the relative location of the center: perhaps earth naturally moves to the nearest center, much as we know now in modern science that objects on Mars fall toward Mars, those on Jupiter fall toward Jupiter, and so on. Then earth in our world would fall toward our—nearer—center, and earth in the proposed second world would fall toward its—nearer—center. However, according to Aristotelian mechanics this cannot be, for it would mean that different samples of earth have strictly distinct proper places. But if they have distinct proper places then they have separate goals, and hence different forms. But the form of an element does not depend on external factors such as relative location, but is internal to the element: "For what is the difference in saying that they are distant to this or that extent?... their form remains the same" (276^b23). Hence if the supposed "earth" in the second world does move naturally to its center then it must have a form different from that of the earth in our world, and so by definition, is not truly earth at all. And in this case, as before, the supposed second "world" is itself not a world at all, for it is not actually composed of the elements.

We have learned a lot about Aristotle's method and science in this chapter, but there are some key ideas that we especially need to bear in mind as we continue. First there is Aristotle's concern with the nature of space (or place): he believed space, or rather place, to be a feature of material objects, not something matter-independent. Second, he sought to describe the interactions between space and matter: he believed that space plays a role in determining the natural motions of objects. Finally, we have seen his arguments for the three-dimensionality of space, and for the uniqueness of the universe. All these points will reappear in the subsequent readings.

Problems

1. Consider further the use of dialectic to establish the first principles of the theory of place. What other common beliefs and puzzles does Aristotle mention? Does he use them to reject any theory? Does he explain how they are consistent with or solved by his theory of place?

2. Aristotle's theory of place seems to conflict with his cosmology. First, a place is the inner surface of a container, but the finite heavens themselves have no container, because there is nothing beyond them to act as a container. And yet in a sense the heavens are somewhere, for they exist in the material world. Second, as he says, "motion in its most general and proper sense is change of place" (208^a31), but even if there is a place for the heavens, they never leave it as they move, but rotate *in situ*. How does Aristotle deal with these difficulties? (See 212^a31-^b21.)

3. We have considered the various natural motions of the elements: the "simple" motions of "simple" bodies. But bodies compounded from the elements will move "according to that [element] which predominates" (269^a5). How might one thus give an Aristotelian account of the motion of a hot air balloon, being inflated on the ground, slowly rising to a certain height, resting there, and then returning to the ground? What other motions can the Aristotelian account explain as natural?

4. How does Aristotle argue for the sphericity of the world in Book II, chapter 4 of *On the Heavens*? (A criticism leveled at Aristotle is that his science is insufficiently quantitative. What does this chapter show about the role he saw for mathematics in science?)

Further Readings and Bibliography

Ackrill, J. L. 1981. *Aristotle the Philosopher*. New York: Oxford University Press. √

Barbour, J. B. 1989. *Absolute or Relative Motion? A Study from a Machian Point of View of the Discovery and Structure of Dynamical Theories,* volume one (see esp. chap. 2). Cambridge, UK: Cambridge University Press. √

Hussey, E., trans. 1983. *Aristotle's Physics: Books III–IV*. New York: Oxford University Press.

Lear, J. 1988. *Aristotle: The Desire to Understand*. Cambridge, UK: Cambridge University Press.

Owen, G. E. L. 1986. *Logic, Science, and Dialectic: Collected Papers in Greek Philosophy*, edited by M. Nussbaum. Ithaca, NY: Cornell University Press.

5 The Aristotelian Tradition

5.1 Introduction

Although the years from Aristotle to Descartes (the fourth century BC to the seventeenth century AD) span—by far—the majority of the period of this book, we will not discuss them in great detail. This is not because it lacks intrinsic interest, nor because no important developments occurred during this time. On the contrary, as we shall glimpse, rich intellectual debates took place then that laid the foundations of modern science. However, before the seventeenth century, scientists had not made the mathematical and physical discoveries necessary for a rigorous and modern understanding of the issues. Since this book primarily aims to explain the modern conception of space—through its origins—it makes sense to concentrate on the period from Descartes onward in the following chapters, and leave more historical treatments to other works (see the references). Hence the brevity of this chapter does not reflect a lack of significance, but rather reflects the goals of this book.

I shall briefly survey some important thinkers to give a general picture of the development of the concept of space, concentrating on those ideas that proved most fruitful in modern science. Although many of these ideas are found in subsequent readings, I am not here claiming that the earlier works necessarily influenced subsequent thought directly. That question is explored in more historical approaches.

5.2 Before Copernicus

Although his philosophy competed for ascendence in Western thought with other approaches—particularly Plato's—Aristotle's views on physics and space dominated science throughout the period. However, thinkers did not slavishly accept all aspects of Aristotelianism, but instead took his general system and sought to develop and clarify it. For instance, several criticized his theory of space, arguing that it was incompatible with other aspects of his physics. It is these criticisms and proposed modifications of the concept of space that interest us here.

The first major critic that we will discuss is John Philoponus, who lived during the sixth century AD. Recall that Aristotle claimed that (ideally) the place of anything is the innermost *motionless* surface containing it. For instance, the place of the terrestrial region—the Earth and surrounding water, air, and fire—is the inner surface of the smallest celestial sphere: the natural "up." That the celestial spheres are made of ether and rotate about the Earth does not concern Aristotle. A rotation does not involve motion out of place and so, he thinks, the inner surface of the heavens counts as a motionless place.

Philoponus rejected this suggestion, pointing out among other things that the place of any part of the inner celestial sphere changes as it rotates: it is bounded to the inside by constantly varying parts of the terrestrial region. And if all its parts are in motion, so is the whole; therefore the inner sphere cannot be motionless. Furthermore, the same reasoning can be applied to all of the celestial spheres, so none of them can be the motionless place of the Earth either. But there is nothing beyond the celestial spheres, so it seems that according to Aristotle's account the terrestrial region has no place; since this is nonsensical, there is something wrong with Aristotle's account.

Philoponus advocated instead one of the views of place rejected by Aristotle, that it is "some sort of extension between the extremities" (*Physics*, 211^{b}8): place is a preexisting three-dimensional region distinct from the objects that occupy it. We can perhaps imagine such a region by thinking of a vacuum as something real—something real that remains even when occupied by matter, as a canvas remains even when covered with paint. In this case we clearly have no problem specifying the place of the Earth, for we do not need to specify any motionless surrounding object. Rather, the place of anything is the region of "filled vacuum" that it occupies. It is this idea, that place (or space) is not just a collection of bodies but something separate, that Newton will ultimately defend. But that is still well over 1,000 years away.

In the early fifteenth century, Hasdai Crescas developed similar arguments against Aristotle's theory of place. For instance, Aristotle's claim that objects are the same size as their places (*Physics*, 211^{a}1) apparently contradicts the theory of place. For instance, remove a narrow cylinder from a sphere; the resulting object is part of the sphere. But this part has a greater surface area than the whole, and hence according to Aristotle's theory has a larger place than the whole. So if the size of an object is equal to the size of its place, this part of the sphere must be larger than the whole sphere, which is a contradiction: no part is greater than the whole.

Crescas also developed Philoponus's conception of place to encompass the larger notion of all space, as we considered it when we discussed the Euclidean hypothesis. He considered space to be much as Philoponus described place—a container, separate from matter—but extended, like the Euclidean plane, to infinity in all directions. When we read Newton we will see this vision developed further and given a central role in mechanics.

The next thinker in our whistle-stop tour is Jean Buridan, who worked during the middle of the fourteenth century. In fact, the aspects of his views that we will discuss were first developed by Philoponus and were the subject of considerable discussion in Buridan's time. So we are considering Buridan not as the originator of this topic, but as giving a mature statement of a standard set of ideas. He objected to Aristotle's theory that unless acted upon by a force, an object moves toward its natural place: the center for earth and water, and the edge of the terrestrial region for air and fire. Such a theory is applicable to a great variety of phenomena, but it is hard to see how it explains the motions of projectiles. Once an arrow leaves the bow it seems that there is no longer any applied force causing it to move forward, so it should move naturally and fall straight to the ground. This problem did not escape Aristotle: he suggested that either the bow string continued to push the air behind the arrow, keeping it in motion; or that the tip of the arrow pushed a column of air that "looped back" to the rear of the arrow, so that it pushed itself forward (*Physics*, Bk. IV, chap. 8).

Buridan objected to these explanations on various grounds. For one thing, if one were to sharpen the tail of a javelin it would have less air resistance and so should be pushed less by the tail wind: it should travel less far than an arrow with a flat end. But we observe no such a phenomenon; it is the forward-facing air resistance that makes a difference.

In place of the Aristotelian account of projectiles Buridan described an "impetus" theory, which was the forerunner of the modern concept of inertia—which we shall discuss at length in the following chapters. According to this theory, as well as (or instead of) moving naturally to natural places, bodies can have "impetus": a tendency to maintain their motion. The arrow shot from the bow receives a quantity of impetus, "filling up" with a kind of internal force that maintains its motion. Against that force, gravity causes the arrow to fall—a qualitative description of the trajectory of an arrow. Of course, this account is *only* qualitative, not answering to the standard of a quantitative, precisely numerical description of motion, but developed conceptually and mathematically, this idea is at the heart of Newtonian mechanics, as we shall soon see.

One crucial feature of Buridan's theory is that a body's impetus can be a tendency to move either in a circle or in a straight line. Given this, impetus theory also suggests an alternative account of the motions of the heavens around the Earth. They need not be made of celestial matter with its own distinct, natural—circular—motion. Instead, as Buridan observed, the heavens might be governed by the same laws of motion as terrestrial matter: perhaps during creation God simply gave them "circular impetus." Buridan did not develop the idea that there might thus be a "universal mechanics," a theory of motion applicable to all matter, but Galileo and Descartes did, and Newton's theory is of this kind.

5.3 Copernicus and Galileo

Philoponus, Buridan, and Crescas offer a brief glimpse of the kinds of problems and solutions developed by thinkers before the development of modern science. And though we cannot here discuss possible direct influences they had on later thinkers, we have at least said enough to see that many of the ideas of modern science did not appear from nowhere, but were "in the air" for a long time. What we will now briefly consider is the period from Copernicus to Descartes, in which these ideas finally began to come together into modern science: the period in which the "scientific revolution" began.

Once again, I will survey only a few highlights of this rich phase in the development of science and discuss only two key figures, Copernicus (1473–1543) and Galileo (1564–1642). It was Copernicus who rejected the Aristotelian or "Ptolemaic" cosmology (after the greatest Aristotelian astronomer, Ptolemy [second century AD]). Copernicus reinvented the model of the universe with the Sun rather than Earth at its center, and he explained the daily motion of the heavens by the Earth's rotation about its axis. Both these ideas were known in antiquity, and Aristotle took the time to explicitly "refute" them (see *On the Heavens*, Bk. II, chaps. 13–14), but after Copernicus they finally took root in science and spurred the development of modern physics. In particular, if the Earth is just another planet in space, then there is no reason why the heavens should be governed by different laws to those applying to terrestrial bodies: thus Copernicus made possible our universal mechanics.

Of course, the idea that the Earth moves rather than maintains an absolutely fixed point in the center of the universe was hard for many to accept, and it took the work of exceptional scientists to reveal its value. We should think of Galileo in this way: in part he was a brilliant developer and experimentalist of, and in part a devastating propagandist for, Copernican science. His works contain a catalogue of arguments that reveal the inadequacies of Aristotle's physics and point clearly to the new physics completed by Newton.

For instance, one of Aristotle's objections to a moving Earth is that if the Earth moved, then objects shot straight in the air would be left behind and fall to the ground at a distance, which obviously doesn't happen on a still day (296^b23). Galileo—borrowing from the earlier impetus theorists—pointed out that this need not be the case. Suppose that its contact with the Earth gives an arrow "circular impetus" in addition to the impetus it derives from the bow. Then it would rotate with the Earth as it rose and fell—to exactly the same spot. (Note that in modern science the only "impetus"—or rather, "inertia"—is in a straight line: there is more to explaining the motion of the arrow.)

Finally, it is worth outlining the reaction of the Christian church in Western Europe to Copernicus. A literal reading of the Bible (for instance, *Ecclesiastes* 1:4–5) seems to entail that the Earth is stationary, as in Ptolemaic but not Copernican cosmology. Perhaps contrary to popular belief, this conflict was not, during the lifetime of Copernicus, seen as problem by the Catholic church, but rather by the fundamentalists of the day, the recently established Protestants. It was not until 1616 that the Catholic church suppressed the Copernican theory, culminating in Galileo's forced recantation in his sixty-ninth year. By this time it was too late to destroy the theory, but not too late to have an important impact on Descartes, as we shall see in the next chapter.

5.4 Omissions

As I indicated at the start of this chapter, I've had to omit many interesting details in order to maintain the narrative of this book. It would, however, be a good idea to mention three topics of special importance that I will not discuss at all. First, these scientific developments took place within a religious framework, particularly within the Judeo-Christian tradition. It is not clear from my brief sketch that within that tradition was the competition between the philosophical Platonists (lead by Augustine in the sixth century) and the Aristotelians (lead by Aquinas in the thirteenth century). Second, these developments also took place in a wide environment, influenced crucially by Jewish and Islamic thought (which was in turn influenced by Aristotle). Finally, I have not discussed the idea of a vacuum as pure, empty, physical space, which was an important part of early thought about the nature of space. For a further discussion of these—and other—matters, the reader should consult the bibliography. Once again I must hope to excuse this sketchy treatment of history on the grounds that here we wish primarily to discuss the modern conception of space.

Despite the limitations of this chapter we have learned some significant lessons. We have seen that many of the important ideas that will confront us in the next chapters did not appear from nowhere, but can be found in thought stretching over centuries. In particular, we have looked more closely at the idea that space is an entity that contains matter but which is separate from matter, seen the origins of the crucial concept of inertia, and seen that there might be a universal science of all matter. These ideas are at work in the physics of Descartes and his contemporaries, and especially in the final development of modern mechanics by Newton, as we shall now discover.

Further Readings and Bibliography

Duhem, P. 1985. *Medieval Cosmology: Theories of Infinity, Place, Time, Void, and the Plurality of Worlds.* Translated by R. Ariew. Chicago, IL: University of Chicago Press.

Grant, E. 1981. *Much Ado About Nothing: Theories of Space and Vacuum from the Middle Ages to the Scientific Revolution.* Cambridge, UK: Cambridge University Press.

Jammer, M. 1993. *Concepts of Space: The History of Theories of Space in Physics,* third edition. Mineola, NY: Dover.

Kuhn, T. S. 1957. *The Copernican Revolution: Planetary Astronomy in the Development of Western Thought.* Cambridge, MA: Harvard University Press. √

Matthews, M. R., ed. 1989. *The Scientific Background to Modern Philosophy: Selected Readings* (see esp. chaps. II and IV). Indianapolis, IN: Hackett Publishing Co. √

Sorabji, R. 1988. *Matter, Space, and Motion: Theories in Antiquity and Their Sequel.* Ithaca, NY: Cornell University Press.

6 Descartes

The Principles of Philosophy

Part One

43

It is certain, however, that we will never mistake the false for the true provided we give our assent only to what we clearly and distinctly perceive. I say that this is certain, because God is not a deceiver, and so the faculty of perception which he has given us cannot incline to falsehood; and the same goes for the faculty of assent, provided its scope is limited to what is clearly perceived. And even if there were no way of proving this, the minds of all of us have been so moulded by nature that whenever we perceive something clearly, we spontaneously give our assent to it and are quite unable to doubt its truth. . . .

48

All the objects of our perception we regard either as things, or affections of things, or else as eternal truths which have no existence outside our thought. The most general items which we regard as things are *substance, duration, order, number* and any other items of this kind which extend to all classes of things. But I recognize only two ultimate classes of things: first, intellectual or thinking things, i.e. those which pertain to mind or thinking substance; and secondly, material things, i.e. those which pertain to extended substance or body. Perception, volition and all the modes both of perceiving and of willing are referred to thinking substance; while to extended substance belong size (that is, extension in length, breadth and depth), shape, motion, position, divisibility of component parts and the like. . . .

53

A substance may indeed be known through any attribute at all; but each substance has one principal property which constitutes its nature and essence, and to which all its other properties are referred. Thus extension in length, breadth and depth constitutes the nature of corporeal substance; and thought constitutes the nature of

Excerpts from René Descartes, "Principles of Philosophy," in *The Philosophical Writings of Descartes* (vol. 1, pp. 207–252), translated and edited by J. Cottingham, R. Stoothoff, and D. Murdoch. © 1985 by Cambridge University Press. Reprinted with the permission of Cambridge University Press.

thinking substance. Everything else which can be attributed to body presupposes extension, and is merely a mode of an extended thing; and similarly, whatever we find in the mind is simply one of the various modes of thinking. For example, shape is unintelligible except in an extended thing; and motion is unintelligible except as motion in an extended space; while imagination, sensation and will are intelligible only in a thinking thing. By contrast, it is possible to understand extension without shape or movement, and thought without imagination or sensation, and so on; and this is quite clear to anyone who gives the matter his attention....

Part Two

4

If we ["make use of the intellect alone, carefully attending to the ideas implanted in it by nature": II.3], we shall perceive that the nature of matter, or body considered in general, consists not in its being something which is hard or heavy or coloured, or which affects the senses in any way, but simply in its being something which is extended in length, breadth and depth. For as regards hardness, our sensation tells us no more than that the parts of a hard body resist the motion of our hands when they come into contact with them. If, whenever our hands moved in a given direction, all the bodies in that area were to move away at the same speed as that of our approaching hands, we should never have any sensation of hardness. And since it is quite unintelligible to suppose that, if bodies did move away in this fashion, they would thereby lose their bodily nature, it follows that this nature cannot consist in hardness. By the same reasoning it can be shown that weight, colour, and all other such qualities that are perceived by the senses as being in corporeal matter, can be removed from it, while the matter itself remains intact; it thus follows that its nature does not depend on any of these qualities....

11

It is easy for us to recognize that the extension constituting the nature of a body is exactly the same as that constituting the nature of a space. There is no more difference between them than there is between the nature of a genus or species and the nature of an individual. Suppose we attend to the idea we have of some body, for example a stone, and leave out everything we know to be non-essential to the nature of body: we will first of all exclude hardness, since if the stone is melted or pulverized it will lose its hardness without thereby ceasing to be a body; next we will exclude colour, since we have often seen stones so transparent as to lack colour; next we will exclude heaviness, since although fire is extremely light it is still thought of as being corporeal; and finally we will exclude cold and heat and all other such qualities, either because they are not thought of as being in the stone, or because if they change, the stone is not on that account reckoned to have lost its bodily nature. After all this, we will see that nothing remains in the idea of the stone except that it is something extended in length, breadth and depth. Yet this is just what is comprised in the idea of a space—not merely a space which is full of bodies, but even a space which is called "empty."

12

There is, however, a difference in the way in which we conceive of space and corporeal substance. For if a stone is removed from the space or place where it is, we think that its extension has also been removed from that place, since we regard the extension as something particular and inseparable from the stone. But at the same time we think that the extension of the place where the stone used to be remains, and is the same as before, although the place is now occupied by wood or water or air or some other body, or is even supposed to be empty. For we are now considering extension as something general, which is thought of as being the same, whether it is the extension of a stone or of wood, or of water or of air or of any other body—or even of a vacuum, if there is such a thing—provided only that it has the same size and shape, and keeps the same position relative to the external bodies that determine the space in question.

13

The terms "place" and "space," then, do not signify anything different from the body which is said to be in a place; they merely refer to its size, shape and position relative to other bodies. To determine the position, we have to look at various other bodies which we regard as immobile; and in relation to different bodies we may say that the same thing is both changing and not changing its place at the same time. For example, when a ship is under way, a man sitting on the stern remains in one place relative to the other parts of the ship with respect to which his position is unchanged; but he is constantly changing his place relative to the neighbouring shores, since he is constantly receding from one shore and approaching another. Then again, if we believe the earth moves, and suppose that it advances the same distance from west to east as the ship travels from east to west in the corresponding period of time, we shall again say that the man sitting on the stern is not changing his place; for we are now determining the place by means of certain fixed points in the heavens. Finally, if we suppose that there are no such genuinely fixed points to be found in the universe (a supposition which will be shown below to be probable) we shall conclude that nothing has a permanent place, except as determined by our thought....

15

Thus we always take a space to be an extension in length, breadth and depth. But with regard to place, we sometimes consider it as internal to the thing which is in the place in question, and sometimes as external to it. Now internal place is exactly the same as space; but external place may be taken as being the surface immediately surrounding what is in the place. It should be noted that "surface" here does not mean any part of the surrounding body but merely the boundary between the surrounding and surrounded bodies, which is no more than a mode. Or rather what is meant is simply the common surface, which is not a part of one body rather than the other but is always reckoned to be the same, provided it keeps the same size and shape. For if there are two bodies, one surrounding the other, and the entire surrounding body changes, surface and all, the surrounded body is not therefore thought of as changing its place, provided that during this time it keeps the same position relative to the external bodies which are regarded as immobile. If, for example, we suppose that a ship on a river is being pulled equally in one direction by the current and in the opposite direction by the wind, so that it does not change its position relative to the banks, we will all readily admit that it stays in the same place, despite the complete change in the surrounding surface....

21

What is more we recognize that this world, that is, the whole universe of corporeal substance, has no limits to its extension. For no matter where we imagine the boundaries to be, there are always some indefinitely extended spaces beyond them, which we not only imagine but also perceive to be imaginable in a true fashion, that is, real. And it follows that these spaces contain corporeal substance which is indefinitely extended. For, as has already been shown very fully, the idea of the extension which we conceive to be in a given space is exactly the same as the idea of corporeal substance.

22

It can also easily be gathered from this that celestial matter is no different from terrestrial matter. And even if there were an infinite number of worlds, the matter of which they were composed would have to be identical; hence, there cannot in fact be a plurality of worlds, but only one. For we very clearly understand that the matter whose nature consists simply in its being an extended substance already occupies absolutely all the imaginable space in which the alleged additional worlds would have to be located; and we cannot find within us an idea of any other sort of matter.

23

The matter existing in the entire universe is thus one and the same, and it is always recognized as matter simply in virtue of its being extended. All the properties which we clearly perceive in it are reducible to its divisibility and consequent mobility in respect of its parts, and its resulting capacity to be affected in all the ways which we perceive as being derivable from the movement of the parts. If the division into parts occurs simply in our thought, there is no resulting change; any variation in matter or diversity in its many forms depends on motion. This seems to have been widely recognized by the philosophers, since they have stated that nature is the principle of motion and rest. And what they meant by "nature" in this context is what causes all corporeal things to take on the characteristics of which we are aware in experience....

25

If, on the other hand, we consider what should be understood by *motion*, not in common usage but in accordance with the truth of the matter, and if our aim is to assign a determinate nature to it, we may say that *motion is the transfer of one piece of matter, or one body, from the vicinity of the other bodies which are in immediate contact with it, and which are regarded as being at rest, to the vicinity of other bodies.* By "one body" or "one piece of matter" I mean whatever is transferred at a given time, even though this may in fact consist of many parts which have different motions relative to each other. And I say "the transfer" as opposed to the force or action which brings about the transfer, to show that motion is always in the moving body as opposed to the body which brings about the movement. The two are not normally distinguished with sufficient care; and I want to make it clear that the motion of something that moves is, like the lack of motion in a thing which is at rest, a mere mode of that thing and not itself a subsistent thing, just as shape is a mere mode of the thing which has shape.

26

It should be noted that in this connection we are in the grip of a strong preconceived opinion, namely the belief that more action is needed for motion than for rest. We have been convinced of this since early childhood owing to the fact that our bodies move by our will, of which we have inner awareness, but remain at rest simply in virtue of sticking to the earth by gravity, the force of which we do not perceive through the senses. And because gravity and many other causes of which we are unaware produce resistance when we try to move our limbs, and make us tired, we think that a greater action or force is needed to initiate a motion than to stop it; for we take *action* to be the effort we expend in moving our limbs and moving other bodies by the use of our limbs. We will easily get rid of this preconceived opinion if we consider that it takes an effort on our part not only to move external bodies, but also, quite often, to stop them, when gravity and other causes are insufficient to arrest their movement. For example, the action needed to move a boat which is at rest in still water is no greater than that needed to stop it suddenly when it is moving—or rather it is not much greater, for one must subtract the weight of the water displaced by the ship and the viscosity of the water, both of which could gradually bring it to a halt. . . .

29

I further specified that the transfer occurs from the vicinity not of *any* contiguous bodies but from the vicinity of those which "are regarded as being at rest." For transfer is in itself a reciprocal process: we cannot understand that a body AB is transferred from the vicinity of a body CD without simultaneously understanding that CD is transferred from the vicinity of AB. Exactly the same force and action is needed on both sides. So if we wished to characterize motion strictly in terms of its own nature, without reference to anything else, then in the case of two contiguous bodies being transferred in opposite directions, and thus separated, we should say that there was just as much motion in the one body as in the other. But this would clash too much with our ordinary way of speaking. For we are used to standing on the earth and regarding it as at rest; so although we may see some of its parts, which are contiguous with other smaller bodies, being transferred out of their vicinity, we do not for that reason think of the earth itself as in motion. . . .

37

From God's immutability we can also know certain rules or laws of nature, which are the secondary and particular causes of the various motions we see in particular bodies. The first of these laws is that each thing, in so far as it is simple and undivided, always remains in the same state, as far as it can, and never changes except as a result of external causes. Thus, if a particular piece of matter is square, we can be sure without more ado that it will remain square for ever, unless something coming from outside changes its shape. If it is at rest, we hold that it will never begin to move unless it is pushed into motion by some cause. And if it moves, there is equally no reason for thinking it will ever lose this motion of its own accord and without being checked by something else. Hence we must conclude that what is in motion always, so far as it can, continues to move. But we live on the Earth, whose composition is such that all motions occurring near it are soon halted, often by causes undetectable by our senses. Hence from our earliest years we have often judged that such motions, which are in fact stopped by causes unknown to us, come to an end of their own accord. And we tend to believe that what we have apparently experienced in many cases holds good in all cases—namely that it is in the very nature of motion to come to an end, or to tend towards a state of rest. This, of course, [is a false preconceived opinion which] is utterly at variance with the laws of nature; for rest is the opposite of motion, and nothing can by its own nature tend towards its opposite, or towards its own destruction.

38

Indeed, our everyday experience of projectiles completely confirms this first rule of ours. For there is no other reason why a projectile should persist in motion for some time after it leaves the hand that throws it, except that what is once in motion continues to move until it is slowed down by bodies that are in the way. And it is clear that projectiles are normally slowed down, little by little, by the air or other fluid bodies in which they are moving, and that this is why their motion cannot persist for long. The fact that air offers resistance to other moving bodies may be confirmed either by our own experience, through the sense of touch if we beat the air with a fan, or by the flight of birds. And in the case of any other fluid, the resistance offered to the motion of a projectile is even more obvious than in the case of air.

39

The second law is that every piece of matter, considered in itself, always tends to continue moving, not in any oblique path but only in a straight line. This is true despite the fact that many particles are often forcibly deflected by the impact of other bodies; and, as I have said above, in any motion the result of all the matter moving simultaneously is a kind of circle. The reason for this second rule is the same as the reason for the first rule, namely the immutability and simplicity of the operation by which God preserves motion in matter. For he always preserves the motion in the precise form in which it is occurring at the very moment when he preserves it, without taking any account of the motion which was occurring a little while earlier. It is true that no motion takes place in a single instant of time; but clearly whatever is in motion is determined, at the individual instants which can be specified as long as the motion lasts, to continue moving in a given direction along a straight line, and never in a curve. . . .

Part Three

28

Here we must bear in mind what I said above about the nature of motion, namely that if we use the term "motion" in the strict sense and in accordance with the truth of things, then motion is simply the transfer of one body from the vicinity of the other bodies which are in immediate contact with it, and which are regarded as being at rest, to the vicinity of other bodies. But it often happens that, in accordance with ordinary usage, any action whereby a body travels from one place to another is called "motion"; and in this sense it can be said that the same thing moves and does not move at the same time, depending on how we determine its location. It follows from this that in the strict sense there is no motion occurring in the case of the earth or even the other planets, since they are not transferred from the vicinity of those parts of the heaven with which they are in immediate contact, in so far as these parts are considered as being at rest. Such a transfer would require them to move away from all these parts at the same time, which does not occur. But since the celestial material is fluid, at any given time different groups of particles move away from the planet with which they are in contact, by a motion which should be attributed solely to the particles, not to the planet. In the same way, the partial transfers of water and air which occur on the surface of the earth are not normally attributed to the earth itself, but to the parts of water and air which are transferred. . . .

COMMENTARY

6.1   Introduction

The French philosopher René Descartes, who lived from 1596–1650, is best known for his dictum *cogito ergo sum* ("I think, therefore I am"). To summarize briefly, his philosophical work was a search for secure knowledge that began with the decision "to doubt everything which we find to contain even the smallest suspicion of uncertainty" (I. 1*). Descartes's standard of suspicion was of the very highest: our senses can trick us, so they are not to be trusted, and since we also make errors in calculations even mathematical knowledge is to be doubted. The principal item that Descartes found to be trustworthy was the *cogito*: the one thing that it is impossible to doubt is *that you are doubting*; but if you are doubting then you are certainly thinking; and if you are thinking then your own existence is certain. Using this one tiny foothold of reliable knowledge on a mountain of uncertainties, he then went about reestablishing an entire system of the world. He established the existence of a perfect (and therefore honest) god, who must have given us some means for distinguishing true and certain knowledge from false or doubtful beliefs. As Descartes explains, God made us so that we can trust what we "clearly and distinctly perceive" (I. 43). *Clear* perception of some concept, say $2 + 2 = 4$, can be thought of as analogous to the clear sight of an object held in front of the eyes in good light. And a *distinct* perception is one in which the concept is not somehow confused by other unclear ideas.

The central assumption behind this methodology is that knowledge is achieved through an act of mind, not through experience: we contemplate various ideas and use our mental powers to determine which are true. Such a methodology, emphasized in Plato and Leibniz, is known as *rationalism*; its opposite is the *empiricism* that we find in Aristotle and especially in Berkeley and Mach, which takes experience to be the sole foundation of knowledge. It emerges in the readings in this collection that thought about space has swung from one tradition to the other, and that both have been important for the development of our modern concept. It also becomes apparent that experience informs rationalists far more than they acknowledge, and that empiricists rely on nonexperiential assumptions far more than they acknowledge. (Or, to put it another way, rationalism and empiricism cannot in practice be defined quite as cleanly as we have done here.) For all these reasons, although Descartes's

---

*All references are to *The Principles of Philosophy* (part and section number).

professed methodology is diametrically opposed to the successful empirical methods of modern science, his views contributed greatly to the formation of our modern conception of space. In our discussion I will focus on two key issues: the nature of space, and the role of space in the theory of motion.

6.2   The Nature of Space

At the base of Descartes's world system is the distinction between mind and matter (or "corporeal substance")—between the stuff that thinks and the stuff that fills up space (I. 48). Ultimately, everything (except God) is made of these two substances, or (as in the case of numbers) is understood in terms of them. As he explains in I. 53 and II. 4 and 11, Descartes believes that the defining or essential characteristic of matter is that it is "extended" in three directions. He rejects hardness, weight, color, and other familiar properties as definitional of matter, on the grounds that if we think carefully about our idea of matter, we see that we could have had the idea of matter without having the idea of hardness, weight, and so on. For instance, we can imagine a world in which material objects moved away at the slightest touch, so that we never came to have an idea of hardness; yet we would still have our idea of matter. So the idea of hardness is not essential to the idea of matter: if X is essential to Y, then it is impossible to be or have Y without also having X. The only characteristic that our idea of matter must have, according to Descartes, is that it is extended. Since our ideas, if clear and distinct when carefully attended to, must be accurate, matter itself must have extension as its essence: what it is to be matter is to be extended.

This account of matter is important for understanding Descartes's view of space (II. 11–13, 15), because space too is pure extension—a volume with no properties— and so space and matter are the same thing. We saw Plato propose and Aristotle reject a similar theory in their investigations. Clearly the view implies that there is no such thing as a vacuum, for a vacuum is a volume that contains no matter, and on the current view, any volume is material. This theory of space is opposed to the idea that space is an independent "arena" in which matter is located: according to Descartes, space just is matter, not a separate entity containing matter. On his view Euclidean geometry correctly describes space so conceived, and indeed, we owe to him (and Leibniz) the familiar idea of using straight—Cartesian—coordinate axes to distinguish points of space.

Still, Descartes must face in some way the obvious objection raised by Aristotle against the material theory of space, namely, that objects move from one place to another and so place and matter are separable. Descartes's response (II. 12) is to argue that the difference lies in the two ways in which we can conceive the situation: on the one hand, we might think of the extension of a moving rock as attached to it, and hence moving with it. This is our usual notion when we speak of matter. On the other hand, we could also think of the volume, fixed by its position relative to other objects, from which the rock has moved. This is how we usually conceptualize space. Descartes explains that in the former case we think of the extension as particular to the rock, and in the latter, we think of it as generic, belonging to any object that happens to fill the place. In one sense, then, namely, the particular, the extension is inseparable from an object; but in the other, namely, the generic sense, it is separable.

One might wonder how this can be, for it is one thing to say that we can think of the extension *alternately* as separable or inseparable from an object, but it seems contradictory for it actually to be both at once. We can put this problem as a question: when a rock moves, does it remain composed of the same matter, or does the matter stay behind so that the properties move and become attached to successive pieces of matter? Descartes proposes a way out of this dilemma: "place and space ... merely refer to [a body's] size, shape, and position relative to other bodies" (II. 13). It seems that he is suggesting that although an object's matter and place are made up of the same "stuff" at any given time, its place is to be identified by its shape and relative location. Thus, assuming that a "piece of matter" exists over a period of time, it seems that pieces of space/matter move through various places—places whose matter changes, but whose relative position stays fixed.

Crucial, therefore, to the generic, separable notion of extension—the notion of a space or place—is that a place is picked out by its position relative to "bodies which we regard as immobile" (II. 13). Places might be made of matter in some sense, but really they are relative locations (perhaps of some specific shape); things are not located in a matter-independent space, but in various relations to one another. If one believed in an independent space then she would say that the Earth is located 150,000,000km from the Sun, because the Earth and Sun occupy points of space that are 150,000,000km apart. For a "relationist" such as Descartes, the two bodies themselves simply are that far apart, and that is all there is to say.

The next few chapters will present a study of the debate between those who subscribe to relationism and their opponents who argue for a matter-independent "container" view of space. The two views can take a while to become clear, and so our approach will be to study the arguments to sharpen our understanding. For the present, we should just realize that this debate concerns two competing answers to our metaphysical question, "What kind of thing is space?" Is it just matter, or is it something else?

The first thing to realize about a relational account of location is that there are many such equal and competing accounts. For instance, the Earth is on average 384,000km from the Moon, and one could also say that that constitutes its location, rather than its Sun-relative position. Of course, the Earth is at both distances, so in that sense the two accounts are compatible. Conflict only arises when one wants to talk of *the* position of things: for instance, if we want to compare the positions of the Earth and Mars we want to know their locations according to one system, relative either to the Sun or to the Moon.

Or again, as Descartes points out (II. 13), the possibility of picking out distinct objects as reference points depending on the relational scheme means that a single thing can have many motions at once: relative to the boat he is sitting on, a sailor is stationary, but relative to the shore, he is moving rapidly. And of course, relative motion is reciprocal as well (II. 29): the shore moves relative to the ship. There is no logical problem here for relationism, as one can reckon position from any point, but as we shall see, there is a question of whether a relational account of space is sufficient for the science of motion. In particular, are all "frames of reference"—to use a modern term—truly equal, as Descartes suggests when he says "nothing has a permanent place, except as determined by our thoughts" (II. 13)? Behind this claim is the modern picture—opposed to Aristotle's—of an unbounded universe full of objects in permanent motion: a universe with no fixed point from which to determine fixed locations. On the face of it, relationism seems committed to the complete equality of all reference bodies, for all equally can be said to be in motion relative to something. The issue, which is considered in the next three chapters, is whether this equality is scientifically true.

I should note that the relationism outlined in these passages of the *Principles* differs from the position that Descartes took in his earlier works (for instance, *The World*), which implicitly assume a matter-independent space. It seems probable that his change of heart was influenced by a concern not to cross the Church, which had condemned Galileo and banned his work in 1633, only 11 years before the publication of the *Principles*. Relationism offered Descartes a way to adopt simultaneously the Copernican Sun-centered account of the solar system with an orbiting Earth, and yet maintain the Aristotelian—and Church—position that the Earth was stationary! His trick was to adopt two notions of place: first, as we have seen, he adopted a theory in which place is extension; second, he adopted, as the "external" notion of place, an Aristotelian view of place as the surface surrounding an object (II. 15) (fixed relative to separate, immobile bodies). According to the first account, a body has many relative motions, but the second theory allows him to define out of these a body's "true motion": its "transfer . . . from the vicinity of the other bodies which are in immediate contact with it, and which are regarded as being at rest, to the vicinity of other bodies" (II. 25). Now, on the Cartesian worldview the Earth orbits the Sun because it is held in a vortex of rotating "celestial matter," like a leaf in a whirlpool. Hence the Earth is stationary in the body and surface surrounding it (III. 28), even though it orbits the Sun relative to the fixed stars (the stars we see around us in the heavens).

6.3   The Theory of Motion

As we have seen previously, a scientific theory of space is important because space is presupposed by a theory of motion, which in turn (since Descartes, II. 23) explains all the changes and processes that occur in the physical world. For us, the most significant feature of Cartesian mechanics is that it contains the first fully recognizably modern notion of inertia, derived from the impetus theories of the previous chapter. This idea is presented in Descartes's first and second laws of motion (II. 37 and 39), and concerns the distinction between *natural* and *constrained* motions.

In Aristotelian mechanics, the natural motion of an object was to its appropriate place; all other motions were constrained, requiring forces to maintain them. In Descartes, the notion of proper place is rejected, so natural motions are not toward particular locations. Instead, it is natural for bodies to keep moving in exactly the way that they are, and forces are required only to change the state of motion, say to slow it down or to deflect an object. Once again the Aristotelian account seems to accord most closely with immediate experience: for instance, a ball rolled up a hill by an unnatural force loses its speed as it moves from the source of the force, and "naturally" rolls back down. It takes extraordinary powers of abstraction to think of a continued movement up the hill as natural and to see unnatural forces such a gravity as causing the observed motion (II. 26 and 38). We are educated to see things Descartes's way, but a little reflection on how common it is to see things falling suggests how hard it was to see such motions as "unnatural."

On the modern conception that we owe to Descartes, then, objects tend to move in (i) straight lines, at (ii) constant speeds (the two together mean that they tend to maintain the same velocity), and only forces can either change the speed or direction of motion. We say that this tendency is their *inertia*, that forces are needed to overcome inertia, and that natural motions are *inertial*. "The principle of inertia"— Descartes's first and second laws—states that objects will maintain a constant velocity until acted upon by a force. It is not hard to see that this principle will collide with relationism: as we saw above, an object's relative velocity depends on the reference frame, and so its velocity is ambiguous. But if so, what can it mean to say it tends to keep the same velocity? Which velocity is supposed to remain the same? Consider an illustration of the problem.

Imagine three spaceships, A, B, and C, in deep space, far away from any stars. Taking A as the reference body, let B and C accelerate away so that B is always moving 10m/s faster than C. Relative to A, A stays at rest—a natural motion—and B and C gain speed; according to the principle of inertia there should be forces on B and C, but none on A. But now consider things relative to B: B is stationary and C moves at a constant 10m/s—both natural motions—and A accelerates away. Relative to B, the law of inertia requires that A has a force on it, and that B and C do not. But if Descartes's laws of motion are to make sense, then (at most) one of these simultaneous descriptions can make sense: either there are forces on A (or B or C) or there are not. The two descriptions are not equivalent.

The problem is that dynamics (the science of objects in forced motion) distinguishes inertial from *noninertial* motions, whereas relationism cannot make sense of this distinction, because what accelerates relative to one object need not accelerate relative to others. This observation (of Newton's) is the basis of one of the most influential arguments for the existence of a matter-independent space, for in such a space one can define an "absolute" velocity and hence make an unequivocal distinction between inertial and noninertial motions.

Descartes does not comment on this collision between his relationism and the principle of inertia that forms a central part of his mechanics, so it is not clear what his view of the matter was. Perhaps he intended that the principle applied only to "true motions," so that objects would move constantly relative to their immediate surroundings unless acted on by forces. Or perhaps he felt that he could separate the use of "true motion"—to explain the Earth's rest—from his mechanics, so that he could invoke a separate, absolute notion of "true mechanical motion" in that context. He doesn't say. However, as we will see in the next chapter on Newton, Descartes is in serious trouble: constant "true motions" do not coincide with inertial motions, and the appropriate notion of planetary motion is surely the mechanical one.

Problems

1. Aristotle's planets orbited the Sun because they were made of ether, and so followed their natural motion with the rest of the heavens. Descartes's planets also rotated around the Sun in a mass of celestial matter, but for him the motion was not in a straight line, and so was unnatural. How then might he have qualitatively

explained the motion of the vortex carrying the planets? (He denied the existence of a gravitational force.)

2. Find those places where Descartes makes implicit reference to the ideas of Aristotle. Are his views really compatible with Aristotle's?

3. Give another example to show that relative position, speed, and acceleration are ambiguous. How might one single out a "preferred" frame in which to define these quantities? (This question is hard and speculative—and addressed in various ways in the following chapters.)

Further Reading and Bibliography

Barbour, J. B. 1989. *Absolute or Relative Motion? A Study from a Machian Point of View of the Discovery and Structure of Dynamical Theories,* volume one (esp. chap. 8). Cambridge, UK: Cambridge University Press. √

Cottingham, J. 1986. *Descartes.* New York: Basil Blackwell. √

Garber, D. 1992. *Descartes's Metaphysical Physics.* Chicago, IL: University of Chicago Press.

7 Newton

READING

On the Gravity and Equilibrium of Fluids (De Gravitatione)

... For the rest, when I suppose in these definitions that space is distinct from body, and when I determine that motion is with respect to the parts of that space, and not with respect to the position of neighbouring bodies, lest this should be taken as being gratuitously contrary to the Cartesians, I shall venture to dispose of his fictions. ...

Indeed, not only do its absurd consequences convince us how confused and incongruous with reason this doctrine is, but Descartes by contradicting himself seems to acknowledge the fact. For he says that speaking properly and according to philosophical sense the Earth and the other Planets do not move, and that he who declares it to be moved because of its translation with respect to the fixed stars speaks without reason and only in the vulgar fashion (III. 26, 27, 28, 29).* Yet later he attributes to the Earth and Planets a tendency to recede from the Sun as from a centre about which they are revolved, by which they are balanced at their [due] distances from the Sun by a similar tendency of the gyrating vortex (III. 140). What then? Is this tendency to be derived from the (according to Descartes) true and philosophical rest of the planets, or rather from [their] common and non-philosophical motion? But Descartes says further that a Comet has a lesser tendency to recede from the Sun when it first enters the vortex, and keeping practically the same position among the fixed stars does not yet obey the impetus of the vortex, but with respect to it is transferred from the neighbourhood of the contiguous aether and so philosophically speaking whirls round the Sun, while afterwards the matter of the vortex carries the comet along with it and so renders it at rest, according to philosophical sense. (III. 119, 120.) The philosopher is hardly consistent who uses as the basis of Philosophy the motion of the vulgar which he had rejected a little before, and now rejects that motion as fit for nothing which alone was formerly said to be true and philosophical, according to the nature of things. And since the whirling of the comet around the Sun in his philosophic sense does not cause a tendency to recede from the centre, which a gyration in the vulgar sense can do, surely motion in the vulgar sense should be acknowledged, rather than the philosophical. ...

... Unless it is conceded that there can be a single physical motion of any body, and that the rest of its changes of relation and position with respect to other bodies

Excerpts from Isaac Newton, *"De Gravitatione,"* in *Unpublished Papers of Isaac Newton: A Selection from the Portsmouth Collection in the University Library, Cambridge* (pp. 123–146), translated and edited by A. R. Hall and M. B. Hall. © 1962 by Cambridge University Press. Reprinted by permission of Cambridge University Press.
*Descartes's *Principles of Philosophy*.

are so many external designations, it follows that the Earth (for example) endeavours to recede from the centre of the Sun on account of a motion relative to the fixed stars, and endeavours the less to recede on account of a lesser motion relative to Saturn and the aetherial orb in which it is carried, and still less relative to Jupiter and the swirling aether which occasions its orbit, and also less relative to Mars and its aetherial orb, and much less relative to other orbs of aetherial matter which, although not bearing planets, are closer to the annual orbit of the Earth; and indeed relative to its own orb it has no endeavour, because it does not move in it. Since all these endeavours and non-endeavours cannot absolutely agree, it is rather to be said that only the motion which causes the Earth to endeavour to recede from the Sun is to be declared the Earth's natural and absolute motion. Its translations relative to external bodies are but external designations....

Fourthly. It also follows from the same doctrine that God himself could not generate motion in some bodies even though he impelled them with the greatest force. For example, if God urged the starry heaven together with all the most remote part of creation with any very great force so as to cause it to revolve about the Earth (suppose with a diurnal motion): yet from this, according to Descartes, the Earth alone and not the sky would be truly said to move (III. 38). As if it would be the same whether, with a tremendous force, He should cause the skies to turn from east to west, or with a small force turn the Earth in the opposite direction. But who will imagine that the parts of the Earth endeavour to recede from its centre on account of a force impressed only upon the heavens? Or is it not more agreeable to reason that when a force imparted to the heavens makes them endeavour to recede from the centre of the revolution thus caused, they are for that reason the sole bodies properly and absolutely moved; and that when a force impressed upon the Earth makes its parts endeavour to recede from the centre of revolution thus caused, for that reason it is the sole body properly and absolutely moved, although there is the same relative motion of the bodies in both cases. And thus physical and absolute motion is to be defined from other considerations than translation, such translation being designated as merely external....

Lastly, that the absurdity of this position may be disclosed in full measure, I say that thence it follows that a moving body has no determinate velocity and no definite line in which it moves. And, what is worse, that the velocity of a body moving without resistance cannot be said to be uniform, nor the line said to be straight in which its motion is accomplished. On the contrary, there cannot be motion since there can be no motion without a certain velocity and determination.

But that this may be clear, it is first of all to be shown that when a certain motion is finished it is impossible, according to Descartes, to assign a place in which the body was at the beginning of the motion; it cannot be said whence the body moved. And the reason is that according to Descartes the place cannot be defined or assigned except by the position of the surrounding bodies, and after the completion of a certain motion the position of the surrounding bodies no longer stays the same as it was before. For example, if the place of the planet Jupiter a year ago be sought, by what reason, I ask, can the Cartesian philosopher define it? Not by the positions of the particles of the fluid matter, for the positions of these particles have greatly changed since a year ago. Nor can he define it by the positions of the Sun and fixed stars. For the unequal influx of subtle matter through the poles of the vortices towards the central stars (III. 104), the undulation (III. 114), inflation (III. 111) and absorption of the vortices, and other more true causes, such as the rotation of the Sun and stars around their own centres, the generation of spots, and the passage of comets through the heavens, change both the magnitude and positions of the stars so much that perhaps they are only adequate to designate the place sought with an error of several miles; and still less can the place be accurately defined and determined by their help, as a Geometer would require. Truly there are no bodies in the world whose relative positions remain unchanged with the passage of time, and certainly none which do not move in the Cartesian sense: that is, which are neither trans- ported from the vicinity of contiguous bodies nor are parts of other bodies so trans- ferred. And thus there is no basis from which we can at the present pick out a place which was in the past, or say that such a place is any longer discoverable in nature. For since, according to Descartes, place is nothing but the surface of surrounding bodies or position among some other more distant bodies, it is impossible (according to his doctrine) that it should exist in nature any longer than those bodies maintain the same positions from which he takes the individual designation. And so, reason- ing as in the question of Jupiter's position a year ago, it is clear that if one follows Cartesian doctrine, not even God himself could define the past position of any moving body accurately and geometrically now that a fresh state of things prevails, since in fact, due to the changed positions of the bodies, the place does not exist in nature any longer.

Now as it is impossible to pick out the place in which a motion began (that is, the beginning of the space passed over), for this place no longer exists after the motion is completed, so the space passed over, having no beginning, can have no length; and hence, since velocity depends upon the distance passed over in a given time, it fol- lows that the moving body can have no velocity, just as I wished to prove at first. Moreover, what was said of the beginning of the space passed over should be applied to all intermediate points too; and thus as the space has no beginning nor interme- diate parts it follows that there was no space passed over and thus no determinate motion, which was my second point. It follows indubitably that Cartesian motion is not motion, for it has no velocity, no definition, and there is no space or distance traversed by it. So it is necessary that the definition of places, and hence of local motion, be referred to some motionless thing such as extension alone or space in so far as it is seen to be truly distinct from bodies. And this the Cartesian philosopher may the more willingly allow, if only he notices that Descartes himself had an idea of extension as distinct from bodies, which he wished to distinguish from corporeal extension by calling it generic (II. 10, 12, 18). And also that the rotations of the vortices, from which he deduced the force of the aether in receding from their centres and thus the whole of his mechanical philosophy, are tacitly referred to generic extension.

In addition, as Descartes in Part II, Art. 4 and 11 seems to have demonstrated that body does not differ at all from extension, abstracting hardness, colour, weight, cold, heat and the remaining qualities which body can lack, so that at last there remains only its extension in length, width and depth which hence alone appertain to its essence;* and as this has been taken as proved by many, and is in my view the only reason for having confidence in this opinion; lest any doubt should remain about the nature of motion, I shall reply to this argument by explaining what extension and body are, and how they differ from each other. For since the distinction of substances into thinking and extended [entities], or rather, into thoughts and extensions, is the principal foundation of Cartesian philosophy, which he contends to be even better known than mathematical demonstrations: I consider it most important to overthrow [that philosophy] as regards extension, in order to lay truer foundations of the mechanical sciences.

Perhaps now it may be expected that I should define extension as substance or accident or else nothing at all. But by no means, for it has its own manner of existence which fits neither substances nor accidents. It is not substance; on the one hand, because it is not absolute in itself, but is as it were an emanent effect of God, or a disposition of all being; on the other hand, because it is not among the proper dispositions that denote substance, namely actions, such as thoughts in the mind and motions in body. For although philosophers do not define substance as an entity that can act upon things, yet all tacitly understand this of substances, as follows from the fact that they would readily allow extension to be substance in the manner of body if only it were capable of motion and of sharing in the actions of body. And on the contrary they would hardly allow that body is substance if it could not move nor

* Descartes's *Principles of Philosophy* (II. 4 and II. 11).

excite in the mind any sensation or perception whatever. Moreover, since we can clearly conceive extension existing without any subject, as when we may imagine spaces outside the world or places empty of body, and we believe [extension] to exist wherever we imagine there are no bodies, and we cannot believe that it would perish with the body if God should annihilate a body, it follows that [extension] does not exist as an accident inherent in some subject. And hence it is not an accident. And much less may it be said to be nothing, since it is rather something, than an accident, and approaches more nearly to the nature of substance. There is no idea of nothing, nor has nothing any properties, but we have an exceptionally clear idea of extension, abstracting the dispositions and properties of a body so that there remains only the uniform and unlimited stretching out of space in length, breadth and depth. And furthermore, many of its properties are associated with this idea; these I shall now enumerate not only to show that it is something, but what it is.

1. In all directions, space can be distinguished into parts whose common limits we usually call surfaces; and these surfaces can be distinguished in all directions into parts whose common limits we usually call lines; and again these lines can be distinguished in all directions into parts which we call points. And hence surfaces do not have depth, nor lines breadth, nor points dimension, unless you say that coterminous spaces penetrate each other as far as the depth of the surface between them, namely what I have said to be the boundary of both or the common limit; and the same applies to lines and points. Furthermore spaces are everywhere contiguous to spaces, and extension is everywhere placed next to extension, and so there are everywhere common boundaries to contiguous parts; that is, there are everywhere surfaces acting as a boundary to solids on this side and that; and everywhere lines in which parts of the surfaces touch each other; and everywhere points in which the continuous parts of lines are joined together. And hence there are everywhere all kinds of figures, everywhere spheres, cubes, triangles, straight lines, everywhere circular, elliptical, parabolical and all other kinds of figures, and those of all shapes and sizes, even though they are not disclosed to sight. For the material delineation of any figure is not a new production of that figure with respect to space, but only a corporeal representation of it, so that what was formerly insensible in space now appears to the senses to exist. For thus we believe all those spaces to be spherical through which any sphere ever passes, being progressively moved from moment to moment, even though a sensible trace of the sphere no longer remains there. We firmly believe that the space was spherical before the sphere occupied it, so that it could contain the sphere; and hence as there are everywhere spaces that can adequately contain any material sphere, it is clear that space is everywhere spherical. And so of other figures.

In the same way we see no material shapes in clear water, yet there are many in it which merely introducing some colour into its parts will cause to appear in many ways. However, if the colour were introduced, it would not constitute material shapes but only cause them to be visible.

2. Space extends infinitely in all directions. For we cannot imagine any limit anywhere without at the same time imagining that there is space beyond it. . . .

3. The parts of space are motionless. If they moved, it would have to be said either that the motion of each part is a translation from the vicinity of other contiguous parts, as Descartes defined the motion of bodies; and that this is absurd has been sufficiently shown; or that it is a translation out of space into space, that is out of itself, unless perhaps it is said that two spaces everywhere coincide, a moving one and a motionless one. Moreover the immobility of space will be best exemplified by duration. For just as the parts of duration derive their individuality from their order, so that (for example) if yesterday could change places with today and become the later of the two, it would lose its individuality and would no longer be yesterday, but today; so the parts of space derive their character from their positions, so that if any two could change their positions, they would change their character at the same time and each would be converted numerically into the other. The parts of duration and space are only understood to be the same as they really are because of their mutual order and position; nor do they have any hint of individuality apart from that order and position which consequently cannot be altered.

4. Space is a disposition of being *qua* being. No being exists or can exist which is not related to space in some way. God is everywhere, created minds are somewhere, and body is in the space that it occupies; and whatever is neither everywhere nor anywhere does not exist. And hence it follows that space is an effect arising from the first existence of being, because when any being is postulated, space is postulated. And the same may be asserted of duration: for certainly both are dispositions of being or attributes according to which we denominate quantitatively the presence and duration of any existing individual thing. So the quantity of the existence of God was eternal, in relation to duration, and infinite in relation to the space in which he is present; and the quantity of the existence of a created thing was as great, in relation to duration, as the duration since the beginning of its existence, and in relation to the size of its presence as great as the space belonging to it.

Moreover, lest anyone should for this reason imagine God to be like a body, extended and made of divisible parts, it should be known that spaces themselves are not actually divisible, and furthermore, that any being has a manner proper to itself of being in spaces. For thus there is a very different relationship between space and body, and space and duration. For we do not ascribe various durations to the different parts of space, but say that all endure together. The moment of duration is the same at Rome and at London, on the Earth and on the stars, and throughout all the heavens. And just as we understand any moment of duration to be diffused throughout all spaces, according to its kind, without any thought of its parts, so it is no more contradictory that Mind also, according to its kind, can be diffused through space without any thought of its parts.

5. The positions, distances and local motions of bodies are to be referred to the parts of space. And this appears from the properties of space enumerated as 1. and 4. above, and will be more manifest if you conceive that there are vacuities scattered between the particles, or if you pay heed to what I have formerly said about motion. To that it may be further added that in space there is no force of any kind which might impede or assist or in any way change the motions of bodies. And hence projectiles describe straight lines with a uniform motion unless they meet with an impediment from some other source. But more of this later.

6. Lastly, space is eternal in duration and immutable in nature, and this because it is the emanent effect of an eternal and immutable being. If ever space had not existed, God at that time would have been nowhere; and hence he either created space later (in which he was not himself), or else, which is not less repugnant to reason, he created his own ubiquity. Next, although we can possibly imagine that there is nothing in space, yet we cannot think that space does not exist, just as we cannot think that there is no duration, even though it would be possible to suppose that nothing whatever endures. This is manifest from the spaces beyond the world, which we must suppose to exist (since we imagine the world to be finite), although they are neither revealed to us by God, nor known from the senses, nor does their existence depend upon that of the spaces within the world. But it is usually believed that these spaces are nothing; yet indeed they are true spaces. Although space may be empty of body, nevertheless it is not in itself a void; and *something* is there, because spaces are there, although nothing more than that. Yet in truth it must be acknowledged that space is no more space where the world is, than where no world is, unless perchance you say that when God created the world in this space he at the same time created space in itself, or that if God should annihilate the world in this space, he would also annihilate the space in it. Whatever has more reality in one space than in another space must belong to body rather than to space; the same thing will appear more clearly if we lay aside that puerile and jejune prejudice according to which extension is inherent in bodies like an accident in a subject without which it cannot actually exist. . . .

... It must be agreed that God, by the sole action of thinking and willing, can prevent a body from penetrating any space defined by certain limits.

If he should exercise this power, and cause some space projecting above the Earth, like a mountain or any other body, to be impervious to bodies and thus stop or reflect light and all impinging things, it seems impossible that we should not consider this space to be truly body from the evidence of our senses (which constitute our sole judges in this matter); for it will be tangible on account of its impenetrability, and visible, opaque and coloured on account of the reflection of light, and it will resonate when struck because the adjacent air will be moved by the blow.

Thus we may imagine that there are empty spaces scattered through the world, one of which, defined by certain limits, happens by divine power to be impervious to bodies, and *ex hypothesi* it is manifest that this would resist the motions of bodies and perhaps reflect them, and assume all the properties of a corporeal particle, except that it will be motionless. If we may further imagine that that impenetrability is not always maintained in the same part of space but can be transferred hither and thither according to certain laws, yet so that the amount and shape of that impenetrable space are not changed, there will be no property of body which this does not possess. It would have shape, be tangible and mobile, and be capable of reflecting and being reflected, and no less constitute a part of the structure of things than any other corpuscle, and I do not see that it would not equally operate upon our minds and in turn be operated upon, because it is nothing more than the product of the divine mind realized in a definite quantity of space. For it is certain that God can stimulate our perception by his own will, and thence apply such power to the effects of his will. ...

Moreover, so that I may respond more concisely to Descartes's argument: let us abstract from body (as he commands) gravity, hardness and all sensible qualities, so that nothing remains except what pertains to its essence. Will extension alone then remain? By no means. For we may also reject that faculty or power by which they [the qualities] stimulate the perceptions of thinking beings. For since there is so great a distinction between the ideas of thinking and of extension that it is impossible there should be any basis of connection or relation [between them] except that which is caused by divine power, the above faculty of bodies can be rejected without violating extension, but not without violating their corporeal nature. Clearly the changes which can be induced in bodies by natural causes are only accidental and they do not denote a true change of substance. But if any change is induced that transcends natural causes, it is more than accidental and radically affects the substance. And according to the sense of the demonstration, only those things are to be rejected which bodies can be deprived of, and made to lack, by the force of nature. But should anyone object that bodies not united to minds cannot directly arouse perceptions in minds, and that hence since there are bodies not united to minds, it follows that this power is not essential to them: it should be noticed that there is no question here of an actual union, but only of a faculty in bodies by which they are capable of a union through the forces of nature. From the fact that the parts of the brain, especially the more subtle ones to which the mind is united, are in a continual flux, new ones succeeding to those which fly away, it is manifest that that faculty is in all bodies. And, whether you consider divine action or corporeal nature, to remove this is no less than to remove that other faculty by which bodies are enabled to transfer mutual actions from one to another, that is, to reduce body into empty space. . . .

READING

The Mathematical Principles of Natural Philosophy (*The* Principia)

Newton's Preface to the First Edition

Since the ancients (as we are told by *Pappus*) esteemed the science of mechanics of greatest importance in the investigation of natural things, and the moderns, rejecting substantial forms and occult qualities, have endeavored to subject the phenomena of nature to the laws of mathematics, I have in this treatise cultivated mathematics as far as it relates to philosophy. The ancients considered mechanics in a twofold respect; as rational, which proceeds accurately by demonstration, and practical. To practical mechanics all the manual arts belong, from which mechanics took its name. But as artificers do not work with perfect accuracy, it comes to pass that mechanics is so distinguished from geometry that what is perfectly accurate is called geometrical; what is less so, is called mechanical. However, the errors are not in the art, but in the artificers. He that works with less accuracy is an imperfect mechanic; and if any could work with perfect accuracy, he would be the most perfect mechanic of all, for the description of right lines and circles, upon which geometry is founded, belongs to mechanics. Geometry does not teach us to draw these lines, but requires them to be drawn, for it requires that the learner should first be taught to describe these accurately before he enters upon geometry, then it shows how by these operations problems may be solved. To describe right lines and circles are problems, but not geometrical problems. The solution of these problems is required from mechanics, and by geometry the use of them, when so solved, is shown; and it is the glory of geometry that from those few principles, brought from without, it is able to produce so many things. Therefore geometry is founded in mechanical practice, and is nothing but that part of universal mechanics which accurately proposes and demonstrates the art of measuring. But since the manual arts are chiefly employed in the moving of bodies, it happens that geometry is commonly referred to their magnitude, and mechanics to their motion. In this sense rational mechanics will be the science of motions resulting from any forces whatsoever, and of the forces required to produce any motions, accurately proposed and demonstrated. This part of mechanics, as far

Excerpts from Isaac Newton, *Principia*, translated by A. Motte, in *Sir Isaac Newton's* Mathematical Principles of Natural Philosophy *and His System of the World* (pp. xvii–xviii, 6–14), edited by F. Cajori. © 1934 by the Regents of the University of California. Reprinted by permission of University of California Press.

as it extended to the five powers which relate to manual arts, was cultivated by the ancients, who considered gravity (it not being a manual power) no otherwise than in moving weights by those powers. But I consider philosophy rather than arts and write not concerning manual but natural powers, and consider chiefly those things which relate to gravity, levity, elastic force, the resistance of fluids, and the like forces, whether attractive or impulsive; and therefore I offer this work as the mathematical principles of philosophy, for the whole burden of philosophy seems to consist in this—from the phenomena of motions to investigate the forces of nature, and then from these forces to demonstrate the other phenomena; and to this end the general propositions in the first and second Books are directed. In the third Book I give an example of this in the explication of the System of the World; for by the propositions mathematically demonstrated in the former Books, in the third I derive from the celestial phenomena the forces of gravity with which bodies tend to the sun and the several planets. Then from these forces, by other propositions which are also mathematical, I deduce the motions of the planets, the comets, the moon, and the sea. I wish we could derive the rest of the phenomena of Nature by the same kind of reasoning from mechanical principles, for I am induced by many reasons to suspect that they may all depend upon certain forces by which the particles of bodies, by some causes hitherto unknown, are either mutually impelled towards one another, and cohere in regular figures, or are repelled and recede from one another. These forces being unknown, philosophers have hitherto attempted the search of Nature in vain; but I hope the principles here laid down will afford some light either to this or some truer method of philosophy.

In the publication of this work the most acute and universally learned Mr. *Edmund Halley* not only assisted me in correcting the errors of the press and preparing the geometrical figures, but it was through his solicitations that it came to be published; for when he had obtained of me my demonstrations of the figure of the celestial orbits, he continually pressed me to communicate the same to the *Royal Society*, who afterwards, by their kind encouragement and entreaties, engaged me to think of publishing them. But after I had begun to consider the inequalities of the lunar motions, and had entered upon some other things relating to the laws and measures of gravity and other forces; and the figures that would be described by bodies attracted according to given laws; and the motion of several bodies moving among themselves; the motion of bodies in resisting mediums; the forces, densities, and motions, of mediums; the orbits of the comets, and such like, I deferred that publication till I had made a search into those matters, and could put forth the whole together. What relates to the lunar motions (being imperfect), I have put all together in the corollaries of Prop. LXVI, to avoid being obliged to propose and dis-

tinctly demonstrate the several things there contained in a method more prolix than
the subject deserved and interrupt the series of the other propositions. Some things,
found out after the rest, I chose to insert in places less suitable, rather than change
the number of the propositions and the citations. I heartily beg that what I have here
done may be read with forbearance; and that my labors in a subject so difficult may
be examined, not so much with the view to censure, as to remedy their defects.

                                                                                                          Is. Newton

Cambridge, Trinity College, May 8, 1686.

Scholium

Hitherto I have laid down the definitions of such words as are less known, and
explained the sense in which I would have them to be understood in the following
discourse. I do not define time, space, place, and motion, as being well known to all.
Only I must observe, that the common people conceive those quantities under no
other notions but from the relation they bear to sensible objects. And thence arise
certain prejudices, for the removing of which it will be convenient to distinguish
them into absolute and relative, true and apparent, mathematical and common.

I. Absolute, true, and mathematical time, of itself, and from its own nature, flows
equably without relation to anything external, and by another name is called duration: relative, apparent, and common time, is some sensible and external (whether
accurate or unequable) measure of duration by the means of motion, which is commonly used instead of true time; such as an hour, a day, a month, a year.

II. Absolute space, in its own nature, without relation to anything external, remains
always similar and immovable. Relative space is some movable dimension or
measure of the absolute spaces; which our senses determine by its position to bodies;
and which is commonly taken for immovable space; such is the dimension of a sub-
terraneous, an aerial, or celestial space, determined by its position in respect of the
earth. Absolute and relative space are the same in figure and magnitude; but they do
not remain always numerically the same. For if the earth, for instance, moves, a
space of our air, which relatively and in respect of the earth remains always the
same, will at one time be one part of the absolute space into which the air passes; at
another time it will be another part of the same, and so, absolutely understood, it
will be continually changed.

III. Place is a part of space which a body takes up, and is according to the space,
either absolute or relative. I say, a part of space; not the situation, nor the external

surface of the body. For the places of equal solids are always equal; but their surfaces, by reason of their dissimilar figures, are often unequal. Positions properly have no quantity, nor are they so much the places themselves, as the properties of places. The motion of the whole is the same with the sum of the motions of the parts; that is, the translation of the whole, out of its place, is the same thing with the sum of the translations of the parts out of their places; and therefore the place of the whole is the same as the sum of the places of the parts, and for that reason, it is internal, and in the whole body.

IV. Absolute motion is the translation of a body from one absolute place into another; and relative motion, the translation from one relative place into another. Thus in a ship under sail, the relative place of a body is that part of the ship which the body possesses; or that part of the cavity which the body fills, and which there-fore moves together with the ship: and relative rest is the continuance of the body in the same part of the ship, or of its cavity. But real, absolute rest, is the continuance of the body in the same part of that immovable space, in which the ship itself, its cavity, and all that it contains, is moved. Wherefore, if the earth is really at rest, the body, which relatively rests in the ship, will really and absolutely move with the same velocity which the ship has on the earth. But if the earth also moves, the true and absolute motion of the body will arise, partly from the true motion of the earth, in immovable space, partly from the relative motion of the ship on the earth; and if the body moves also relatively in the ship, its true motion will arise, partly from the true motion of the earth, in immovable space, and partly from the relative motions as well of the ship on the earth, as of the body in the ship; and from these relative motions will arise the relative motion of the body on the earth. As if that part of the earth, where the ship is, was truly moved towards the east, with a velocity of 10010 parts; while the ship itself, with a fresh gale, and full sails, is carried towards the west, with a velocity expressed by 10 of those parts; but a sailor walks in the ship towards the east, with 1 part of the said velocity; then the sailor will be moved truly in immovable space towards the east, with a velocity of 10001 parts, and relatively on the earth towards the west, with a velocity of 9 of those parts.

Absolute time, in astronomy, is distinguished from relative, by the equation or correction of the apparent time. For the natural days are truly unequal, though they are commonly considered as equal, and used for a measure of time; astronomers correct this inequality that they may measure the celestial motions by a more accu-rate time. It may be, that there is no such thing as an equable motion, whereby time may be accurately measured. All motions may be accelerated and retarded, but the flowing of absolute time is not liable to any change. The duration or perseverance of the existence of things remains the same, whether the motions are swift or slow, or none at all: and therefore this duration ought to be distinguished from what are only sensible measures thereof; and from which we deduce it, by means of the astronomical equation. The necessity of this equation, for determining the times of a phenomenon, is evinced as well from the experiments of the pendulum clock, as by eclipses of the satellites of Jupiter.

As the order of the parts of time is immutable, so also is the order of the parts of space. Suppose those parts to be moved out of their places, and they will be moved (if the expression may be allowed) out of themselves. For times and spaces are, as it were, the places as well of themselves as of all other things. All things are placed in time as to order of succession; and in space as to order of situation. It is from their essence or nature that they are places; and that the primary places of things should be movable, is absurd. These are therefore the absolute places; and translations out of those places, are the only absolute motions.

But because the parts of space cannot be seen, or distinguished from one another by our senses, therefore in their stead we use sensible measures of them. For from the positions and distances of things from any body considered as immovable, we define all places; and then with respect to such places, we estimate all motions, considering bodies as transferred from some of those places into others. And so, instead of absolute places and motions, we use relative ones; and that without any inconvenience in common affairs; but in philosophical disquisitions, we ought to abstract from our senses, and consider things themselves, distinct from what are only sensible measures of them. For it may be that there is no body really at rest, to which the places and motions of others may be referred.

But we may distinguish rest and motion, absolute and relative, one from the other by their properties, causes, and effects. It is a property of rest, that bodies really at rest do rest in respect to one another. And therefore as it is possible, that in the remote regions of the fixed stars, or perhaps far beyond them, there may be some body absolutely at rest; but impossible to know, from the position of bodies to one another in our regions, whether any of these do keep the same position to that remote body, it follows that absolute rest cannot be determined from the position of bodies in our regions.

It is a property of motion, that the parts, which retain given positions to their wholes, do partake of the motions of those wholes. For all the parts of revolving bodies endeavor to recede from the axis of motion; and the impetus of bodies moving forwards arises from the joint impetus of all the parts. Therefore, if surrounding bodies are moved, those that are relatively at rest within them will partake of their motion. Upon which account, the true and absolute motion of a body cannot be determined by the translation of it from those which only seem to rest; for the external bodies ought not only to appear at rest, but to be really at rest. For otherwise, all included bodies, besides their translation from near the surrounding ones, partake likewise of their true motions; and though that translation were not made, they would not be really at rest, but only seem to be so. For the surrounding bodies stand in the like relation to the surrounded as the exterior part of a whole does to the interior, or as the shell does to the kernel; but if the shell moves, the kernel will also move, as being part of the whole, without any removal from near the shell.

A property, near akin to the preceding, is this, that if a place is moved, whatever is placed therein moves along with it; and therefore a body, which is moved from a place in motion, partakes also of the motion of its place. Upon which account, all motions, from places in motion, are no other than parts of entire and absolute motions; and every entire motion is composed of the motion of the body out of its first place, and the motion of this place out of its place; and so on, until we come to some immovable place, as in the before-mentioned example of the sailor. Wherefore, entire and absolute motions can be no otherwise determined than by immovable places; and for that reason I did before refer those absolute motions to immovable places, but relative ones to movable places. Now no other places are immovable but those that, from infinity to infinity, do all retain the same given position one to another; and upon this account must ever remain unmoved; and do thereby constitute immovable space.

The causes by which true and relative motions are distinguished, one from the other, are the forces impressed upon bodies to generate motion. True motion is neither generated nor altered, but by some force impressed upon the body moved; but relative motion may be generated or altered without any force impressed upon the body. For it is sufficient only to impress some force on other bodies with which the former is compared, that by their giving way, that relation may be changed, in which the relative rest or motion of this other body did consist. Again, true motion suffers always some change from any force impressed upon the moving body; but relative motion does not necessarily undergo any change by such forces. For if the same forces are likewise impressed on those other bodies, with which the comparison is made, that the relative position may be preserved, then that condition will be preserved in which the relative motion consists. And therefore any relative motion may be changed when the true motion remains unaltered, and the relative may be preserved when the true suffers some change. Thus, true motion by no means consists in such relations.

The effects which distinguish absolute from relative motion are, the forces of receding from the axis of circular motion. For there are no such forces in a circular motion purely relative, but in a true and absolute circular motion, they are greater or less, according to the quantity of the motion. If a vessel, hung by a long cord, is so often turned about that the cord is strongly twisted, then filled with water, and held at rest together with the water; thereupon, by the sudden action of another force, it is whirled about the contrary way, and while the cord is untwisting itself, the vessel continues for some time in this motion; the surface of the water will at first be plain, as before the vessel began to move; but after that, the vessel, by gradually communicating its motion to the water, will make it begin sensibly to revolve, and recede by little and little from the middle, and ascend to the sides of the vessel, forming itself into a concave figure (as I have experienced), and the swifter the motion becomes, the higher will the water rise, till at last, performing its revolutions in the same times with the vessel, it becomes relatively at rest in it. This ascent of the water shows its endeavor to recede from the axis of its motion; and the true and absolute circular motion of the water, which is here directly contrary to the relative, becomes known, and may be measured by this endeavor. At first, when the relative motion of the water in the vessel was greatest, it produced no endeavor to recede from the axis; the water showed no tendency to the circumference, nor any ascent towards the sides of the vessel, but remained of a plain surface, and therefore its true circular motion had not yet begun. But afterwards, when the relative motion of the water had decreased, the ascent thereof towards the sides of the vessel proved its endeavor to recede from the axis; and this endeavor showed the real circular motion of the water continually increasing, till it had acquired its greatest quantity, when the water rested relatively in the vessel. And therefore this endeavor does not depend upon any translation of the water in respect of the ambient bodies, nor can true circular motion be defined by such translation. There is only one real circular motion of any one revolving body, corresponding to only one power of endeavoring to recede from its axis of motion, as its proper and adequate effect; but relative motions, in one and the same body, are innumerable, according to the various relations it bears to external bodies, and, like other relations, are altogether destitute of any real effect, any otherwise than they may perhaps partake of that one only true motion. And therefore in their system who suppose that our heavens, revolving below the sphere of the fixed stars, carry the planets along with them; the several parts of those heavens, and the planets, which are indeed relatively at rest in their heavens, do yet really move. For they change their position one to another (which never happens to bodies truly at rest), and being carried together with their heavens, partake of their motions, and as parts of revolving wholes, endeavor to recede from the axis of their motions.

Wherefore relative quantities are not the quantities themselves, whose names they bear, but those sensible measures of them (either accurate or inaccurate), which are commonly used instead of the measured quantities themselves. And if the meaning of words is to be determined by their use, then by the names time, space, place, and motion, their [sensible] measures are properly to be understood; and the expression will be unusual, and purely mathematical, if the measured quantities themselves are meant. On this account, those violate the accuracy of language, which ought to be kept precise, who interpret these words for the measured quantities. Nor do those less defile the purity of mathematical and philosophical truths, who confound real quantities with their relations and sensible measures.

It is indeed a matter of great difficulty to discover, and effectually to distinguish, the true motions of particular bodies from the apparent; because the parts of that immovable space, in which those motions are performed, do by no means come under the observation of our senses. Yet the thing is not altogether desperate; for we have some arguments to guide us, partly from the apparent motions, which are the differences of the true motions; partly from the forces, which are the causes and effects of the true motions. For instance, if two globes, kept at a given distance one from the other by means of a cord that connects them, were revolved about their common centre of gravity, we might, from the tension of the cord, discover the endeavor of the globes to recede from the axis of their motion, and from thence we might compute the quantity of their circular motions. And then if any equal forces should be impressed at once on the alternate faces of the globes to augment or diminish their circular motions, from the increase or decrease of the tension of the cord, we might infer the increment or decrement of their motions; and thence would be found on what faces those forces ought to be impressed, that the motions of the globes might be most augmented; that is, we might discover their hindmost faces, or those which, in the circular motion, do follow. But the faces which follow being known, and consequently the opposite ones that precede, we should likewise know the determination of their motions. And thus we might find both the quantity and the determination of this circular motion, even in an immense vacuum, where there was nothing external or sensible with which the globes could be compared. But now, if in that space some remote bodies were placed that kept always a given position one to another, as the fixed stars do in our regions, we could not indeed determine from the relative translation of the globes among those bodies, whether the motion did belong to the globes or to the bodies. But if we observed the cord, and found that its tension was that very tension which the motions of the globes required, we might conclude the motion to be in the globes, and the bodies to be at rest; and then, lastly, from the translation of the globes among the bodies, we should find the determination of their motions. But how we are to obtain the true motions from their causes, effects, and apparent differences, and the converse, shall be explained more at large in the following treatise. For to this end it was that I composed it.

Axioms, or Laws of Motion

Law I

Every body continues in its state of rest, or of uniform motion in a right line, unless it is compelled to change that state by forces impressed upon it.

Projectiles continue in their motions, so far as they are not retarded by the resistance of the air, or impelled downwards by the force of gravity. A top, whose parts by their cohesion are continually drawn aside from rectilinear motions, does not cease its rotation, otherwise than as it is retarded by the air. The greater bodies of the planets and comets, meeting with less resistance in freer spaces, preserve their motions both progressive and circular for a much longer time.

Law II

The change of motion is proportional to the motive force impressed; and is made in the direction of the right line in which that force is impressed.

If any force generates a motion, a double force will generate double the motion, a triple force triple the motion, whether that force be impressed altogether and at once, or gradually and successively. And this motion (being always directed the same way with the generating force), if the body moved before, is added to or subtracted from the former motion, according as they directly conspire with or are directly contrary to each other; or obliquely joined, when they are oblique, so as to produce a new motion compounded from the determination of both.

Law III

To every action there is always opposed an equal reaction: or, the mutual actions of two bodies upon each other are always equal, and directed to contrary parts.

Whatever draws or presses another is as much drawn or pressed by that other. If you press a stone with your finger, the finger is also pressed by the stone. If a horse draws a stone tied to a rope, the horse (if I may so say) will be equally drawn back towards the stone; for the distended rope, by the same endeavor to relax or unbend itself, will draw the horse as much towards the stone as it does the stone towards the horse, and will obstruct the progress of the one as much as it advances that of the other. If a body impinge upon another, and by its force change the motion of the other, that body also (because of the equality of the mutual pressure) will undergo an equal change, in its own motion, towards the contrary part. The changes made by these actions are equal, not in the velocities but in the motions of bodies; that is to say, if the bodies are not hindered by any other impediments. For, because the motions are equally changed, the changes of the velocities made towards contrary parts are inversely proportional to the bodies. This law takes place also in attractions, as will be proved in the next Scholium.

COMMENTARY

7.1   Introduction

We can gain insight into the significance of the work of Sir Isaac Newton (1643–1727) by comparing him with Euclid, and more specifically by comparing Newton's great work the *Principia* (or "The Mathematical Principles of Natural Philosophy," to give its full English title) with the *Elements*. The former book, first published in 1687, is the source of classical mechanics, as the latter is the source of classical geometry, and familiar student textbooks are designed to teach the ideas that they contain.

Euclid was the great synthesizer of geometry, and Newton served an analogous role in mechanics, as the preface to the *Principia* makes clear. The format of the book itself fits the pattern of the *Elements:* definitions and axioms are given, followed by proofs of propositions concerning various kinds of motion. Not only is the logic of their work comparable, but so too are their historical positions. As I noted in the chapter on Euclid, neither produced new science entirely out of the blue, but rather completed in a single system developments initiated by earlier scientists. This in no way denigrates their respective achievements—rather it reveals the nature of their creative geniuses: thinkers before them discovered important clues to the new science, but it was Euclid and Newton who finally solved the riddles.

Mechanics is a theory of motion, and intuitively motion is change of position, so space—the collection of all possible positions—is an integral element of mechanics. Not surprisingly then, Newton, like Aristotle, wrote about the nature of space and its role within his theory. He took the Euclidean hypothesis literally: he accepted that space had a (three-dimensional) Euclidean structure, and, contrary to the relationist, that it served as a distinct container for material objects. The account is laid out in the two readings reprinted here: *De Gravitatione* (or, "On the Gravity and Equilibrium of Fluids") and the later *Scholium* (following definition eight of the *Principia*). The former was unpublished in its time and was only discovered in the 1940s, and so it was unknown to those who wrote the essays in this anthology. It is interesting reading, however, for although the later *Scholium* advances new and perhaps stronger arguments, *De Gravitatione* develops certain points more clearly.

One might wonder why Newton felt it necessary to discuss apparently philosophical questions in a physics text. The answer, as we shall see, is that not all questions can be so neatly pigeon-holed: this issue, like many others, is neither strictly philosophical nor strictly scientific. Indeed, before the twentieth century, the distinction was made far less rigidly than it is now. In the next section, we will follow Newton in explicating the notion of absolute space as an alternative to Descartes's views and then consider the role that he believed it to play within his mechanics. The topic of this chapter is the subtle concept of inertia. To facilitate understanding we will look at the same basic ideas several times, from different angles and with increasing depth.

7.2   Absolute Space and True Motion

In *De Gravitatione*, Newton seeks to dispute Descartes's identification of matter with space and to describe his alternative account of matter-independent, absolute space. We will consider in particular Newton's criticisms of two components of Descartes's theory: the claim that "true" motion is motion relative to immediate surroundings (*Principles*, II. 25), and the view that position—a crucial aspect of place—is a relational notion (*Principles*, II. 13).

As we will soon see, the distinction—implicit in the principle of inertia—between objects in constant versus accelerated motion is often sharply detectable: you feel pushed to the floor of an elevator as you accelerate upward, or thrown forward when your bus comes to an abrupt halt, for instance. And in particular, rotating objects seem to pull away from the center of the rotation: for example, on those funfair rides in which a circular room is spun at speed, you are pressed against the wall and don't slide down when the floor is lowered. A similar phenomenon is observed in all rotating bodies, including the planets, since they rotate both about the sun and on their own axes.

So it seems that Descartes is committed to three things that are, if not inconsistent, difficult to reconcile: First, since on his view the Earth is at rest in its surroundings, it is at true rest. Second, the Earth exhibits a tendency to recede from the Sun, which, third, according to the principle of inertia, means that it is accelerating. In other words, the Earth accelerates and yet is truly at rest. It seems that the real, observable effect of recession must be due to some "false" motion, for instance, relative to the fixed stars: "Is this tendency to be derived from the ... true and philosophical rest of the planets, or rather from [their] common and nonphilosophical motion?" (*De Grav.*, this vol., p. 107). The problem here is one that we will see again later: objects can simultaneously be at true rest and yet detectably accelerate. It seems that Descartes's notion is demonstrably inapplicable in the science of mechanics; and if we accept Aristotle's view that the study of space is only important for the study of motion, it follows that Cartesian "true motion" is of no fundamental significance.

It doesn't make sense to explain the planets' tendency to recede in terms of their true rest, but what about in terms of their "common"—or "nonphilosophical"—relative motions? This sense of motion is the second of Descartes's views that Newton attacks, using a generalization of the first argument. For a single body will have many relative motions, relative to distinct objects "regarded at rest": for instance, the Earth has different motions relative to the distant stars, to Saturn, to Jupiter, and so on. But suppose (correctly) that the Earth's tendency to recede from the Sun depends on its motion, so that the faster it accelerates, the more it pulls away; then, relative to each of the bodies "regarded at rest," the Earth will exhibit a different tendency to recede. But this is impossible: the Earth pulls away in exactly one way, not many. Otherwise it would be as if you were pushed into the wall of the funfair ride with different forces relative to the ground, the Moon, the Sun or whatever; no, you are pushed with just one force. The point is that in a theory of mechanics, such as Newton's (and Descartes's), which explains *inertial effects* such as the tendency to recede, one of an object's motions must be *absolute:* the motion that determines the strength of the tendency, for example. So, not all relative motions are equal: relationism cannot be the whole truth about mechanics.

Newton has already rejected Descartes's true motion as a candidate for absolute motion within mechanics, so we should now consider just what account he gives of absolute motion. This is the second subject of *De Gravitatione:* the theory of absolute space. This theory is often called the "container view," and this metaphor is quite useful as a first approximation. Just as your breakfast cereal and the box it comes in are distinct and equally real, so the material universe and its container—space—are supposed to be distinct but equally real things. And just as the pieces of cereal will be at different relative distances from one another, but at unique places in the box, so objects will have various relative positions but a unique absolute position in space. (On the other hand, absolute space is infinite and unbounded, quite unlike a cereal box.) Consider then the several senses in which Newton suggests that space is absolute.

Substantivalism.   Newton makes clear (*De Grav.*, this vol., p. 111) that he takes space to be a geometric object, just as we conceived it in the Euclidean hypothesis. It is composed of points, collections of which comprise lines, surfaces and "solids" (in the sense of having volume, not solidity) as in geometry. These geometric objects are possible "absolute places" for material objects, over and above their relative locations. The points, then, exist independently of material objects: first in the sense that locations exist before they are occupied—"We firmly believe that the space was spherical before the sphere occupied it..." (*De Grav.*, this vol., p. 111); and second in the sense that space would exist even if there were no matter—"we can possibly imagine that there is nothing in space, yet we cannot think that space does not exist ..." (*De Grav.*, this vol., p. 113). Existence independent from matter is the first sense in which Newton thinks space is absolute, not relative; in contrast, if there were no material objects then there would be no relative distances between objects, and hence no space, according to the relationist.

Of course, such matter-independence makes space hard to understand, for familiar objects are material, and if space is not, it must have some unfamiliar nature. Newton is aware of this problem and attempts to address it, somewhat unsatisfactorily, in *De Gravitatione* (this vol., p. 113). His view is that space is a necessary precondition of the existence, not just of matter but of God, who is everywhere. That is, space is an immediate consequence of God's presence. This is an interesting idea, but it neither fits comfortably with modern science, nor helps us much in understanding how space can be physical and yet immaterial. Newton puts the problem this way (*De Grav.*, this vol., p. 110): he thinks that any object is composed of matter, or "substance," in which the various properties, or "accidents," of the object are manifested. Hence if space is something then it should either be substance—as Descartes said—or a property. But, it seems to be neither: space is not substance because it depends on God's presence for its existence, and space is not a property of substance because there can be empty space, without substance. And yet space is *something*, rather than nothing: it "approaches more nearly the nature of substance" (*De Grav.*, this vol., p. 111). Roughly, Newton's view is that absolute space is "stuff" rather than a "property," but not as substantial as matter. This part of his view has become known as *substantivalism*: it asserts that absolute space is something as real as matter and whose existence does not require matter, but which is not the same stuff as matter. Many philosophers and scientists have found this notion hard to swallow and have adopted relationism instead, which denies the existence of a matter-independent space and replaces it with a system of relations between objects.

Immutability.   Not only does Newton believe space to be distinct from matter, in much the way that objects are distinct from one another, he believes it to be unaffected by matter or by anything else (*De Grav.*, this vol., p. 113, *Principia*, this vol., p. 118). Thus points, lines, surfaces, and "solids" persist through time and remain the same sizes and distances apart: absolute space is an infinite, three-dimensional, rigid, Euclidean "box" that exists, unchanging through all time.

Absolute motion.   Immutability is important to Newton's view in that it allows the specification of one absolute motion, over and above motions relative to material objects. For, as he says, "the positions, distances and local motions of bodies are to be referred to the parts of space" (*De Grav.*, this vol., p. 113). Thus the absolute motion of a body is its motion relative to the unchanging points of absolute space. For example: An object is at absolute rest just in case it remains at the same point of space; if a body moves in a straight line in space between two points 5m apart in 1s, then it has an average absolute velocity of 5m/s; and an object's absolute rotation is given by the size of the circle it traverses in absolute space and the time it takes to return to the same absolute point on the orbit.

Here, three points should be emphasized: First, strictly speaking, absolute motion is motion *relative* to absolute space! However, we will for simplicity use "relative motion" to mean motion relative to material objects. Second, relationists can be absolutist in some ways: for instance, Leibniz denied that there is a substantival, matter-independent space, but he did believe that between any two objects there is a definite distance, which is independent of how it is measured. Such a notion is, in some sense, absolute too, and Poincaré will be seen to question this sense later.

Third, we have given one account of absolute motion, as motion in absolute space; but, as we shall see, other accounts are possible, perhaps even "relational" ones. (Indeed, one can see Descartes's true motion as a—failed—proposal for absolute motion.) In other words, the terminology at this point is a little confusing: potentially, a motion could be absolute, even if there were no absolute space.*

Newton attacked Descartes's theories of true place and his relational account of position on the grounds that they yielded, respectively, either incorrect or ambiguous senses of motion. It seems that mechanics requires an absolute standard of motion, and Newton's absolute space can provide it. For the rest of this chapter we will study this argument in more detail: first developing the idea of relationism in more sophisticated terms than Descartes, and then studying what familiar mechanical phenomena might require an absolute standard of motion.

---

*Those familiar with the topics in this book will probably realize that there is an ambiguity in the term "absolute motion," and in particular in "absolute acceleration." Some, such as Sklar (1976) and Friedman (1983), define the term to refer to noninertial motions revealed by inertial effects. Others, such as Earman (1989), define the term to refer to nongeodesic motions in the appropriate spacetime. Of course, in the space-time picture one identifies inertial and geodesic motions, making the uses coextensional, but that identification begs the important question raised in the current discussion: "What is absolute acceleration (in the first sense)?" I will thus use the expression in the former sense: objects that exhibit inertial effects are absolutely accelerating by definition.

7.3 Relative Spaces

In this section we will consider the relational view more carefully. It is important to bear in mind that "relational" or "relative" space is *not* the "relativistic space" of Einstein's theory of relativity. The two views of space are closely linked historically and logically, but relativistic space resembles both absolute and relative space in certain aspects (though it is different from both). Until the final reading, we will discuss only relative/relational space and relationism, not relativistic space or relativity; though part of the mission of the book is to introduce some of the key ideas needed to understand relativity.

What is relative space? When considering the position or motion of something, we need to know where it is located with reference to other things: to drive to work we need to know the position of our house relative to our destination, to land a plane we need to know our location relative to the runway, in high-energy physics experiments we want to know the position of particles relative to the laboratory, to send rockets to the moon we need to know the relative places of the Earth and Moon, and so on. In each of these examples, we define a "frame of reference" (or simply a "frame") relative to some object, called the "reference body." Sometimes the object is yourself (as when you wonder if a car will hit you), sometimes the object is the Earth's surface (as when we measure the speed of a runner), and sometimes it is the Sun or our galaxy (as when we study the Earth's orbit). It is such reference frames that Newton has in mind when he discusses relative spaces (e.g., *Principia*, this vol., pp. 118–119).

Given such a frame, we can introduce relative motion as the change of position relative to the reference body. Recall Descartes's nice example in the *Principles* (II. 13) of a sailor sitting on the deck of a moving ship (see also *Principia*, this vol., p. 119). The sailor does not change his position relative to the ship, so in the ship frame he is stationary; but relative to the shore, since the ship moves, so does the sailor. We can distinguish states of relative motion in a reference frame more precisely: a body is said to be *at rest* in a frame if it remains at a fixed distance in a fixed direction (so that it is not orbiting) from the reference body, and it is said to be in *constant relative motion* in a frame when it moves in a straight line and covers equal distances in equal times in that frame. Otherwise—that is, if an object changes its speed or travels along a curved trajectory relative to the reference body—it is *relatively accelerating*.

Four objects at mutual rest—or four distinct points of a single object—can define a relative reference frame: one for the origin, and one to define the direction of each of three axes, x, y, and z. We will take the axes to be at right angles to one another.

Each axis defines a vector of unit length. Let unit vector $\mathbf{i}$ point in the direction of the x-axis, $\mathbf{j}$ the y-axis, and $\mathbf{k}$ the z-axis. Between the origin and an object at coordinates (x, y, z) lies its relative *position vector*, $\mathbf{r} \equiv x\mathbf{i} + y\mathbf{j} + z\mathbf{k}$.

In a frame of reference the relative *velocity vector* of an object is its change of position per unit time: $\mathbf{v} \equiv d\mathbf{r}/dt = dx/dt \cdot \mathbf{i} + dy/dt \cdot \mathbf{j} + dz/dt \cdot \mathbf{k}$ m/s. (See section 3.4.)

The relative acceleration of an object is its change of velocity per unit time: $\mathbf{a} \equiv d\mathbf{v}/dt = d^2\mathbf{r}/dt^2 = d^2x/dt^2 \cdot \mathbf{i} + d^2y/dt^2 \cdot \mathbf{j} + d^2z/dt^2 \cdot \mathbf{k}$ m/s^2.

If an object has a constant velocity, then its velocity along each axis is constant over time, so dx/dt, dy/dt, and dz/dt are constant and $\mathbf{a} = 0$.

If $\mathbf{a} \neq 0$ and $\mathbf{a}$ and $\mathbf{v}$ are parallel, then the object changes speed but not direction over time, and the acceleration is *linear*. If $\mathbf{a} \neq 0$ but $\mathbf{a}$ and $\mathbf{v}$ are not parallel, then the trajectory is not straight, and the acceleration is *nonlinear*.

We can similarly define an absolute frame of reference by taking four points of absolute space: one for the origin, and one to define the direction of each of three axes, x, y, and z. Position, velocity, and acceleration of an object can then be defined exactly as are relative position, velocity, and acceleration, except with respect to the absolute frame, and hence with respect to space itself, not other material objects.

At this point we can discuss thoroughly our common notions of relational positions and motions: as the examples show, we are usually concerned with locations and movements of objects relative to one another. In fact, one might well wonder if relative spaces are sufficient for all cases, not just everyday ones. Given a relative frame, one can specify unequivocally the location of any object at any time, and what more need be said? In particular, why hypothesize the existence of Newton's absolute space, which is supposed to exist independently of matter? The relationist claims that since such a separate "background" space is unnecessary, it simply does not exist; instead there are only relative positions (and motions), and no further positions in a matter-independent space.

If one wants an unambiguous way to describe the location of an object along its trajectory, then it is true that any relative frame is entirely adequate (this fact is often called *kinematic relativity*). However, spatial notions, such as position and motion, must do more work then this, for they provide the framework for mechanics. And as we have seen (and are attempting to understand), not all relative frames are mechanically equivalent: Newton pointed out that the magnitude of a rotating object's tendency to recede must be determined by one relative motion, not by all of them. (In other words, dynamic relativity does not hold generally.)

As we shall discuss in the next section, this phenomenon is a direct result of the principle of inertia. As we noted in the previous chapter, according to this principle—Newton's first law—"Every body continues in its state of rest, or of uniform motion in a right line, unless it is compelled to change that state by forces impressed upon it" (*Principia*, this vol., p. 124). According to the law there is a genuine distinction between uniform and accelerated motions—revealed by the effects of impressed forces—but there seems to be no unequivocal relative motion: the same body accelerates relatively in some frames and moves uniformly in others. If all frames are equal, then "the velocity of a body moving without resistance cannot be said to be uniform, nor the line said to be straight in which its motion is accomplished" (*De Grav.*, this vol., p. 108). According to the law of inertia, every object has a unique, definite "absolute acceleration" (equal to zero for an object in uniform motion). An acceleration, our thinkers suppose, is a kind of motion relative to something—the question is, "relative to what?" What should fill the blank in the statement "absolute acceleration is acceleration relative to _____"? Newton filled in "absolute space," but what is the relationist to say? Unless a particular frame is specified, the notion of absolute acceleration is left unacceptably ambiguous; but what reason might a relationist give for selecting one specific frame?

To put the problem another way, the law of inertia cannot hold in every relative frame. Suppose two objects, X and Y, accelerate equally in a relative frame in which the law holds, X and Y must have forces on them. Then the law of inertia fails in the frame that Y defines: X does not accelerate in the frame, even though it has forces acting on it; and a third object with no forces acting on it will move constantly in the given frame, and hence accelerate in Y's frame. The principle of inertia cannot be true in every relative frame, so, referring to those frames in which it does hold as *inertial frames*, the problem for the relationist is to give a principled account of which of the many frames are inertial. Of course, Newton provided an answer to this question: absolute space itself defines an inertial frame.

One final point: among the problematic features of absolute space is that it cannot be seen and that its parts are all exactly alike. For this reason it is not generally possible to use an absolute frame of reference, and instead the absolutist uses relative spaces to describe motions. This is why Newton calls relative reference frames such things as the "sensible measures" of absolute space (*Principia*, this vol., p. 120). He means that we have to use observable material objects to describe locations. There is nothing wrong with this, for the absolutist does not deny the existence of relative spaces, but rather postulates absolute space in addition to them. The role of absolute space is not to provide a practical frame of reference, but to ground the absolute distinction between uniform and accelerated motions.

We have so far treated this distinction at a theoretical level, in terms of the law of inertia; now we will consider its practical consequences, and how Newton uses them against the relationist and in favor of absolute space.

7.4   Inertia

Stir your tea in the morning and then remove the spoon. The surface of the still spinning liquid will be curved up the sides of the cup. The phenomenon is familiar, but why does it occur? The first level of explanation is the same as for the deformation of any object: there are forces acting on the tea (similarly, the car is dented because something hit it). But what are these forces? It doesn't seem as if something is depressing the liquid from above (as when you blow on the surface perhaps), so what is happening? The answer lies in the principle of inertia: the tea is moving in circles inside the cup, and circular motions are not straight. The curvature of the water reveals the forces that produce this nonuniform motion.

Another familiar phenomenon should make this clearer: if you whirl a rock around your head on a rope, you will feel a pull outward—a "centrifugal force"—through the rope. Why? Suddenly left to itself (let go of the rope), the rock will have a straight uniform motion (don't try this indoors), so to prevent the rock from flying off you must exert a force on it by pulling the rope. According to Newton's third law, action and reaction are equal and opposite, so the rock pulls on you just as much as you pull on it. What seems slightly confusing is that if you release it, the rock will fly off at a tangent to the circle in which it moves, at right angles to the tension in the rope. But this is not so hard to understand: tangential motion is the natural straight motion for the rock, and the force towards the center is required to keep it curving inward. (From Newton's second law, an object accelerates in the direction of the force acting on it.) In general, one should think of circular motion as occurring when an object is constantly pulled towards the center, overcoming its inertial tendency to move tangentially.

Aristotle said that rotation was a simple motion, and there is something uncomplicated about a circle, but in fact the mechanics of rotation are not simple to work out and have tripped up many great scientists. Our treatment will be fairly heuristic, though accurate. The reader should also think through these ideas carefully to make sure that they are clear. For instance, if you've followed to this point you should be bothered by what has just been said in the previous two paragraphs, for forces causing rotation are directed toward the center, but when tea has been stirred in a cup, the surface curves outward and not inward. Even Newton would describe the curving effect as the tea's "tendency to recede from ... [the] centre about which [it revolves]" (*De Grav.*, this vol., p. 107), though he knew full well that rotating objects "tend" naturally to move tangentially.

The answer to this puzzle is that when an insufficiently large central force is applied to a rotating object, its inertial tendency to move tangentially is not fully

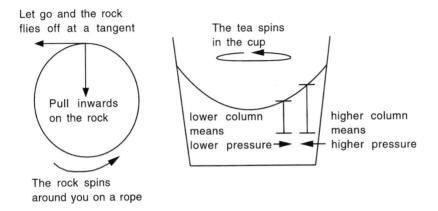

Figure 7.1
Rotation: objects rotating are acted upon by central forces.

overcome, and it spirals outward, rather than moving in a circle. When the spoon starts to stir there are no central forces on the tea, so it flows outward, curving up the sides of the cup. At this stage, at any point within the tea (see figure 7.1) the surface will be higher toward the edge than the center; consequently there will be a greater weight of tea above the outer side. The greater weight in turn implies that the pressure in the tea will be greater to the outer side of any point: there will be a net inward—that is, central—force on the tea at any point. That is, once stirred, the tea moves outward until its shape supplies the correct central forces to maintain its noninertial rotation.

It might be difficult to get comfortable with the concepts here, but the lesson that we need to draw is simple. The surface of the tea curves because it is rotating, and rotation requires a force directed toward the center. This fact is significant for it means that we can tell whether something is rotating without having to see it spinning, by looking for the presence of such central forces. A similar consideration applies to accelerations in general. For example, think of the way in which you are thrust back into your seat as you speed away at a green light: you would know that you were moving even if you had your eyes closed. As the law of inertia states, any time an object deviates from a constant straight motion there must be a force involved, and such forces generally have observable inertial effects: for instance, your being squashed into the back of the car seat. Thus the kind of effects seen in the bucket and globes discussed by Newton in the *Scholium* are representative of accelerations in general, not just rotations.

Accelerometer
at rest

Accelerometer
accelerating forward

Figure 7.2
The accelerometer: the displacement of the weight reveals the magnitude of the acceleration.

Lest it should seem that inertial effects are some kind of phantom that appear in accelerating bodies, we should examine a simple model that clarifies their origin. Consider an "accelerometer," a device designed to measure acceleration. It is a rigid box containing a weight that is attached by identical springs to the front and back ends. When there is no tension in the springs, the weight sits in the middle, but when the box is accelerated by a force applied to one side, the weight is displaced in that direction, just as you are "pushed" back into the seat of an accelerating car. Both your and the weight's movements are inertial effects associated with accelerations, and both provide a measure of the acceleration: the greater the displacement, the greater the acceleration. (As Newton points out [*Principia*, this vol., p. 122] the water in his bucket is also an accelerometer, for the height it reaches up the sides measures the rate of rotation.)

But there is nothing phantasmic about the weight's displacement (or yours). The box is rigid and so the force applied to it is instantaneously transmitted throughout, and obeying the law of inertia, it accelerates without deformation. On the other hand, the weight is not attached rigidly to the box, but through the springs. Thus the force is not transmitted instantaneously to the weight, which thus does not initially accelerate: the box accelerates forward but the weight does not, and it is displaced backward relative to the box. But as the weight is displaced, the spring in front is stretched and that behind compressed, pulling and pushing on the weight, until the force on it causes it to accelerate at the same rate as the box (if oscillations are suppressed). That is, the weight is displaced to a position in which the springs are stretched and compressed to transmit the applied force to the weight.

The accelerometer is just a simple model of what happens when a force is applied to any body. If the force is not applied in a way that makes every part accelerate at the same rate, then as it is transmitted through the body the various parts are deformed and placed under tension. But as we've just seen, there is nothing mysterious about these displacements and tensions: Any displaced part of a complex body is just like the weight in the accelerometer. We call these displacements and tensions *inertial effects,* for they result when a force overcomes the inertia of the body. Since

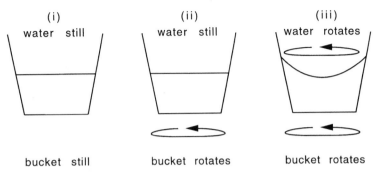

Figure 7.3
Newton's bucket experiment: the three stages observed.

such displacements are in principle observable, they are visible indications that a body is absolutely accelerating, as we understood earlier through the law of inertia. We will now see how Newton attempted to demonstrate the existence of absolute space using such phenomena.

7.5 Space and Inertia

Consider the experiment proposed by Newton (*Principia*, this vol., p. 122). He describes a bucket hung from a cord by its handle: before the experiment, the bucket is spun around, twisting the cord. With the apparatus prepared, the following three stages are observed.

(i)   The bucket of water is held still.
        Then it is released, and because of the tension in the cord ...

(ii)   the bucket starts to turn about its central axis, though the water sits still.
        Then, due to friction between the sides of the bucket and the water, the water starts to rotate as well, until ...

(iii)   finally, the water and bucket rotate at the same rate.

Why does the surface of the water curve? For the same reason the surface of the tea curves when stirred: because it is rotating. But it is clear, as Newton demonstrates, that the rotation revealed by the curvature is not rotation relative to the bucket: in stage (ii) the water rotates relative to the bucket but does not curve, and in stage (iii), when it is curved, the water is at rest relative to the bucket. This example is intended as a direct attack on Descartes's claim that objects—such as the Earth in its surrounding vortex of celestial matter—are truly at rest when they rest relative to their immediate surroundings. Immediately after describing this experiment Newton explicitly claims to have refuted the Cartesian account of the Earth's motion: those "who suppose that our heavens ... carry the planets along with them" must accept that the planets really move (*Principia*, this vol., p. 122). The water spinning in the bucket is just like the vortices that carry the planets around in Descartes's system, and just as (a "piece" of) the water "truly rotates" without moving from its immediate surroundings, so must Descartes's planets. In the first place, then, Newton has shown that true rotation is not absolute rotation: in particular, the curving of the water in stage (iii) reveals its absolute rotation even though it is in a state of true rest.

But Newton shows more, since he has revealed a weakness in any relational account of space. For the relationist, all motions are relational, and so if the curvature of the water reveals rotation, it must reveal a relative rotation. But relative to what? Not to the bucket, as we have just seen. Does the water rotate relative to itself? No, in all three stages, every part of the water is at rest with respect to every other, just like the points on a CD. (Moreover, the water does not rotate "relative to" a one-dimensional line through the axis of rotation, for that would require the line to have a determinate rotation about itself, which is incoherent.)

Does the curvature, then, reveal rotation relative to us, the observers standing around the bucket? The water is flat when at rest relative to us, but curved when rotating in front of us. But we can make exactly the same argument for observers as for the bucket. Running around a stationary bucket of water does not make its surface curve, and running around a rotating bucket of water does not make it flat: the curvature is independent of, and hence does not reveal, motion relative to us. And a similar argument applies to the suggestion that it is rotation relative to the room that the curvature reveals. Place the building on a giant turntable and attach the bucket by its cord through a hole in the roof to a crane overhead; spinning the building around the bucket can neither produce nor cancel curvature.

Let's try again. Perhaps it is rotation relative to the Earth that produces the curvature. This is no good either. In the first place, this suggestion reproduces the mistake of the previous proposals: there is no (suitable) interaction between the observers and the water, or the building and water, to explain the curvature, and neither is there between the Earth and the water. (Of course, there is the gravitational attraction of the Earth on the water, but classical gravity doesn't change when an object spins so that it is stronger at the center than the edges.) In the second place, observation tells us that the Earth is itself rotating: for instance, it is measurably bulged around the equator, just as the surface of the water curved. But if the Earth is rotating, it is not a fixed point for defining true rotations. For similar reasons, the Sun does not define a suitable reference frame either.

Newton himself does not explicitly refute the possibility that the curvature of the water indicates rotation relative to something other than the bucket. However, the globes thought experiment (*Principia*, this vol., p. 123) makes almost the same point against the relationist. If a pair of spheres are joined by a rod and set spinning, they will exert a central force through the rod on each other toward the axis of rotation. And, assuming Newtonian mechanics, such a force would be present—and measurable as a tension in the rod—even if there were no other material objects. But if there were no other material objects then the globes would not move relatively at all: tension in the rod would reveal an absolute rotation that could not be a relative one. Note that this argument takes us further than Newton's rejection of relationism in *De Gravitatione*: there he complained that relationism was ambiguous about motion, and here it seems that no relative frame at all can specify absolute acceleration.

The general point against the relationist is that there seem to be detectable motions that are not comprehensible as relative motions. To follow the logic through: At the heart of Newtonian mechanics is the principle of inertia, according to which accelerations are produced by forces; the effects of forces are generally detectable, so the question of whether an object is accelerating can be settled by observation; on the other hand, an object that accelerates in one relative frame might not accelerate in another, so apparently there is no relational notion of absolute acceleration; thus the principle of inertia does not make sense in relational terms, and objects that are detectably accelerating might not be in relative motion at all. It seems that the relationist cannot explain inertial effects, because the relationist has no proper notion of constant—inertial—motion. In the next two chapters we will see some relationist attempts to respond to Newton, but for now remember how he took absolute space to clarify these issues.

Newton believes that absolute space helps explain inertial effects because it provides an absolute standard of motion and a determinate acceleration for every object. In his mechanics, inertial motion is motion in a straight line at a constant speed "relative" to absolute space, and forces and inertial effects will be present when objects accelerate through absolute space: absolute space is an inertial frame. Looking at his view this way, we might say that Newton believes that absolute space is required by the best explanation of inertial effects, and hence that the bucket experiment provides abductive support for the hypothesis that space is absolute.

Before we close this discussion let us acknowledge two nagging doubts. First, consider the reasons given for rejecting relational accounts of the water's behavior. We did not deny that there was relative motion between the water and the observers, the Earth and the Sun; instead we pointed out that these motions could not adequately *explain* the curvature (either because there is no suitable interaction, or because the reference body itself rotates). We are not looking for just anything as a fixed reference, but the kind of thing that—very loosely—might "cause" spinning liquids to curve; we want an acceptable theory of mechanics in which there is a natural standard of constant motion. For example, a theory that simply postulates the existence of some arbitrary body to define an inertial reference frame would arguably be unsatisfactory, because it postulates that the body affects other objects—determining their inertial motions—without postulating a specific interaction between them. Newton's solution does seem satisfactory: by determining which trajectories are constant, absolute space determines the natural, unforced, inertial motions of objects, so the theory can explain deformations under applied forces.

But is this really an appealing position? It seems that there is an unpleasant lack of symmetry in what we have just described. Space acts on matter, keeping it on the "straight and narrow," but there is no reciprocal effect: matter can have no effect on space, because it is "always similar and immovable." Of course this is not a proof that the theory is wrong, but it does point to tension between the theory and the plausible principle that all action should be matched by some reaction. (Note too that a similar problem applies for Aristotle: the center of his universe can determine natural motions, but arguably the arrangement of matter cannot affect the center.)

The second worry will be made clear to us by Leibniz in the next chapter. Although it is generally possible to measure accelerations by inertial effects, there is no corresponding way to determine the absolute position and velocity of a material object. But if these absolute quantities are not detectable in any way, is there really any reason to think that they exist? And if not, why think that absolute space exists?

Problems

1. How does Newton's example involving the ship and the sailor help clarify the notion of absolute space? Of relative space?

2. Carry out Newton's bucket experiment and write it up as you would a piece of lab work, with a description of the apparatus, the method, the results, and conclusion. Does Newton draw the correct conclusion? What other explanations could there be of the phenomena observed?

3. Show that a rock, with a mass of $m$kg, circling a point at a distance of rm, with an instantaneous velocity of magnitude vm/s, will remain in the orbit if the force on

it toward the center is $F = mv^2/r$. Explain why the "endeavor to recede" of an object in rotation increases as it moves faster.

4. Compare Newton's arguments in *De Gravitatione* and the *Scholium*. In what ways does the earlier work foreshadow the ideas of the second? For instance, how do the arguments against Descartes's relationism develop between the two works?

Further Readings and Bibliography

Barbour, J. B. 1989. *Absolute or Relative Motion? A Study from a Machian Point of View of the Discovery and Structure of Dynamical Theories*, volume one (esp. chaps. 10–11). Cambridge, UK: Cambridge University Press. $\sqrt{}$

Earman, J. 1989. *World Enough and Space-Time*. Cambridge, MA: MIT Press.

Friedman, M. 1983. *Foundations of Space-Time Theories: Relativistic Physics and Philosophy of Science*. Princeton, NJ: Princeton University Press.

Laymon, R. "Newton's Bucket Experiment." *Journal of the History of Philosophy* 16, no. 3 (July 1978): 399–413.

Sklar, L. 1976. *Space, Time, and Space-Time* (chap. II, A–C). Berkeley, CA: University of California Press. $\sqrt{}$

Stein, H. "Newtonian Space-Time." *The Texas Quarterly* 10, no. 3 (Autumn 1967): 174–200.

Westfall, R. 1993. *The Life of Isaac Newton*. Cambridge, UK: Cambridge University Press. $\sqrt{}$

8 Leibniz and Clarke

READING

The Leibniz-Clarke Correspondence

Mr. Leibniz's First Paper

1. Natural religion itself, seems to decay (in England) very much. Many will have human souls to be material: others make God himself a corporeal being.

2. Mr. Locke, and his followers, are uncertain at least, whether the soul be not material, and naturally perishable.

3. Sir Isaac Newton says, that space is an organ, which God makes use of to perceive things by. But if God stands in need of any organ to perceive things by, it will follow, that they do not depend altogether upon him, nor were produced by him.

4. Sir Isaac Newton, and his followers, have also a very odd opinion concerning the work of God. According to their doctrine, God Almighty wants to wind up his watch from time to time: otherwise it would cease to move. He had not, it seems, sufficient foresight to make it a perpetual motion. Nay, the machine of God's making, is so imperfect, according to these gentlemen; that he is obliged to clean it now and then by an extraordinary concourse, and even to mend it, as a clockmaker mends his work; who must consequently be so much the more unskilful a workman, as he is oftener obliged to mend his work and to set it right. According to my opinion, the same force and vigour remains always in the world, and only passes from one part of matter to another, agreeably to the laws of nature, and the beautiful pre-established order. And I hold, that when God works miracles, he does not do it in order to supply the wants of nature, but those of grace. Whoever thinks otherwise, must needs have a very mean notion of the wisdom and power of God.

Dr. Clarke's First Reply

1. That there are some in England, as well as in other countries, who deny or very much corrupt even natural religion itself, is very true, and much to be lamented. But (next to the vicious affections of men) this is to be principally ascribed to the false philosophy of the materialists, to which the mathematical principles of philosophy

Excerpts from G. W. Leibniz and S. Clarke, *The Leibniz-Clarke Correspondence* (pp. 11–77), edited by H. G. Alexander. Reprinted by permission of Barnes and Noble Books and Peter Gray-Lucas.

are the most directly repugnant. That some make the souls of men, and others even God himself to be a corporeal being; is also very true: but those who do so, are the great enemies of the mathematical principles of philosophy; which principles, and which alone, prove matter, or body, to be the smallest and most inconsiderable part of the universe.

2. That Mr. Locke doubted whether the soul was immaterial or no, may justly be suspected from some parts of his writings: but herein he has been followed only by some materialists, enemies to the mathematical principles of philosophy; and who approve little or nothing in Mr. Locke's writings, but his errors.

3. Sir Isaac Newton doth not say, that space is the organ which God makes use of to perceive things by; nor that he has need of any medium at all, whereby to perceive things: but on the contrary, that he, being omnipresent, perceives all things by his immediate presence to them, in all space wherever they are, without the intervention or assistance of any organ or medium whatsoever. In order to make this more intelligible, he illustrates it by a similitude: that as the mind of man, by its immediate presence to the pictures or images of things, form'd in the brain by the means of the organs of sensation, sees those pictures as if they were the things themselves; so God sees all things, by his immediate presence to them; he being actually present to the things themselves, to all things in the universe; as the mind of man is present to all the pictures of things formed in his brain. Sir Isaac Newton considers the brain and organs of sensation, as the means by which those pictures are formed: but not as the means by which the mind sees or perceives those pictures, when they are so formed. And in the universe, he doth not consider things as if they were pictures, formed by certain means, or organs; but as real things, form'd by God himself, and seen by him in all places wherever they are, without the intervention of any medium at all. And this similitude is all that he means, when he supposes infinite space to be (as it were) the *sensorium* of the Omnipresent Being.*...

Mr. Leibniz's Second Paper

1. It is rightly observed in the paper delivered to the Princess of Wales, which Her Royal Highness has been pleased to communicate to me, that, next to corruption of manners, the principles of the materialists do very much contribute to keep up impiety. But I believe the author had no reason to add, that the mathematical principles of philosophy are opposite to those of the materialists. On the contrary, they are

---

* See Newton's *Optics*, Query 28.

the same; only with this difference, that the materialists, in imitation of Democritus, Epicurus, and Hobbes, confine themselves altogether to mathematical principles, and admit only bodies; whereas the Christian mathematicians admit also immaterial substances. Wherefore, not mathematical principles (according to the usual sense of that word) but metaphysical principles ought to be opposed to those of the materialists. Pythagoras, Plato, and Aristotle in some measure, had a knowledge of these principles; but I pretend to have established them demonstratively in my *Theodicy*, though I have done it in a popular manner. The great foundation of mathematics is the principle of contradiction, or identity, that is, that a proposition cannot be true and false at the same time; and that therefore A is A, and cannot be not A. This single principle is sufficient to demonstrate every part of arithmetic and geometry, that is, all mathematical principles. But in order to proceed from mathematics to natural philosophy, another principle is requisite, as I have observed in my *Theodicy*: I mean, the principle of a sufficient reason, viz. that nothing happens without a reason why it should be so, rather than otherwise. And therefore Archimedes being to proceed from mathematics to natural philosophy, in his book *De Æquilibrio*, was obliged to make use of a particular case of the great principle of a sufficient reason. He takes it for granted, that if there be a balance, in which everything is alike on both sides, and if equal weights are hung on the two ends of that balance, the whole will be at rest. 'Tis because no reason can be given, why one side should weigh down, rather than the other. Now, by that single principle, viz. that there ought to be a sufficient reason why things should be so, and not otherwise, one may demonstrate the being of a God, and all the other parts of metaphysics or natural theology; and even, in some measure, those principles of natural philosophy, that are independent upon mathematics: I mean, the dynamical principles, or the principles of force....

Dr. Clarke's Second Reply

1. When I said that the mathematical principles of philosophy are opposite to those of the materialists; the meaning was, that whereas materialists suppose the frame of nature to be such as could have arisen from mere mechanical principles of matter and motion, of necessity and fate; the mathematical principles of philosophy show on the contrary, that the state of things (the constitution of the sun and planets) is such as could not arise from any thing but an intelligent and free cause. As to the propriety of the name; so far as metaphysical consequences follow demonstratively from mathematical principles, so far the mathematical principles may (if it be thought fit) be called metaphysical principles.

'Tis very true, that nothing is, without a sufficient reason why it is, and why it is thus rather than otherwise. And therefore, where there is no cause, there can be no effect. But this sufficient reason is oft-times no other, than the mere will of God. For instance: why this particular system of matter, should be created in one particular place, and that in another particular place; when, (all place being absolutely indifferent to all matter,) it would have been exactly the same thing *vice versa*, supposing the two systems (or the particles) of matter to be alike; there can be no other reason, but the mere will of God. Which if it could in no case act without a predetermining cause, any more than a balance can move without a preponderating weight; this would tend to take away all power of choosing, and to introduce fatality....

Mr. Leibniz's Third Paper

1. According to the usual way of speaking, mathematical principles concern only mere mathematics, viz. numbers, figures, arithmetic, geometry. But metaphysical principles concern more general notions, such as are cause and effect.

2. The author grants me this important principle; that nothing happens without a sufficient reason, why it should be so, rather than otherwise. But he grants it only in words, and in reality denies it. Which shows that he does not fully perceive the strength of it. And therefore he makes use of an instance, which exactly falls in with one of my demonstrations against real absolute space, which is an idol of some modern Englishmen. I call it an idol, not in a theological sense, but in a philosophical one; as Chancellor Bacon says, that there are *idola tribus, idola specus*.

3. These gentlemen maintain therefore, that space is a real absolute being. But this involves them in great difficulties; for such a being must needs be eternal and infinite. Hence some have believed it to be God himself, or, one of his attributes, his immensity. But since space consists of parts, it is not a thing which can belong to God.

4. As for my own opinion, I have said more than once, that I hold space to be something merely relative, as time is; that I hold it to be an order of coexistences, as time is an order of successions. For space denotes, in terms of possibility, an order of things which exist at the same time, considered as existing together; without enquiring into their manner of existing. And when many things are seen together, one perceives that order of things among themselves.

5. I have many demonstrations, to confute the fancy of those who take space to be a substance, or at least an absolute being. But I shall only use, at the present, one demonstration, which the author here gives me occasion to insist upon. I say then,

that if space was an absolute being, there would something happen for which it would be impossible there should be a sufficient reason. Which is against my axiom. And I prove it thus. Space is something absolutely uniform; and, without the things placed in it, one point of space does not absolutely differ in any respect whatsoever from another point of space. Now from hence it follows, (supposing space to be something in itself, besides the order of bodies among themselves,) that 'tis impossible there should be a reason, why God, preserving the same situations of bodies among themselves, should have placed them in space after one certain particular manner, and not otherwise; why every thing was not placed the quite contrary way, for instance, by changing East into West. But if space is nothing else, but that order or relation; and is nothing at all without bodies, but the possibility of placing them; then those two states, the one such as it now is, the other supposed to be the quite contrary way, would not at all differ from one another. Their difference therefore is only to be found in our chimerical supposition of the reality of space in itself. But in truth the one would exactly be the same thing as the other, they being absolutely indiscernible; and consequently there is no room to enquire after a reason of the preference of the one to the other. . . .

7. It appears from what I have said, that my axiom has not been well understood; and that the author denies it, tho' he seems to grant it. 'Tis true, says he, that there is nothing without a sufficient reason why it is, and why it is thus, rather than otherwise: but he adds, that this sufficient reason, is often the simple or mere will of God: as, when it is asked why matter was not placed otherwhere in space; the same situations of bodies among themselves being preserved. But this is plainly maintaining, that God wills something, without any sufficient reason for his will: against the axiom, or the general rule of whatever happens. This is falling back into the loose indifference, which I have confuted at large, and showed to be absolutely chimerical even in creatures, and contrary to the wisdom of God, as if he could operate without acting by reason. . . .

Dr. Clarke's Third Reply

. . .

2. Undoubtedly nothing is, without a sufficient reason why it is, rather than not; and why it is thus, rather than otherwise. But in things in their own nature indifferent; mere will, without any thing external to influence it, is alone that sufficient reason. As in the instance of God's creating or placing any particle of matter in one place rather than in another, when all places are originally alike. And the case is the same,

even though space were nothing real, but only the mere order of bodies: for still it would be absolutely indifferent, and there could be no other reason but mere will, why three equal particles should be placed or ranged in the order *a*, *b*, *c*, rather than in the contrary order. And therefore no argument can be drawn from this indifferency of all places, to prove that no space is real. For different spaces are really different or distinct one from another, though they be perfectly alike. And there is this evident absurdity in supposing space not to be real, but to be merely the order of bodies; that, according to that notion, if the earth and sun and moon had been placed where the remotest fixed stars now are, (provided they were placed in the same order and distance they now are with regard one to another,) it would not only have been, (as this learned author rightly says,) *la même chose*, the same thing in effect; which is very true: but it would also follow, that they would then have been in the same place too, as they are now: which is an express contradiction.

The ancients[a] did not call all space which is void of bodies, but only extramundane space, by the name of imaginary space. The meaning of which, is not, that such space is not real;[b] but only that we are wholly ignorant what kinds of things are in that space. Those writers, who by the word, *imaginary*, meant at any time to affirm that space was not real; did not thereby prove, that it was not real.

3. Space is not a being, an eternal and infinite being, but a property, or a consequence of the existence of a being infinite and eternal. Infinite space, is immensity: but immensity is not God: and therefore infinite space, is not God. Nor is there any difficulty in what is here alleged about space having parts. For infinite space is one, absolutely and essentially indivisible: and to suppose it parted, is a contradiction in terms; because there must be space in the partition itself; which is to suppose it parted, and yet not parted at the same time. The immensity or omnipresence of God, is no more a dividing of his substance into parts; than his duration, or continuance of existing, is a dividing of his existence into parts. There is no difficulty here, but what arises from the figurative abuse of the word, *parts*.

4. If space was nothing but the order of things coexisting; it would follow, that if God should remove in a straight line the whole material world entire, with any swiftness whatsoever; yet it would still always continue in the same place: and that nothing would receive any shock upon the most sudden stopping of that motion. And if time was nothing but the order of succession of created things; it would follow, that if God had created the world millions of ages sooner than he did, yet it

a. This was occasioned by a passage in the private letter wherein Mr. Leibniz's third paper came inclosed.
b. Of nothing, there are no dimensions, no magnitudes, no quantity, no properties.

would not have been created at all the sooner. Further: space and time are quantities; which situation and order are not.

5. The argument in this paragraph, is; that because space is uniform or alike, and one part does not differ from another; therefore the bodies created in one place, if they had been created in another place, (supposing them to keep the same situation with regard to each other,) would still have been created in the same place as before: which is a manifest contradiction. The uniformity of space, does indeed prove, that there could be no (external) reason why God should create things in one place rather than in another: but does that hinder his own will, from being to itself a sufficient reason of acting in any place, when all places are indifferent or alike, and there be good reason to act in some place?...

7 and 8. Where there is any difference in the nature of things, there the consideration of that difference always determines an intelligent and perfectly wise agent. But when two ways of acting are equally and alike good, (as in the instances before mentioned;) to affirm in such case, that God cannot act at all, or that 'tis no perfection in him to be able to act, because he can have no external reason to move him to act one way rather than the other, seems to be denying God to have in himself any original principle or power of beginning to act, but that he must needs (as it were mechanically) be always determined by things extrinsic....

Mr. Leibniz's Fourth Paper

...

3. 'Tis a thing indifferent, to place three bodies, equal and perfectly alike, in any order whatsoever; and consequently they will never be placed in any order, by him who does nothing without wisdom. But then he being the author of things, no such things will be produced by him at all; and consequently there are no such things in nature.

4. There is no such thing as two individuals indiscernible from each other. An ingenious gentleman of my acquaintance, discoursing with me, in the presence of Her Electoral Highness the Princess Sophia, in the garden of Herrenhausen; thought he could find two leaves perfectly alike. The Princess defied him to do it, and he ran all over the garden a long time to look for some; but it was to no purpose. Two drops of water, or milk, viewed with a microscope, will appear distinguishable from each other. This is an argument against atoms; which are confuted, as well as a vacuum, by the principles of true metaphysics.

5. Those great principles of a *sufficient reason*, and of the *identity of indiscernibles*, change the state of metaphysics. That science becomes real and demonstrative by means of these principles; whereas before, it did generally consist in empty words.

6. To suppose two things indiscernible, is to suppose the same thing under two names. And therefore to suppose that the universe could have had at first another position of time and place, than that which it actually had; and yet that all the parts of the universe should have had the same situation among themselves, as that which they actually had; such a supposition, I say, is an impossible fiction.

7. The same reason, which shows that extramundane space is imaginary, proves that all empty space is an imaginary thing; for they differ only as greater and less.

8. If space is a property or attribute, it must be the property of some substance. But what substance will that bounded empty space be an affection or property of, which the persons I am arguing with, suppose to be between two bodies?

9. If infinite space is immensity, finite space will be the opposite to immensity, that is, 'twill be mensurability, or limited extension. Now extension must be the affection of some thing extended. But if that space be empty, it will be an attribute without a subject, an extension without any thing extended. Wherefore by making space a property, the author falls in with my opinion, which makes it an order of things, and not any thing absolute.

10. If space is an absolute reality; far from being a property or an accident opposed to substance, it will have a greater reality than substances themselves. God cannot destroy it, nor even change it in any respect. It will be not only immense in the whole, but also immutable and eternal in every part. There will be an infinite number of eternal things besides God.

11. To say that infinite space has no parts, is to say that it does not consist of finite spaces; and that infinite space might subsist, though all finite spaces should be reduced to nothing. It would be, as if one should say, in the Cartesian supposition of a material extended unlimited world, that such a world might subsist, though all the bodies of which it consists, should be reduced to nothing. . . .

13. To say that God can cause the whole universe to move forward in a right line, or in any other line, without making otherwise any alteration in it; is another chimerical supposition. For, two states indiscernible from each other, are the same state; and consequently, 'tis a change without any change. Besides, there is neither rhyme nor reason in it. But God does nothing without reason; and 'tis impossible there should be any here. Besides, it would be *agendo nihil agere*, as I have just now said, because of the indiscernibility.

14. These are *idola tribus*, mere chimeras, and superficial imaginations. All this is only grounded upon the supposition, that imaginary space is real....

16. If space and time were any thing absolute, that is, if they were any thing else, besides certain orders of things; then indeed my assertion would be a contradiction. But since it is not so, the hypothesis [that space and time are any thing absolute] is contradictory, that is, 'tis an impossible fiction.

17. And the case is the same as in geometry; where by the very supposition that a figure is greater than it really is, we sometimes prove that it is not greater. This indeed is a contradiction; but it lies in the hypothesis, which appears to be false for that very reason.

18. Space being uniform, there can be neither any external nor internal reason, by which to distinguish its parts, and to make any choice among them. For, any external reason to discern between them, can only be grounded upon some internal one. Otherwise we should discern what is indiscernible, or choose without discerning. A will without reason, would be the chance of the Epicureans. A God, who should act by such a will, would be a God only in name. The cause of these errors proceeds from want of care to avoid what derogates from the divine perfections.

19. When two things which cannot both be together, are equally good; and neither in themselves, nor by their combination with other things, has the one any advantage over the other; God will produce neither of them.

20. God is never determined by external things, but always by what is in himself; that is, by his knowledge of things, before any thing exists without himself....

41. The author contends, that space does not depend upon the situation of bodies. I answer: 'tis true, it does not depend upon such or such a situation of bodies; but it is that order, which renders bodies capable of being situated, and by which they have a situation among themselves when they exist together; as time is that order, with respect to their successive position. But if there were no creatures, space and time would be only in the ideas of God....

Dr. Clarke's Fourth Reply

1 and 2. This notion leads to universal necessity and fate, by supposing that motives have the same relation to the will of an intelligent agent, as weights have to a balance;[a] so that of two things absolutely indifferent, an intelligent agent can no more choose

---

a. See above, Mr. Leibniz's Second Paper, §1.

either, than a balance can move itself when the weights on both sides are equal. But the difference lies here. A balance is no agent, but is merely passive and acted upon by the weights; so that, when the weights are equal, there is nothing to move it. But intelligent beings are agents; not passive, in being moved by the motives, as a balance is by weights; but they have active powers and do move themselves, sometimes upon the view of strong motives, sometimes upon weak ones, and sometimes where things are absolutely indifferent. In which latter case, there may be very good reason to act, though two or more ways of acting may be absolutely indifferent. This learned writer always supposes the contrary, as a principle; but gives no proof of it, either from the nature of things, or the perfections of God.

3 and 4. This argument, if it was true, would prove that God neither has created, nor can possibly create any matter at all. For the perfectly solid parts of all matter, if you take them of equal figure and dimensions (which is always possible in supposition,) are exactly alike; and therefore it would be perfectly indifferent if they were transposed in place; and consequently it was impossible (according to this learned author's argument,) for God to place them in those places wherein he did actually place them at the creation, because he might as easily have transposed their situation. 'Tis very true, that no two leaves, and perhaps no two drops of water are exactly alike; because they are bodies very much compounded. But the case is very different in the parts of simple solid matter. And even in compounds, there is no impossibility for God to make two drops of water exactly alike. And if he should make them exactly alike, yet they would never the more become one and the same drop of water, because they were alike. Nor would the place of the one, be the place of the other; though it was absolutely indifferent, which was placed in which place. The same reasoning holds likewise concerning the original determination of motion, this way or the contrary way.

5 and 6. Two things, by being exactly alike, do not cease to be two. The parts of time, are as exactly like to each other, as those of space: yet two points of time, are not the same point of time, nor are they two names of only the same point of time. Had God created the world but this moment, it would not have been created at the time it was created. And if God has made (or can make) matter finite in dimensions, the material universe must consequently be in its nature moveable; for nothing that is finite, is immoveable. To say therefore that God could not have altered the time or place of the existence of matter, is making matter to be necessarily infinite and eternal, and reducing all things to necessity and fate.

7. Extra-mundane space, (if the material world be finite in its dimensions,) is not imaginary, but real. Nor are void spaces in the world, merely imaginary. In an

exhausted receiver,[a] though rays of light, and perhaps some other matter, be there in an exceeding small quantity; yet the want of resistance plainly shows, that the greatest part of that space is void of matter. For subtleness or fineness of matter, cannot be the cause of want of resistance. Quicksilver is as subtle, and consists of as fine parts and as fluid, as water; and yet makes more than ten times the resistance: which resistance arises therefore from the quantity, and not from the grossness of the matter.

8. Space void of body, is the property of an incorporeal substance. Space is not bounded by bodies, but exists equally within and without bodies. Space is not inclosed between bodies; but bodies, existing in unbounded space, are, themselves only, terminated by their own dimensions.

9. Void space, is not an attribute without a subject; because, by void space, we never mean space void of every thing, but void of body only. In all void space, God is certainly present, and possibly many other substances which are not matter; being neither tangible, nor objects of any of our senses.

10. Space is not a substance, but a property; and if it be a property of that which is necessary, it will consequently (as all other properties of that which is necessary must do,) exist more necessarily, (though it be not itself a substance,) than those substances themselves which are not necessary. Space is immense, and immutable, and eternal; and so also is duration. Yet it does not at all from hence follow, that any thing is eternal *hors de Dieu*. For space and duration are not *hors de Dieu*, but are caused by, and are immediate and necessary consequences of his existence. And without them, his eternity and ubiquity (or omnipresence) would be taken away.

11 and 12. Infinites are composed of finites, in no other sense, than as finites are composed of infinitesimals. In what sense space has or has not parts, has been explained before, Reply III, §3. Parts, in the corporeal sense of the word, are separable, compounded, ununited, independent on, and moveable from, each other: but infinite space, though it may by us be partially apprehended, that is, may in our imagination be conceived as composed of parts; yet those parts (improperly so called) being essentially indiscernible and immoveable from each other, and not partable without an express contradiction in terms, (see above, Reply II, §4 and Reply III, §3;) space consequently is in itself essentially one, and absolutely indivisible.

13. If the world be finite in dimensions, it is moveable by the power of God and therefore my argument drawn from that moveableness is conclusive. Two places,

---

a. This was occasioned by a passage in the private letter wherein Mr. Leibniz's paper came inclosed.

though exactly alike, are not the same place. Nor is the motion or rest of the universe, the same state; any more than the motion or rest of a ship, is the same state, because a man shut up in the cabin cannot perceive whether the ship sails or not, so long as it moves uniformly. The motion of the ship, though the man perceives it not, is a real different state, and has real different effects; and, upon a sudden stop, it would have other real effects; and so likewise would an indiscernible motion of the universe. To this argument, no answer has ever been given. It is largely insisted on by Sir Isaac Newton in his *Mathematical Principles*, (Definit. 8.) where, from the consideration of the properties, causes, and effects of motion, he shows the difference between real motion, or a body's being carried from one part of space to another; and relative motion, which is merely a change of the order or situation of bodies with respect to each other. This argument is a mathematical one; showing, from real effects, that there may be real motion where there is none relative; and relative motion, where there is none real: and is not to be answered, by barely asserting the contrary.

14. The reality of space is not a supposition, but is proved by the foregoing arguments, to which no answer has been given. Nor is any answer given to that other argument, that space and time are quantities, which situation and order are not....

Mr. Leibniz's Fifth Paper

. . .

29. I have demonstrated, that space is nothing else but an order of the existence of things, observed as existing together; and therefore the fiction of a material finite universe, moving forward in an infinite empty space, cannot be admitted. It is altogether unreasonable and impracticable. For, besides that there is no real space out of the material universe; such an action would be without any design in it: it would be working without doing any thing, *agendo nihil agere*. There would happen no change, which could be observed by any person whatsoever. These are imaginations of philosophers who have incomplete notions, who make space an absolute reality. Mere mathematicians, who are only taken up with the conceits of imagination, are apt to forge such notions; but they are destroyed by superior reasons.

30. Absolutely speaking, it appears that God can make the material universe finite in extension; but the contrary appears more agreeable to his wisdom.

31. I don't grant, that every finite is moveable. According to the hypothesis of my adversaries themselves, a part of space, though finite, is not moveable. What is moveable, must be capable of changing its situation with respect to something else,

and to be in a new state discernible from the first: otherwise the change is but a fiction. A moveable finite, must therefore make part of another finite, that any change may happen which can be observed....

47. I will here show, how men come to form to themselves the notion of space. They consider that many things exist at once and they observe in them a certain order of co-existence, according to which the relation of one thing to another is more or less simple. This order, is their *situation* or distance. When it happens that one of those co-existent things changes its relation to a multitude of others, which do not change their relation among themselves; and that another thing, newly come, acquires the same relation to the others, as the former had; we then say, it is come into the place of the former; and this change, we call a motion in that body, wherein is the immediate cause of the change. And though many, or even all the co-existent things, should change according to certain known rules of direction and swiftness; yet one may always determine the relation of situation, which every co-existent acquires with respect to every other co-existent; and even that relation which any other co-existent would have to this, or which this would have to any other, if it had not changed, or if it had changed any otherwise. And supposing, or feigning, that among those co-existents, there is a sufficient number of them, which have undergone no change; then we may say, that those which have such a relation to those fixed existents, as others had to them before, have now the *same place* which those others had. And that which comprehends all those places, is called *space*. Which shows, that in order to have an idea of place, and consequently of space, it is sufficient to consider these relations, and the rules of their changes, without needing to fancy any absolute reality out of the things whose situation we consider. And, to give a kind of a definition: *place* is that, which we say is the same to A and, to B, when the relation of the co-existence of B, with C, E, F, G, etc. agrees perfectly with the relation of the co-existence, which A had with the same C, E, F, G, etc. supposing there has been no cause of change in C, E, F, G, etc. It may be said also, without entering into any further particularity, that *place* is that, which is the same in different moments to different existent things, when their relations of co-existence with certain other existents, which are supposed to continue fixed from one of those moments to the other, agree entirely together. And *fixed existents* are those, in which there has been no cause of any change of the order of their co-existence with others; or (which is the same thing,) in which there has been no motion. Lastly, *space* is that, which results from places taken together. And here it may not be amiss to consider the difference between place, and the relation of situation, which is in the body that fills up the place. For, the place of A and B, is the same; whereas the relation of A to fixed

bodies, is not precisely and individually the same, as the relation which B (that comes into its place) will have to the same fixed bodies; but these relations agree only. For, two different subjects, as A and B, cannot have precisely the same individual affection; it being impossible, that the same individual accident should be in two subjects, or pass from one subject to another. But the mind not contented with an agreement, looks for an identity, for something that should be truly the same; and conceives it as being extrinsic to the subjects: and this is what we call *place* and *space*. But this can only be an ideal thing; containing a certain order, wherein the mind conceives the application of relations. In like manner, as the mind can fancy to itself an order made up of genealogical lines, whose bigness would consist only in the number of generations, wherein every person would have his place; and if to this one should add the fiction of a *metempsychosis*, and bring in the same human souls again; the persons in those lines might change place; he who was a father, or a grandfather, might become a son, or a grandson, etc. And yet those genealogical places, lines, and spaces, though they should express real truth, would only be ideal things. I shall allege another example, to show how the mind uses, upon occasion of accidents which are in subjects, to fancy to itself something answerable to those accidents, out of the subjects. The ratio or proportion between two lines L and M, may be conceived three several ways; as a ratio of the greater L, to the lesser M; as a ratio of the lesser M, to the greater L; and lastly, as something abstracted from both, that is, as the ratio between L and M, without considering which is the antecedent, or which the consequent; which the subject, and which the object. And thus it is, that proportions are considered in music. In the first way of considering them, L the greater; in the second, M the lesser, is the subject of that accident, which philosophers call relation. But, which of them will be the subject, in the third way of considering them? It cannot be said that both of them, L and M together, are the subject of such an accident; for it so, we should have an accident in two subjects, with one leg in one, and the other in the other; which is contrary to the notion of accidents. Therefore we must say, that this relation, in this third way of considering it, is indeed out of the subjects; but being neither a substance, nor an accident, it must be a mere ideal thing, the consideration of which is nevertheless useful. To conclude: I have here done much like Euclid, who not being able to make his readers well understand what *ratio* is absolutely in the sense of geometricians; defines what are the *same ratios*. Thus, in like manner, in order to explain what *place* is, I have been content to define what is the *same place*. Lastly; I observe, that the traces of moveable bodies, which they leave sometimes upon the immoveable ones on which they are moved; have given men occasion to form in their imagination such an idea, as if some trace did still remain, even when there is nothing unmoved. But this is a mere ideal thing, and imports only, that if there was any unmoved thing there, the trace might be marked out upon it. And 'tis this analogy, which makes men fancy places, traces and spaces; though those things consist only in the truth of relations, and not at all in any absolute reality.

48. To conclude. If the space (which the author fancies) void of all bodies, is not altogether empty; what is it then full of? Is it full of extended spirits perhaps, or immaterial substances, capable of extending and contracting themselves; which move therein, and penetrate each other without any inconveniency, as the shadows of two bodies penetrate one another upon the surface of a wall? Methinks I see the revival of the odd imaginations of Dr. Henry More (otherwise a learned and well-meaning man,) and of some others who fancied that those spirits can make themselves impenetrable whenever they please. Nay, some have fancied, that man, in the state of innocency, had also the gift of penetration; and that he became solid, opaque, and impenetrable by his fall. Is it not overthrowing our notions of things, to make God have parts, to make spirits have extension? The principle of the want of a sufficient reason does alone drive away all these spectres of imagination. Men easily run into fictions, for want of making a right use of that great principle. . . .

52. In order to prove that space, without bodies, is an absolute reality; the author objected, that a finite material universe might move forward in space. I answered, it does not appear reasonable that the material universe should be finite; and, though we should suppose it to be finite; yet 'tis unreasonable it should have motion any otherwise, than as its parts change their situation among themselves; because such a motion would produce no change that could be observed, and would be without design. 'Tis another thing, when its parts change their situation among themselves; for then there is a motion in space; but it consists in the order of relations which are changed. The author replies now, that the reality of motion does not depend upon being observed; and that a ship may go forward, and yet a man, who is in the ship, may not perceive it. I answer, motion does not indeed depend upon being observed; but it does depend upon being possible to be observed. There is no motion, when there is no change that can be observed. And when there is no change that can be observed, there is no change at all. The contrary opinion is grounded upon the supposition of a real absolute space, which I have demonstratively confuted by the principle of the want of a sufficient reason of things.

53. I find nothing in the Eighth Definition of the *Mathematical Principles of Nature*, nor in the Scholium belonging to it, that proves, or can prove, the reality of space

in itself. However, I grant there is a difference between an absolute true motion of a body, and a mere relative change of its situation with respect to another body. For when the immediate cause of the change is in the body, that body is truly in motion; and then the situation of other bodies, with respect to it, will be changed consequently, though the cause of that change be not in them. 'Tis true that, exactly speaking, there is not any one body, that is perfectly and entirely at rest; but we frame an abstract notion of rest, by considering the thing mathematically. Thus have I left nothing unanswered, of what has been alleged for the absolute reality of space. And I have demonstrated the falsehood of that reality, by a fundamental principle, one of the most certain both in reason and experience; against which, no exception or instance can be alleged. Upon the whole, one may judge from what has been said that I ought not to admit a moveable universe; nor any place out of the material universe....

62. I don't say that matter and space are the same thing. I only say, there is no space, where there is no matter; and that space in itself is not an absolute reality. Space and matter differ, as time and motion. However, these things, though different, are inseparable.

COMMENTARY

8.1 Introduction

The *Correspondence* is a series of letters written in the years 1715–1716 by Newton's spokesperson, Samuel Clarke, and Newton's longtime critic, Leibniz, in the last two years of his life. In them, a range of philosophical, theological, and physical issues are hotly debated, and a clear picture of the competing views of absolute and relative space emerge.

Before we analyze these letters, let me offer a few points of background. First, it is often claimed that Newton helped Clarke draft his replies to Leibniz, and we will take it that, for the most part, Clarke's letters express the official Newtonian position. Also, note that the tone of the letters seems sometimes to reveal personal animosity: for instance, Leibniz's opening accusation that Newton's science was leading to the decay of religion. This is probably because Newton and Leibniz were engaged in a bitter priority dispute concerning the invention of the calculus (we still use Leibniz's ∫ symbol for integration), since both discovered key ideas roughly simultaneously. It is, however, worth noting that the writers saw the correspondence as worthwhile, and that Clarke regarded Leibniz highly enough to publish the *Correspondence* as early as 1717.

One thing that might stand in our way when reading these letters is that many of the arguments center on considerations of God's nature and what God can or cannot do. Though many people today think that the relation of religion to science is an important issue, in the eighteenth century it was a ubiquitous one, and we can see that it is an integral part of the *Correspondence*. Such arguments are of a different kind from those we have considered: we have been focusing solely on physical, rather than religious, issues. We need not say much about the two approaches—theological and scientific—except to point out that it is harder to give the religious approach a solid foundation. For instance, Leibniz had a very clear conception of God, but how can we tell whether his notion was right? As such, we will concentrate on the physical aspects of his arguments.

Finally, Leibniz, like Descartes, belonged to the *rationalist* school of philosophy, which holds that reason alone, not empirical science, can reliably discover the nature of reality. One might wonder how they thought that such a thing was possible, but it is not so far-fetched. In the first place, as Descartes pointed out, any of our experiences can be mistaken, and so none are completely trustworthy. Second, pure geometry is a science of reason alone, requiring no experience for its justification: valid deductions, not experiments, are required to show that the theorems follow from the axioms. The rationalist suggestion is that a similar model can be applied to all knowledge: start from basic axioms, and derive all the facts about the world. In his second letter Leibniz makes just this claim: "Now, by that single principle, viz. that *there ought to be some sufficient reason why things should be so, and not otherwise*, one may demonstrate the being of a God, and all other parts of metaphysics or natural theology; and even in some measure ... principles of natural philosophy" (LII.1*: my emphasis). This is heady stuff: just as Euclid systematized all of geometry with his axioms, so Leibniz claims to derive all (nonmathematical) knowledge from this axiom, which we shall call the *Principle of Sufficient Reason*, or the PSR for short. Leibniz also gives us an example of the principle in action: if one side of a pair of scales is lower than the other, then there must be a sufficient reason for this, namely, that that side is heavier. Not surprisingly we shall see him make use of the PSR in his arguments with Clarke. (Note that Clarke assents to the principle, but has a rather different conception of its meaning.)

8.2 Leibniz's Relationism

Clarke proposes arguments for absolute space, but since none seems any more forceful than those given by Newton in the last readings, we will concentrate on Leibniz's arguments for the relational conception of space. Indeed, Leibniz is often thought to give both the classic statement of relationism and the definitive objections to absolutism.

Thus far we have understood relationism mostly negatively, as the idea that there is no absolute reference frame separate from all the relative reference frames defined by material objects. It is worth considering whether there is a more positive gloss to be put on the doctrine: if space is not an absolute substance, what is it? According to Leibniz, relational space is "an order of coexistences" (LIII.4) or a "situation of bodies among themselves" (LIII.5). The point is this: in a relative reference frame, one determines the relative locations of all bodies from some reference body. But any object can, in principle, be a reference body, so collectively one has a collection of objects at various relative distances from one another. So, although either the Sun or the Earth can define reference frames for the planets, these are just different ways of describing the relative distances between all of the members of the solar system. Or

---

* References in this chapter are to the *Correspondence* unless otherwise noted, and are given by letter and section number: for example, LII.1 = Leibniz's second letter, section one, and CIV.7 = Clarke's fourth letter, section seven.

perhaps it helps to start with the image of space as a Euclidean plane with various figures drawn in it; mentally subtract the plane away, leaving only the figures themselves, still arranged at various distances from each other. By analogy, material objects are the figures, and they are "ordered" or "situated" at various distances relative to one another as a brute fact, not because they are located those distances from one another in absolute places. This view is the opposite of Newton's position that space is a substance separate from matter: on the relational view, without matter there would be no "situation of objects" and hence no relational space.

8.3   Leibniz's Arguments

To understand Leibniz's arguments for relationism, we need to discuss two important facts. First of all, every point of absolute space is exactly like every other. All points are identical, and absolute space is Euclidean: utterly flat and featureless. Thus there is no way to distinguish experimentally one absolute place from any other. Second, for similar reasons, there is no way to determine how fast any object is moving in absolute space. This point might sound contrary to Newton's demonstration that inertial effects—such as the concave surface of spinning water—reveal absolute acceleration, so we need some clarification.

What we saw in the previous chapter is that inertial effects reveal the magnitude of an object's absolute acceleration, but from this it by no means follows that they reveal its velocity in absolute space. Indeed, suppose two identical objects differ in their velocities: let X be at rest in absolute space and Y move uniformly at 1m/s in a straight line. If the same forces now act on them, they will exhibit identical inertial effects: none at all if no forces are applied, and identical internal tensions if they are. The result is quite general: objects whose motions differ by a constant amount will exhibit identical inertial effects. That is, their inertial effects do not distinguish their motions, and hence do not offer a measure of their velocities in absolute space. This phenomenon is familiar: if a car is smooth and quiet, 10mph feels the same as 100mph. Of course you can look out the window and determine your velocity relative to the road, but not relative to absolute space.

Generally, no mechanical experiment can measure the absolute velocity of a system—only its velocity relative to other systems if they exist. This fact was recognized by Newton: "The motions of bodies included in a given space are the same among themselves, whether that space is at rest, or moves uniformly forwards in a right line without any circular motion" (*Principia*, Corollary V). What Newton means is that if his laws of motion are true in one frame, then they are true in every frame moving with a constant relative velocity. Take the first law, for example:

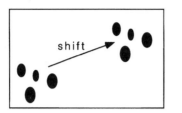
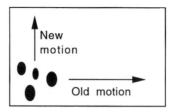

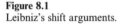

Static shift: move
everything from one
absolute place to another

Kinematic shift: change the
velocity of everything by a fixed
amount—e.g., from motion to the
right to vertical motion

Figure 8.1
Leibniz's shift arguments.

suppose that relative to a particular reference body, objects only accelerate when
acted on by forces, so that the law of inertia holds in the given frame. Now consider
a second reference body moving constantly relative to the first; objects will move
constantly in its reference frame just in case they also move constantly in the first
frame (but at different speeds and directions). Therefore, objects that accelerate in
the second frame also accelerate in the first and hence experience forces: the first law
holds in both frames. Since we are calling frames in which the first law holds *inertial
frames*, we have just shown that there is a family of inertial frames that move constantly relative to one another.

   The equivalence, with respect to Newton's laws, of frames in constant relative
motion is at the root of the undetectability of absolute velocities. For suppose that
the laws only held in frames at rest in absolute space; we could find such a frame
experimentally by testing the laws in various frames. Having found the "rest frame,"
we could then determine the absolute velocity of any object, as the velocity in the
rest frame. But the laws in fact hold in every inertial frame (including the frame of
absolute space), so the best we can do is find the family of frames that move constantly with respect to absolute space. And since we don't know which frame is at
rest in absolute space, we cannot measure the absolute velocity of any object.

   Given the unmeasurability of absolute position and velocity, we can now understand the so-called *shift arguments* that Leibniz offered as refutations of Newton's
conception of absolute space. These are indirect proofs, so we first suppose for argument that space is absolute, and then see what consequences follow.

The static shift.   Imagine a second universe just like ours except that all the matter
is located in (i.e., shifted to) another place in absolute space, without any change in

the relations of one object to another. Since space is a Euclidean plane, the two places are exactly alike, and so no differences will be seen.

The kinematic shift. Imagine a second universe just like ours except that the absolute velocity of every piece of matter differs by (i.e., is shifted by) a fixed, constant amount, without any change in the relations of one object to another. Since the two velocities differ only by a constant amount, no differences will be seen.

(Just to be clear, bear in mind that in these shifts we are not thinking of two duplicate material universes in a single absolute space, but of two whole universes, each with its own absolute space.)

Both of these thought experiments are usually taken to tell against absolute space, and so it is ironic that they are both first brought up by Clarke (CII.1 and CIII.4). Leibniz turns them around and uses them to hit back at Clarke and Newton. In both cases he argues that because the shifts make no "practical" difference, then— contrary to what would be the case were there absolute space—they make no real difference either. And for the relationist such "shifts" indeed make no difference at all, for, by definition, they leave all relations the same. Let us look at this in more detail.

Leibniz's first line of attack employs his "axiom," the PSR, to argue that the shifts are impossible and hence that absolute space cannot exist. Take the static shift, for instance (LIII.5): since absolute space is exactly the same everywhere, there could be no sufficient reason for the material universe to be located at one absolute place rather than another. Therefore, if the universe was created in absolute space then something would have happened without a sufficient reason, and hence space is not absolute.

Leibniz's argument is an indirect proof; the assumption of absolute space entails that something happens without sufficient reason, which is contrary to the PSR. So if the argument is to have any influence over us, we will have to accept the PSR. But do we? It is clear that Leibniz has in mind the (sufficient) reasons that a thinking creator, God, might have for creating the universe as he did. (We're to imagine God wondering about how to create the world: "Shall I make an absolute space? Better not, because I'd have no reason to put matter one place rather than another.") And hence Leibniz's argument depends on knowing the kind of reasons for action that God might find compelling. That Clarke has a very different view of God's decision-making capacities—". . . this sufficient reason is oft-times no other, than the mere will of God" (CII.1)—and that neither philosopher offers very convincing arguments for one conception or the other suggests that this line of thought is not likely to be fruitful.

A second attack used by Leibniz has found much more favor with commentators of the debate. It is based on the *Principle of the Identity of Indiscernibles*, or PII, which states that "to suppose two things indiscernible, is to suppose the same thing under two names" (LIV.5–6). That is, if two things are alike in every way, then they are really only one thing. Leibniz gives an argument for PII based on PSR (LIV.3), but if we follow this line then PII will only be as strong as PSR. Instead, we will see how the principle is further explained in the debate surrounding the kinematic shift, a way that many philosophers have found convincing. (It is a further irony of the *Correspondence* that Leibniz's rationalistic PII has, as we shall see, found most favor in the twentieth century as an empiricist principle.)

Consider how Leibniz uses the PII to construe the kinematic shift as a problem for the absolutist (LIV.13). The original and shifted universes cannot be told apart, so according to the PII they are one and the same; but if absolute space existed then they would have absolutely different motions: therefore, the postulation of absolute space is contrary to the PII. Clarke points out in reply that there are motions that differ from one another without being detected; for instance (CIV.13), inside a sealed room on a ship, it is impossible to tell whether you are stationary or traveling smoothly at 10 knots, but nevertheless the two motions are distinct. Couldn't the situation of the kinematic shift of the universe be exactly analogous, so that Leibniz is wrong to assume the PII in his argument?

No; Leibniz clarifies just what the principle involves. PII does not say that for objects to be nonidentical a difference must in fact be observed, but rather that the difference "does depend on being possible to be observed" (LV.52)—that is, that one *could* be observed. In the case of the boat one could distinguish the two motions relative to a further reference body, for example, the shore line, and hence they are not, properly speaking, indiscernible, and hence the PII does not apply here. The case is rather different for the kinematic shift. Not only would no one notice the difference between the universes, no one could notice them by any experiment whatsoever: there is no further reference body. In such cases, Leibniz believes, the PII does apply, and so the supposedly distinct motions are one, confuting the existence of absolute space.

Once again, Leibniz's arguments only have force if we accept the PII: that any two things that cannot be distinguished—by any observation at all—must be one and the same thing. To see why one might accept the principle, consider the following parable. Suppose that I claimed to have discovered a new kind of electricity, called "nelectricity," and announced that everything carries a nelectric charge of some strength. You'd be impressed with my Earth-shattering proposal, but then you'd want to know something about nelectricity, perhaps how it affects the movements of nelectrically charged objects. Imagine your reaction if I told you that the nelectric charge makes no difference at all. You would probably conclude that there was no nelectric charge, and if I protested then you might well point out that I had failed to say what it would mean for something to have negative nelectric charge. My assignments of charges would be just so much empty talk: different nelectric charges are indiscernible, and hence nothing at all. One could even have a "nelectric shift": imagine a universe just like ours except that everything has twice its actual nelectric charge. Since nelectricity has no observable consequences, no difference between this universe and ours would be detectable. Then one could criticize the theory of nelectricity for claiming that such indistinguishable universes would be nonidentical: just what would be the point of saying that they differed?

Nelectricity is clearly nothing, but the theory of nelectricity apparently parallels Newton's theory of absolute space. He claims that every object has an absolute position and velocity, but that these have no observable effect on the object whatsoever, and so cannot be determined. What is to stop us from having the same reaction that we had to nelectricity? Since Newton agrees that differences in the absolute position and velocity of an object have no effect, shouldn't we conclude, as the PII entails, that such differences—and absolute space with them—are not real? Shouldn't we also say that Newton has failed in some way to tell us what absolute places and velocities are, if he cannot say how to distinguish them?

The reasoning involved here is that of the philosophy of empiricism. There are many versions of this doctrine—as there are many versions of rationalism—but at the core is the idea that all our knowledge of the world is derived from experience. Any claims that cannot be tested in some way cannot be justified; they are useless, serving no practical or scientific purpose, and perhaps they are even meaningless. We have thus argued for PII as an empiricist principle: it is at best useless, and at worst nonsense, to claim that two situations are distinct if no experiences could ever reveal a difference. And it seems that the PII thus understood is a damaging criticism of Newton's absolute space, for the unmeasurability of absolute position and velocity indeed threaten to make these concepts useless or nonsensical.

But consider a slightly different story: Suppose that I claim that the actual value of the nelectric charge makes no observable difference, but that something observable occurs whenever the value is changing. What if, for example, objects with increasing nelectricity glowed red? Then we might have grounds for believing in nelectricity after all. And of course something exactly analogous might rescue absolute space from the PII: We might not be able to measure absolute positions or velocities, but our work in the previous chapter shows that we can detect absolute accelerations. And if they are detectable, they must be real. So now we can reason as Newton must have: How can absolute acceleration be real? Well, only if absolute position and hence changes in absolute position—that is, absolute velocity—are real, for absolute acceleration just is change in absolute velocity. Actually, as we shall see in chapter 10, Newton was wrong in thinking that a concept of absolute velocity was required to make sense of absolute acceleration, but we will follow his thought for now.

To put things another way: Leibniz is quite correct when he points out that static and kinematic shifts would be undetectable, and his use of the PII against absolute space would be justified if these were the only cases to consider. But it would not be correct to claim that two universes differing only in acceleration would be indistinguishable, and so the PII is not applicable to such a "dynamic shift." In the final section, we will thus see what happens to the arguments when we consider acceleration and inertia.

8.3 Leibniz and Absolute Acceleration

Consider more precisely how one would describe a dynamic shift.

The dynamic shift.   Imagine a second universe just like ours except that the absolute acceleration of every piece of matter differs by (i.e., is shifted by) a fixed amount, by the application of an appropriate force on the center of each body, without any change in the relations of one object to another. New inertial effects would appear, making the new universe discernible from ours (so that the PII is not violated).

Clarke made a rhetorical error when he introduced the static and kinematic shifts—thereby highlighting the weak points of the Newtonian account—rather than the dynamic shift—a problem for Leibniz. Suppose that every object in the universe suddenly experienced stretching, compression, and internal tensions. What account could be given? The Newtonian can explain the effects as inertial, the result of some (possibly miraculous) force causing the entire universe to accelerate in absolute space. However, within the two universes, the relations between bodies are identical, so exactly the same relative accelerations occur within each one. But for the relationist the only accelerations are relative accelerations, so the inertial effects cannot be explained by relative accelerations: the inertial effects differ but the relations don't. Indeed, since the relationist must hold that inertial effects are to be understood relationally, then if the whole universe decelerated, they would have to maintain that "nothing would receive any shock upon the most sudden stopping of motion" (CIII.4). After all, if the *whole* universe decelerated, then no relations would change, and there would be no new relative accelerations. The point that Clarke is making is

Newton's: absolute space itself may not be observable, but it has observable inertial effects. We need it to understand the law of inertia.

The *Correspondence* is rather frustrating on this point: we are eager to hear what Leibniz has to say about the bucket argument, but he gives us very little. Clarke eventually forces the issue and refers Leibniz to the *Scholium* (CIV.13). Leibniz's reply is disappointing in its brevity. He acknowledges that there is a difference between absolute ("true") and merely relative accelerations, but this difference has nothing to do with absolute space, but rather with whether "the immediate cause of the change is in the body" (LV.53). That is, an object is absolutely accelerating if there is a force on it. This is of course true, but it does not tell us what absolute acceleration is in relational terms, which is Newton's challenge.

Did Leibniz have further thoughts that would have clarified this matter and hence given the definitive relationist answer to Newton? Unfortunately, Leibniz died before he could write his fifth letter and never gave a clear response to the bucket argument. So, we cannot pursue Leibniz's thoughts any further here. Instead, in the next chapter we will consider other relationist attempts to come to terms with inertia. For now we should reflect that Leibniz has revealed some deeply troubling aspects of absolute space that relationism avoids, but that the relationist must acknowledge the problem of inertia raised by the bucket experiment.

Problems

1. Read LIII.4 and LV.47 carefully. How are the doctrines of relationism and absolutism explained in them? Members of a family have relationships with one another in the same way that objects have distance relations with one another. What grounds do we have for thinking that there is an absolute space to explain these relationships when we don't believe in any "absolute genealogical space" in which the family is arranged?

2. PSR as we formulated it is not very satisfactory, but is there any hope for a better version? What if we understand it as saying "everything has a cause" (as perhaps Leibniz sometimes does, and as Clarke seems to)? This formulation seems more plausible, for it doesn't presuppose any intelligent creator. What problems might arise for it? Does this principle imply that there could be no reason for objects to occupy one absolute place rather than another?

3. We argued against absolute position and velocity using PII, but what about the following alternative: In good science we should keep everything as simple as possible, discarding anything not strictly necessary (this is often called *Occam's razor*). On

these grounds we should abandon absolute space because absolute positions and velocities serve no function. But is the principle sensible? Why or why not? Is this an effective argument against absolute space?

4. External forces are communicated throughout an object, producing inertial effects; pushing on the back of our accelerometer deforms the springs until they exert a large enough force to accelerate the weight at the same rate. But if an external force accelerated every part of a body at the same rate simultaneously, then no tensions would be produced and no inertial effects observed. First, explain why a dynamic shift of this kind would present another problem for Newton using the PII. Now using Newton's second law (acceleration = force/mass = F/m) explain why a constant gravitational field (so a mass, m, feels a force, $F = g \cdot m$, for some constant, g) produces such a force.

Further Readings and Bibliography

Earman, J. "Who's Afraid of Absolute Space?" *Australasian Journal of Philosophy* 48 (1970): 287–317.

Earman, J. 1989. *World Enough and Space-Time* (see esp. chap. 6). Cambridge, MA: MIT Press.

Mates, B. 1986. *The Philosophy of Leibniz: Metaphysics and Language.* Oxford: Oxford University Press.
√

Reichenbach, H. 1959. "The Theory of Motion According to Newton, Leibniz, and Huygens," pp. 46–66 in *Modern Philosophy of Science: Selected Essays*, edited and translated by M. Reichenbach. London: Routledge and Kegan Paul.

Vailati, E. 1997. *Leibniz and Clarke: A Study of Their Correspondence.* Oxford: Oxford University Press.

van Fraassen, B. C. 1970. *An Introduction to the Philosophy of Time and Space* (see esp. chap. IV. 1). New York: Random House.

9 Berkeley and Mach

READING

Berkeley's De Motu

52. The Peripatetics used to distinguish various kinds of motion corresponding to the variety of changes which a thing could undergo. To-day those who discuss motion understand by the term only local motion. But local motion cannot be understood without understanding the meaning of the *locus* or place. Now *place* is defined by moderns as "the part of space which a body occupies," whence it is divided into relative and absolute following a division of space. For they distinguish between absolute or true space and relative or apparent space. That is they postulate space on all sides measureless, immoveable, insensible, permeating and containing all bodies, which they call absolute space. But space comprehended or defined by bodies, and therefore an object of sense, is called relative, apparent, vulgar space.

53. And so let us suppose that all bodies were destroyed and brought to nothing. What is left they call absolute space, all relation arising from the situation and distances of bodies being removed together with the bodies. Again, that space is infinite, immoveable, indivisible, insensible, without relation and without distinction. That is, all its attributes are privative or negative. It seems therefore to be mere nothing. The only slight difficulty arising is that it is extended, and extension is a positive quality. But what sort of extension, I ask, is that which cannot be divided or measured, no part of which can be perceived by sense or pictured by the imagination? For nothing enters the imagination which from the nature of the thing cannot be perceived by sense, since indeed the imagination is nothing else than the faculty which represents sensible things either actually existing or at least possible. Pure intellect, too, knows nothing of absolute space. That faculty is concerned only with spiritual and inextended things, such as our minds, their states, passions, virtues, and such like. From absolute space then let us take away now the words of the name, and nothing will remain in sense, imagination, or intellect. Nothing else then is denoted by those words than pure privation or negation, *i.e.* mere nothing.

54. It must be admitted that in this matter we are in the grip of the deepest prejudices, and to win free we must exert the whole force of our minds. For many, so far from regarding absolute space as nothing, regard it as the only thing (God excepted)

Excerpts from George Berkeley, *De Motu*, translated by A. A. Luce (with revisions by M. R. Ayers), in *The Works of George Berkeley Bishop of Cloyne* (vol. 4, pp. 45–50), edited by A. A. Luce and T. E. Jessop. © 1946–57 by Thomas Nelson and Sons Ltd. Reprinted by permission of Thomas Nelson and Sons Ltd.

which cannot be annihilated; and they lay down that it necessarily exists of its own nature, that it is eternal and uncreated, and is actually a participant in the divine attributes. But in very truth since it is most certain that all things which we designate by names are known by qualities or relations, at least in part (for it would be stupid, to use words to which nothing known, no notion, idea or concept, were attached), let us diligently inquire whether it is possible to form any idea of that pure, real, and absolute space continuing to exist after the annihilation of all bodies. Now such an idea, when I examine it somewhat more intently, I find to be the purest idea of nothing, if indeed it can be called an idea. This I myself have found on giving the matter my closest attention; this, I think, others will find on doing likewise.

55. We are sometimes deceived by the fact that when we imagine the removal of all other bodies, yet we suppose our own body to remain. On this supposition we imagine the movement of our limbs fully free on every side; but motion without space cannot be conceived. None the less if we reconsider the matter attentively we shall find that what is conceived is, first, relative space defined by the parts of our body; second, a fully free power of moving our limbs obstructed by no obstacle; and besides these two things nothing. It is false to believe that some third thing really exists, *viz.* immense space which confers on us the free power of moving our body; for this purpose the absence of other bodies is sufficient. And we must admit that this absence or privation of bodies is nothing positive.

56. But unless a man has examined these points with a free and keen mind, words and terms avail little. To one who meditates, however, and reflects, it will be manifest, I think, that predications about pure and absolute space can all be predicated about nothing. By this argument the human mind is easily freed from great difficulties, and at the same time from the absurdity of attributing necessary existence to any being except to the good and great God alone.

57. It would be easy to confirm our opinion by arguments drawn, as they say *a posteriori*, by proposing questions about absolute space, *e.g.* Is it substance or accidents? is it created or uncreated? and showing the absurdities which follow from either answer. But I must be brief. I must not omit, however, to state that Democritus of old supported this opinion with his vote. Aristotle is our authority for the statement, *Phys.* Bk. I, where he has these words, "Democritus lays down as principles the solid and the void, of which the one, he says, is as what is, the other is what is not." That the distinction between absolute and relative space has been used by philosophers of great name, and that on it as on a foundation many fine theorems have been built, may make us scruple to accept the argument, but those are empty scruples as will appear from what follows.

58. From the foregoing it is clear that we ought not to define the true place of the body as the part of absolute space which the body occupies, and true or absolute motion as the change of true or absolute place; for all place is relative just as all motion is relative. But to make this appear more clearly we must point out that no motion can be understood without some determination or direction, which in turn cannot be understood unless besides the body in motion our own body also, or some other body, be understood to exist at the same time. For *up, down, left,* and *right* and all places and regions are founded in some relation, and necessarily connote and suppose a body different from the body moved. So that if we suppose the other bodies are annihilated and, for example, a globe were to exist alone, no motion could be conceived in it; so necessary is it that another body should be given by whose situation the motion should be understood to be determined. The truth of this opinion will be very clearly seen if we have correctly conceived of the annihilation of all bodies, including our own, with the sole exception of the globe.

59. Then let two globes be conceived to exist and nothing corporeal besides them. Let forces then be conceived to be applied in some way; whatever we may understand by the application of forces, a circular motion of the two globes round a common centre cannot be conceived by the imagination. The let us suppose that the sky of the fixed stars is created; suddenly from the conception of the approach of the globes to different parts of that sky the motion will be conceived. That is to say that since motion is relative in its own nature, it could not be conceived before the correlated bodies were given. Similarly no other relation can be conceived without correlates.

60. As regards circular motion many think that, as motion truly circular increases, the body necessarily tends ever more and more away from its axis. This belief arises from the fact that circular motion can be seen taking its origin, as it were, at every moment from two directions, one along the radius and the other along the tangent, so that if the impetus be increased in this latter direction only, then the body in motion will retire from the centre, and its orbit will cease to be circular. But if the forces be increased equally in both directions the motion will remain circular though accelerated by *conatus*—which will not argue an increase in the forces of retirement from the axis, any more than in the forces of approach to it. Therefore we must say that the water forced round in the bucket rises to the sides of the vessel, because when new forces are applied in the direction of the tangent to any particle of water, in the same instant new equal centripetal forces are not applied. From which experiment it in no way follows that absolute circular motion is necessarily recognized by the forces of retirement from the axis of motion. Again, how those terms *corporeal*

forces and *conatus* are to be understood is more than sufficiently shown in the fore-going discussion.

61. A curve can be considered as consisting of an infinite number of straight lines, though in fact it does not consist of them. That hypothesis is useful in geometry; and just so circular motion can be regarded as arising from an infinite number of recti-linear directions—which supposition is useful in mechanics. Yet that does not mean that it is impossible that the centre of gravity of any body should exist successively in single points of the circular periphery, no account being taken of any rectilineal direction in the tangent or the radius.

62. We must not omit to point out that the motion of a stone in a sling or of water in a whirled bucket cannot be called truly circular motion as that term is conceived by those who define the true places of bodies by the parts of absolute space, since it is strangely compounded of the motions, not alone of bucket or sling, but also of the daily motion of the earth round her own axis, of her monthly motion round the common centre of gravity of earth and moon, and of her annual motion round the sun. And on that account each particle of the stone or the water describes a line far removed from circular. Nor in fact does that supposed axifugal *conatus* exist, since it is not concerned with some one axis in relation to absolute space, supposing that such a space exists; accordingly I do not see how that can be called a single *conatus* to which a truly circular motion corresponds as to its proper and adequate effect.

63. No motion can be recognized or measured, unless through sensible things. Since then absolute space in no way affects the senses, it must necessarily be quite useless for the distinguishing of motions. Besides, determination or direction is essential to motion; but that consists in relation. Therefore it is impossible that absolute motion should be conceived.

64. Further, since the motion of the same body may vary with the diversity of rela-tive place—indeed a thing can be said in one respect to be in motion and in another respect to be at rest—in order to determine true motion and true rest, for the removal of ambiguity and for those philosophers who take a wider view of the system of things, it would be enough to bring in, instead of absolute space, relative space as confined to the heavens of the fixed stars, considered as at rest. And indeed motion and rest marked out by such relative space can conveniently be substituted in place of the absolutes, which cannot be distinguished from them by any mark. For how-ever forces may be impressed, whatever *conatus* there are, let us grant that motion is distinguished by actions exerted on bodies; never, however, will it follow that that absolute space exists, and absolute place change of which is true motion.

65. The laws of motions and the effects, and theorems containing the proportions and calculations of the same for the different configurations of the paths, likewise for accelerations and different directions, and for mediums resisting in greater or less degree, all these hold without bringing absolute motion into account. As is plain from this that, since according to the principles of those who introduce absolute motion, we cannot know by any indication whether the whole frame of things is at rest, or is moved uniformly in a direction, clearly we cannot know the absolute motion of any body.

66. From the foregoing it is clear that the following rules will be of great service in determining the true nature of motion: (1) to distinguish mathematical hypotheses from the natures of things; (2) to beware of abstractions; (3) to consider motion as something sensible, or at least imaginable; and to be content with relative measures. If we do so, all the famous theorems of the mechanical philosophy by which the secrets of nature are unlocked, and by which the system of the world is reduced to human calculation, will remain untouched; and the study of motion will be freed from a thousand minutiæ, subtleties, and abstract ideas. And let these words suffice about the nature of motion. . . .

READING

Mach's The Science of Mechanics

3. ... *All* masses and *all* velocities, and consequently *all* forces, are relative. There is no decision about relative and absolute which we can possibly meet, to which we are forced, or from which we can obtain any intellectual or other advantage. When quite modern authors let themselves be led astray by the Newtonian arguments which are derived from the bucket of water, to distinguish between relative and absolute motion, they do not reflect that the system of the world is only given *once* to us, and the Ptolemaic or Copernician view is *our* interpretation, but both are equally actual. Try to fix Newton's bucket and rotate the heaven of fixed stars and then prove the absence of centrifugal forces.

4. It is scarcely necessary to remark that in the reflections here presented Newton has again acted contrary to his expressed intention only to investigate *actual facts*. No one is competent to predicate things about absolute space and absolute motion; they are pure things of thought, pure mental constructs, that cannot be produced in experience. All our principles of mechanics are, as we have shown in detail, experimental knowledge concerning the relative positions and motions of bodies. Even in the provinces in which they are now recognized as valid, they could not, and were not, admitted without previously being subjected to experimental tests. No one is warranted in extending these principles beyond the boundaries of experience. In fact, such an extension is meaningless, as no one possesses the requisite knowledge to make use of it.

We must suppose that the change in the point of view from which the system of the world is regarded which was initiated by Copernicus, left deep traces in the thought of Galileo and Newton. But while Galileo, in his theory of the tides, quite naïvely chose the sphere of the fixed stars as the basis of a new system of coördinates, we see doubts expressed by Newton as to whether a given fixed star is at rest only apparently or really. This appeared to him to cause the difficulty of distinguishing between true (absolute) and apparent (relative) motion. By this he was also impelled to set up the conception of *absolute space*. By further investigations in this direction—the discussion of the experiment of the rotating spheres which are

Excerpts from Ernst Mach, *The Science of Mechanics: A Critical and Historical Account of Its Development* (pp. 279–296), translated by T. J. McCormack. © 1893, 1902, 1919, 1942, 1960 by Open Court Publishing Company. Reprinted by permission of Open Court Publishing Company, a division of Carus Publishing.

connected together by a cord and that of the rotating water-bucket—he believed that he could prove an absolute rotation, though he could not prove any absolute translation. By absolute rotation he understood a rotation relative to the fixed stars, and here centrifugal forces can always be found. "But how we are to collect," says Newton in the Scholium at the end of the Definitions, "the true motions from their causes, effects, and apparent differences, and *vice versa*; how from the motions, either true or aparent, we many come to the knowledge of their causes and effects, shall be explained more at large in the following Tract." The resting sphere of fixed stars seems to have made a certain impression on Newton as well. The natural system of reference is for him that which has any uniform motion or translation without rotation (relatively to the sphere of fixed stars).[1] But do not the words quoted in inverted commas give the impression that Newton was glad to be able now to pass over to less precarious questions that could be tested by experience?

Let us look at the matter in detail. When we say that a body K alters its direction and velocity solely through the influence of another body K', we have asserted a conception that it is impossible to come at unless other bodies $A, B, C \ldots$ are present with reference to which the motion of the body K has been estimated. In reality, therefore, we are simply cognizant of a relation of the body K to $A, B, C \ldots$ If now we suddenly neglect $A, B, C \ldots$ and attempt to speak of the deportment of the body K in absolute space, we implicate ourselves in a twofold error. In the first place, we cannot know how K would act in the absence of $A, B, C \ldots$; and in the second place, every means would be wanting of forming a judgment of the behavior of K and of putting to the test what we had predicated—which latter therefore would be bereft of all scientific significance. . . .

The motion of a body K can only be estimated by reference to other bodies $A, B, C \ldots$ But since we always have at our disposal a sufficient number of bodies, that are as respects each other relatively fixed, or only slowly change their positions, we are, in such reference, restricted to no one *definite* body and can alternately leave out of account now this one and now that one. In this way the conviction arose that these bodies are indifferent generally.

It might be, indeed, that the isolated bodies $A, B, C \ldots$ play merely a collateral rôle in the determination of the motion of the body K, and that this motion is determined by a *medium* in which K exists. In such a case we should have to substitute this medium for Newton's absolute space. Newton certainly did not entertain this idea. Moreover, it is easily demonstrable that the atmosphere is not this motion-

---

1. *Principia*, Coroll. V: "The motions of bodies included in a given space are the same among themselves, whether that space is at rest or moves uniformly forwards in a right line without any circular motion."

determinative medium. We should, therefore, have to picture to ourselves some other medium, filling, say, all space, with respect to the constitution of which and its kinetic relations to the bodies placed in it we have at present no adequate knowledge. In itself such a state of things would not belong to the impossibilities. It is known, from recent hydrodynamical investigations, that a rigid body experiences resistance in a frictionless fluid only when its velocity *changes*. True, this result is derived theoretically from the notion of inertia; but it might, conversely, also be regarded as the primitive fact from which we have to start. Although, practically, and at present, nothing is to be accomplished with this conception, we might still hope to learn more in the future concerning this hypothetical medium; and from the point of view of science it would be in every respect a more valuable acquisition than the forlorn idea of absolute space. When we reflect that we cannot abolish the isolated bodies *A*, *B*, *C* ..., that is, cannot determine by experiment whether the part they play is fundamental or collateral, that hitherto they have been the sole and only competent means of the orientation of motions and of the description of mechanical facts, it will be found expedient provisionally to regard all motions as determined by these bodies.

5. Let us now examine the point on which Newton, apparently with sound reasons, rests his distinction of absolute and relative motion. If the earth is affected with an *absolute* rotation about its axis, centrifugal forces are set up in the earth: it assumes an oblate form, the acceleration of gravity is diminished at the equator, the plane of Foucault's pendulum rotates, and so on. All these phenomena disappear if the earth is at rest and the other heavenly bodies are affected with absolute motion round it, such that the same *relative* rotation is produced. This is, indeed, the case, if we start *ab initio* from the idea of absolute space. But if we take our stand on the basis of facts, we shall find we have knowledge only of *relative* spaces and motions. *Relatively*, not considering the unknown and neglected medium of space, the motions of the universe are the same whether we adopt the Ptolemaic or the Copernican mode of view. Both views are, indeed, equally *correct*; only the latter is more simple and more *practical*. The universe is not *twice* given, with an earth at rest and an earth in motion; but only *once*, with its *relative* motions, alone determinable. It is, accordingly, not permitted us to say how things would be if the earth did not rotate. We may interpret the one case that is given us, in different ways. If, however, we so interpret it that we come into conflict with experience, our interpretation is simply wrong. The principles of mechanics can, indeed, be so conceived, that even for relative rotations centrifugal forces arise.

Newton's experiment with the rotating vessel of water simply informs us, that the relative rotation of the water with respect to the sides of the vessel produces *no* noticeable centrifugal forces, but that such forces *are* produced by its relative rotation with respect to the mass of the earth and the other celestial bodies. No one is competent to say how the experiment would turn out if the sides of the vessel increased in thickness and mass till they were ultimately several leagues thick. The one experiment only lies before us, and our business is, to bring it into accord with the other facts known to us, and not with the arbitrary fictions of our imagination.

6. When Newton examined the principles of mechanics discovered by Galileo, the great value of the simple and precise law of inertia for deductive derivations could not possibly escape him. He could not think of renouncing its help. But the law of inertia, referred in such a naïve way to the earth supposed to be at rest, could not be accepted by him. For, in Newton's case, the rotation of the earth was not a debatable point; it rotated without the least doubt. Galileo's happy discovery could only hold approximately for small times and spaces, during which the rotation did not come into question. Instead of that, Newton's conclusions about planetary motion, referred as they were to the fixed stars, appeared to conform to the law of inertia. Now, in order to have a generally valid system of reference, Newton ventured the fifth corollary of the *Principia*. He imagined a momentary terrestrial system of coördinates, for which the law of inertia is valid, held fast in space without any rotation relatively to the fixed stars. Indeed he could, without interfering with its usability, impart to this system any initial position and any uniform translation relatively to the above momentary terrestrial system. The Newtonian laws of force are not altered thereby; only the initial positions and initial velocities—the constants of integration— may alter. By this view Newton gave the *exact* meaning of his hypothetical extension of Galileo's law of inertia. We see that the reduction to absolute space was by no means necessary, for the system of reference is just as relatively determined as in every other case. In spite of his metaphysical liking for the absolute, Newton was correctly led by the *tact of the natural investigator*. This is particularly to be noticed, since, in former editions of this book, it was not sufficiently emphasized. How far and how accurately the conjecture will hold good in future is of course undecided.

The comportment of terrestrial bodies with respect to the earth is reducible to the comportment of the earth with respect to the remote heavenly bodies. If we were to assert that we knew more of moving objects than this their last-mentioned, experimentally-given comportment with respect to the celestial bodies, we should render ourselves culpable of a falsity. When, accordingly, we say, that a body preserves unchanged its direction and velocity *in space*, our assertion is nothing more or less than an abbreviated reference to *the entire universe*. The use of such an abbreviated expression is permitted the original author of the principle, because he knows, that as things are no difficulties stand in the way of carrying out its implied directions. But no remedy lies in his power, if difficulties of the kind mentioned present themselves; if, for example, the requisite, relatively fixed bodies are wanting.

7. Instead, now, of referring a moving body K to space, that is to say to a system of coördinates, let us view directly its relation to the bodies of the universe, by which alone such a system of coördinates can be determined....

Instead of saying, the direction and velocity of a mass μ in space remain constant, we may also employ the expression, the mean acceleration of the mass μ with respect to the masses m, m', m''... at the distances r, r', r''... is $= 0$, or $d^2(\Sigma mr/\Sigma m)/dt^2 = 0$. The latter expression is equivalent to the former, as soon as we take into consideration a sufficient number of sufficiently distant and sufficiently large masses. The mutual influence of more proximate small masses, which are apparently not concerned about each other, is eliminated of itself. That the constancy of direction and velocity is given by the condition adduced, will be seen at once if we construct through μ as vertex cones that cut out different portions of space, and set up the condition with respect to the masses of these separate portions. We may put, indeed, for the *entire* space encompassing μ, $d^2(\Sigma mr/\Sigma m)/dt^2 = 0$. But the equation in this case asserts nothing with respect to the motion of μ, since it holds good for all species of motion where μ is uniformly surrounded by an infinite number of masses....

When we reflect that the time-factor that enters into the acceleration is nothing more than a quantity that is the measure of the distances (or angles of rotation) of the bodies of the universe, we see that even in the simplest case, in which apparently we deal with the mutual action of only *two* masses, the neglecting of the rest of the world is *impossible*. Nature does not begin with elements, as we are obliged to begin with them. It is certainly fortunate for us, that we can, from time to time, turn aside our eyes from the over-powering unity of the All, and allow them to rest on individual details. But we should not omit, ultimately to complete and correct our views by a thorough consideration of the things which for the time being we left out of account.

8. The considerations just presented show, that it is not necessary to refer the law of inertia to a special absolute space. On the contrary, it is perceived that the masses that in the common phraseology exert forces on each other as well as those that exert none, stand with respect to acceleration in quite similar relations. We may, indeed, regard *all* masses as related to each other. That *accelerations* play a prominent part in the relations of the masses, must be accepted as a fact of experience; which does not, however, exclude attempts to *elucidate* this fact by a comparison of it with other facts, involving the discovery of new points of view....

9. We have attempted in the foregoing to give the law of inertia a different expression from that in ordinary use. This expression will, so long as a sufficient number of bodies are apparently fixed in space, accomplish the same as the ordinary one. It is as easily applied, and it encounters the same difficulties. In the one case we are unable to come at an absolute space, in the other a limited number of masses only is within the reach of our knowledge, and the summation indicated can consequently not be fully carried out. It is impossible to say whether the new expression would still represent the true condition of things if the stars were to perform rapid movements among one another. The general experience cannot be constructed from the particular case given us. We must, on the contrary, *wait* until such an experience presents itself. Perhaps when our physico-astronomical knowledge has been extended, it will be offered somewhere in celestial space, where more violent and complicated motions take place than in our environment. The most important result of our reflections is, however, *that precisely the apparently simplest mechanical principles are of a very complicated character, that these principles are founded on uncompleted experiences, nay on experiences that never can be fully completed, that practically, indeed, they are sufficiently secured, in view of the tolerable stability of our environment, to serve as the foundation of mathematical deduction, but that they can by no means themselves be regarded as mathematically established truths but only as principles that not only admit of constant control by experience but actually require it.*

... The surroundings in which we live, with their almost constant angles of direction to the fixed stars, appear to me to be an extremely special case, and I would not dare to conclude from this case to a very different one. Although I expect that astronomical observation will only as yet necessitate very small corrections, I consider it possible that the law of inertia in its simple Newtonian form has only, for us human beings, a meaning which depends on space and time. Allow me to make a more general remark. We measure time by the angle of rotation of the earth, but could measure it just as well by the angle of rotation of any other planet. But, on that account, we would not believe that the *temporal* course of all physical phenomena would have to be disturbed if the earth or the distant planet referred to should suddenly experience an abrupt variation of angular velocity. We consider the dependence as not immediate, and consequently the temporal orientation as *external*. Nobody would believe that the chance disturbance—say by an impact—of one body in a system of uninfluenced bodies which are left to themselves and move uniformly in a straight line, where all the bodies combine to fix the system of coördinates, will immediately cause a disturbance of the others as a consequence. The orientation is external here also. Although we must be very thankful for this, especially when it is purified from meaninglessness, still the natural investigator must feel the need of further insight—of knowledge of the *immediate* connections, say, of the masses of the universe. There will hover before him as an ideal an insight into the principles of the whole matter, from which accelerated and inertial motions result in the *same* way. The progress from Kepler's discovery to Newton's law of gravitation, and the impetus given by this to the finding of a physical understanding of the attraction in the manner in which electrical actions at a distance have been treated, may here serve as a model. We must even give rein to the thought that the masses which we see, and by which we by chance orientate ourselves, are perhaps not those which are really decisive. . . .

COMMENTARY

9.1 Introduction

Berkeley lived from 1685 to 1753 and Mach from 1836 to 1916. Berkeley was two years old when Newton's *Principia* was published, and most of his works were devoted to developing a philosophical system appropriate for the new science of his day. Mach worked during the years before the theories of relativity and quantum mechanics, which supplanted Newtonian mechanics, were developed. It has been claimed that Mach's relationism is an early statement of the key principles of Einstein's relativity; but, it is highly questionable whether relativity theory is a form of relationism in the sense we have used. It is thus worth repeating that "relative" and "relativistic" do not mean the same thing. Our relationists are not arguing for modern relativity theory, but only that there are relative spaces: frames of reference defined by material objects.

I've placed these two thinkers together in this collection because both were relationists who took a particular interest in Newton's *Scholium* and its crucial arguments for absolute space, and because of their similar philosophical outlooks. As we shall see, there are important differences between the two and their relational accounts of inertia, but their arguments are sufficiently similar to justify treating them together. The discussion divides into two parts: first the critique of absolute space, and second the relational account of the bucket.

9.2 Absolute Space

Berkeley and Mach object to absolute space on the empiricist grounds that we discussed in the previous chapter on Leibniz. Absolute space, absolute location, and absolute velocity are all unobservable or unmeasurable, and hence, empiricists claim, talk of them is vacuous or incomprehensible, as in the fictitious case of "nelectricity."

In particular, Berkeley argues that one cannot imagine an object moving without imagining it moving relative to some other object: "no motion can be understood without some determination or direction, which in turn cannot be understood unless ... some other body be understood to exist at the same time" (*De Motu*, sec. 58). In other words, a motion that is purely absolute is inconceivable. This argument strikes at the legitimacy of Newton's globes thought experiment, in which a pair of spheres, connected by a rod, rotate about their center in an otherwise empty absolute space.

Newton's example attempts to show that inertial effects—tension in the connecting rod—could occur even if there were no relative reference frame at all, and hence that no relative motion can explain inertia. Berkeley claims that without a material reference body no motion in the globes can be conceived, and so any forces or inertial effects on the globes simply cannot be understood in terms of their motion. That is, Newton's explanation of tension in the rod joining the globes in terms of rotation in absolute space is wrong—or rather, just plain nonsense.

Similarly, Mach claims that the scientist must stick to the "actual facts" of experience: in mechanics, these are the relative motions of objects. Any speculation beyond what can be thus ascertained is meaningless because "no one possesses the requisite knowledge to make use of it" (*Science of Mechanics*, sec. 4). He too considers how an object might move in a universe with no other bodies. Like Berkeley, he notes that we can only ever experience relative motions, and hence any other kind of motion—such as motion in absolute space—is a meaningless fantasy. Thus we cannot say anything of the behavior of a test body, K, in the absence of reference bodies, labeled $A, B, C, \ldots$, for two reasons: First, "we cannot know how K would act in the absence of $A, B, C, \ldots$"; and second, "every means would be wanting of forming a judgment of the behavior of K and putting to the test what we had predicted...." (*Science of Mechanics*, sec. 4). The first point questions our ability to extrapolate from experiment. Suppose we observe a test body moving in a relative reference frame in some way; how can we legitimately infer that it would behave in the same way without the reference bodies? After all, that would be a rather different situation, especially if we are considering, as Newton did, a case with no reference bodies at all. If no such inference is possible then Newton can make no claim about what would happen to the globes in an otherwise empty universe. The second point is the same as Berkeley's: in the absence of reference bodies, it is impossible to attribute any motion to a body or to test whether it has that motion. The only motions that we can predict or measure are relative, and if there were no reference bodies no such prediction or measurement would be possible. For Mach, Newton can say nothing of scientific significance about motion in an empty universe, and so talk of motion through absolute space is again considered nonsense.

Berkeley and Mach deny the existence of absolute space on the empiricist grounds that positions and motions in absolute space are unobservable and hence incomprehensible. The reader has most likely learned enough to reply that while not itself directly observable, absolute space does have some observable consequences: inertial effects in accelerating bodies. The evidence for absolute space is indirect, not direct, observation. For instance, the bucket experiment demonstrates the existence of inertial effects in the universe as we find it, and so it abductively confirms Newton's absolutist account of such effects. Indeed, one might point out that such indirect evidence is common in science: we don't *directly* observe bacteria or distant galaxies, but rather infer their existence from experiments involving microscopes or telescopes. Don't inertial effects constitute experimental knowledge of absolute space, which makes the concept practical and scientifically meaningful?

To reply, the relationist needs to show that inertial effects can be understood using relative motions alone: that the blank in "absolute acceleration is acceleration relative to____" can be filled in by a relation between material objects that holds in exactly those cases in which inertial effects are observed. An empiricist could argue that a successful relational account would be superior to Newton's in at least two ways: it would be simpler—not postulating absolute space—and it would be fully meaningful—avoiding untestable predictions about absolute velocities. But do Berkeley and Mach give a successful relational theory of inertia?

9.3 The Principle of Inertia

The bucket experiment demonstrates the existence of inertial forces, which, following Newton's laws of motion, we understand as being due to the absolute rotation (i.e., acceleration) of the water. The question that we are interested in is, "What is absolute acceleration?" Newton answered that it is acceleration relative to absolute space, but what could a relationist say? Acceleration means a change in speed or direction, but in which reference frame? An object at rest on the sidewalk will accelerate relative to a braking car, and two carousel horses are at relative rest, but move in circles relative to the ground. Berkeley and Mach give the same answer: absolute motion is not motion in absolute space, but motion relative to the distant "fixed stars." "[T]o determine true motion and true rest ... it would be enough to bring in, instead of absolute space, relative space as confined to the heavens of the fixed stars, considered as at rest" (*De Motu*, sec. 64). In this section, we will consider what led them to this account of absolute acceleration, and whether it can provide a successful understanding of inertia. Since Mach's theory is more complete than Berkeley's, we will consider his views first, and then briefly return to Berkeley in conclusion.

Mach rejected Newton's absolute space because "motion in absolute space" is unobservable and hence "without scientific significance," according to the empiricist. "But," the Newtonian might respond, "in the bucket experiment, we do observe acceleration in absolute space." Mach rejects this claim, arguing that all that is in fact observed is that "[inertial effects] are produced by the [water's] relative rotation with respect to the mass of the earth and other celestial bodies" (*Science of Mechanics*, sec. 5). Of course, Mach is correct about what is seen: the stars stayed fixed for the duration of the experiment, and the surface of the water only curved when it rotated relative to them. According to him, all we can strictly conclude from our experiment is that bodies accelerating in the relative frame of the heavens accelerate absolutely: in our earlier terminology, the stars determine an inertial frame of reference. Hence the only directly testable statement of the law of inertia is that "objects remain in constant motion relative to the distant stars unless acted upon by a force." For a Machian empiricist, only this formulation of the law has scientific significance, not Newton's view that objects naturally move constantly with respect to absolute space. The relational form of the law is given by Mach in section 7, with the clarification that the reference frame is not the distant stars—which are in fact in motion—but the center of mass of the "entire universe." (The center of mass of a system of objects is found by averaging their positions, weighted according to their masses. So, for instance, the center of mass of a 1kg object 1m away from a 3kg object is a point on the line between them, 25cm from the heavier body.) So, for example, Mach's law of inertia says that you will be pushed back in your seat as your car accelerates relative to the universe as a whole, which is true of our experiences.

DEFINITION: Let masses $m_1, m_2, \ldots$ be located at position vectors $\mathbf{r}_1, \mathbf{r}_2, \ldots$ respectively from the origin of some reference frame: the distance from the origin to the center of mass, the *center of mass displacement*, $R = \left| \sum_i m_i \mathbf{r}_i \middle/ \sum_i m_i \right|$.

The *displacement speed* is dR/dt and the *displacement acceleration* d^2R/dt^2. Thus $\left| d^2 \left(\sum_i m_i \mathbf{r}_i \middle/ \sum_i m_i \right) \middle/ dt^2 \right| = 0$ implies that the displacement varies constantly in the given frame.

MACH PROPOSES: Any object defines a reference frame and hence a center of mass displacement for the entire universe, R_U. If $d^2 R_U/dt^2 = 0$ holds, then the center of mass displacement changes constantly; equivalently, the displacement of the object from the center of mass of the universe changes constantly. The principle of inertia states that $d^2 R_U/dt^2 = 0$ for all objects unless acted upon by some force; equivalently, any object for which $d^2 R_U/dt^2 = 0$ determines an inertial frame. (But see problem 2 below.)

Perhaps an example will clarify what it means to say that absolute acceleration is acceleration relative to the stars. Imagine a whole universe with a bucket of water at the center, in rotation relative to the rest of the material universe surrounding it. The absolutist can consider two distinct situations with this description: (a) the bucket is spinning in absolute space, say clockwise, and the surrounding universe, including the distant stars, is at rest; (b) the bucket is stationary, but the surrounding universe rotates around the bucket anticlockwise in absolute space. In case (a), the surface of the water will be concave, but in case (b), the bucket does not spin, so the surface will be flat. We can call the two situations "Copernican" and "Ptolemaic" respectively; Copernicus believed that the Earth rotated about its axis, and Ptolemy believed that the heavens rotated about the Earth. (Note that the two situations are related by a "dynamic shift," in the terms used in sec. 8.3.)

In both cases the relative motions are the same, and so, according to Mach's definition, the absolute acceleration and inertial effects must be the same: the water curves either way. Indeed, since the "two" cases differ in no relational way, they are simply different descriptions of one state of affairs. "The universe is not twice given, with a [bucket] at rest and a [bucket] in motion; but only once, with its relative motions, alone determinable" (*Science of Mechanics*, sec. 5). For Mach an acceptable, testable theory of mechanics can involve only relative positions and motions; hence, in any two situations with the same relative motions and positions, the same objects will experience the same inertial effects. This is not the case in Newtonian mechanics, since systems with the same relative motions can have very different motions through absolute space.

At this point it is important to see where Mach's reasoning has taken us: he starts with the correct claim that all we directly observe is that inertial effects occur in objects accelerating relative to the distant stars; he adds the philosophical claim that only the observable is significant in science; and he concludes that a legitimate science of mechanics must be relational. Mach complains of Newton's "metaphysical liking for the absolute," but his relational physics is just as much—if not more—driven by philosophical considerations, namely, by his brand of empiricism. We thus have to ask whether the physical theory demanded by Mach's philosophy can be given: it is one thing to say that there ought to be such a theory, but it is another to give it. Newton introduced absolute space in order to understand his law of inertia, but what theory does Mach produce to account for his?

Mach does not offer an explicit theory, though he is aware that one is needed and hopes that it can be found (*Science of Mechanics*, sec. 11). However, his idea is that given the complete relative arrangement of matter in the universe, the theory will specify the inertial motion of each object at a time. Furthermore, the entire matter of the universe will act on any object not moving constantly to produce inertial effects in it: the effects would be due to some gravity-like force that acts only on accelerating bodies (accelerating relative to the center of mass of the universe that is). In other words, in a Machian theory, matter would do all the work that absolute space does in Newton's theory.

In a Machian theory, then, the deep distinction between forced and unforced, natural and unnatural motions is erased. Material objects simply interact in various ways, sometimes to produce constant, inertial motion, and sometimes to produce absolute acceleration. Such a theory might in principle take on many forms, but it must predict that objects accelerating relative to a universe arranged like ours experience inertial effects.

Though Mach does not give us a theory, two comments are worth making. First, Newton himself considered the possibility that the rotation of the water in the bucket could be understood as motion relative to the distant stars, but he rejected the idea. To paraphrase: "But who will imagine that the parts of the [water] endeavor to recede from its center on account of a force impressed only on the heavens?" (*De Grav.*, this vol., p. 108). That is, if we set the universe spinning around the bucket, how does that affect the surface of the water, as Mach's theory demands?

Second, has anyone succeeded in constructing a theory along the lines sought by Mach? Unfortunately this is a rather technical question, so we will not explore it in detail. However, we can break it into two parts corresponding to classical and relativistic mechanics. First, there have been attempts to construct a Machian theory for Newtonian mechanics—most recently by Barbour and Bertotti—but these have their problems. (See Earman, 1989, for a review of these attempts; he argues that Barbour and Bertotti's theory is unlikely to match with experiment.)

So is Mach's idea that inertia is a species of relative force shown to be correct by relativity? As we saw in the discussion of Aristotle, in general relativity the "force" of gravity is due to the curving of the straight paths of inertial motion. In a sense, then, Mach's idea that the relative arrangement of distant matter affects which motions are inertial is true in relativity theory. But more is needed if we are to say that Mach was right: if general relativity were the theory that he wanted, then the distribution of matter alone would completely determine which motions were natural. But it does not: even relativity requires an absolute standard of constant motion. What can provide this standard? Modern-day followers of Newton believe that it must be some kind of absolute space, at least in the sense of a "substance" distinct from matter. Whether this is correct or not is a topic still much debated, but to discuss it further would require a knowledge of relativity beyond the scope of this book.

Berkeley and Mach are interesting as relationists because both paid attention to the inertial effects revealed by Newton's bucket. Mach saw the need for a full relational theory of inertia, but it seems that Berkeley had a lesser understanding of the problem posed by Newton. For he only took the fixed stars to provide a "convenient" inertial frame of reference, not to be involved in determining inertial motion. But in fact, the stars only define an inertial frame if they themselves move constantly, and so

Berkeley begs the question of which motions are constant. Furthermore, Berkeley's direct attempt to explain the curvature in the bucket (*De Motu*, sec. 60) does no more than say that the curvature reveals the central forces required to keep the water rotating. As we saw, this is the correct Newtonian explanation, but it in turn presupposes that we have made sense of a notion of absolute acceleration, for the forces only appear when the water rotates absolutely! All this suggests that Berkeley missed the point of Newton's argument, namely, that his mechanics, based on the principle of inertia, requires an absolute notion of acceleration. Berkeley's attempt to define it in terms of motion relative to the stars does not go deep enough.

In the next reading (by Kant) we will leave the question of whether a relational account of inertia is possible and move on to a further argument concerning the absolute and relational conceptions of space. But first a brief coda to our discussion, to show how the debate has been transformed by the modern understanding of the nature of "space-time." We will look at these ideas in the next chapter.

Problems

1. How might Berkeley and Mach respond to the dynamic shift described in the previous chapter? What could they say about the "inertial effects"?

2. As Mach himself acknowledges (in sec. 7), demanding that the center of mass displacement vary constantly is not sufficient for constant motion. Explain why the displacement of an object spiraling out from the center of mass may vary constantly. How does Mach try to modify his definition of constant motion to avoid this problem?

3. We have followed both absolutists and relationists in the assumption that the absolute accelerations revealed by inertial effects are motions relative to something. Can the relationist make any headway with the problem of Newton's bucket by denying this assumption? Is it possible somehow that objects simply exhibit inertial effects in a systematic way without further explanation in absolute or relative terms? This suggestion is made in Sklar (1976) and discussed by Ray (1991).

Further Readings and Bibliography

Earman, J. 1989. *World Enough and Space-Time* (see esp. chaps. 4–5). Cambridge, MA: MIT Press.

Popper, K. 1962. "A Note on Berkeley as a Precursor of Mach and Einstein," reprinted as chap. 6 in *Conjectures and Refutations: The Growth of Scientific Knowledge*. New York: Basic Books.

Ray, C. 1991. *Time, Space, and Philosophy* (see esp. chap. 6). London and New York: Routledge. √

Sklar, L. 1976. *Space, Time, and Space-Time* (see esp. chap. III, E–F). Berkeley, CA: University of California Press. √

10 Space-Time

10.1 Introduction

In the next chapter we will explore a new argument for absolute space, and after that we will leave the absolute/relative controversy to explore other topics in the philosophy of space. But first we need to consider the modern conception in which space and time are not considered distinct, but as forming a single entity, "space-time." The space-time picture was forced upon us by relativity theory, but it is also applicable to prerelativistic, Newtonian physics, and hence to the debates that we have studied so far. On the space-time conception, important new facts are revealed about the nature of inertia and the absolute/relative debate, which is why we need to discuss it.

10.2 From Space to Space-Time

Space is the collection of all possible places, and time the collection of all possible instants, so space-time is the collection of all possible "place-instants": every "where-and-when" anything might exist. On this new view, in which space and time are taken to be a single unified whole, we think of one space-time which can be cut into slices of "space-at-an-instant" much as a stack of pancakes can be sliced up into individual pancakes. This view is opposed to Newton's conception of a single entity, space, that exists from one time to the next.

We can view space-time as obtained by adding an extra dimension to space, much as one goes from plane to three-dimensional geometry by adding a third direction, up-and-down. In reality, space is three-dimensional, and space-time four-dimensional, which is a little hard to comprehend without some practice, and always difficult to draw. We will maintain the harmless fiction that space is two-dimensional and take space-time to be three-dimensional: picture it as having two horizontal space dimensions, and one vertical dimension representing the passage of time. Each point on the time axis represents an instant of time, and if we take all the points with the same time coordinate then we have a space slice of space-time: points on the slice are separated in space, but not in time. But again, these slices—technically called "space-like hypersurfaces"—are as pancakes in a stack, not a single space that exists at all times.

The smallest parts of space-time are points, but now a point picks out not just a location in space, but also a particular time: space-time points have both space and time coordinates. Since all occurrences take place somewhere at some time, points of space-time are known as *events*. Because an object exists over a region of space and

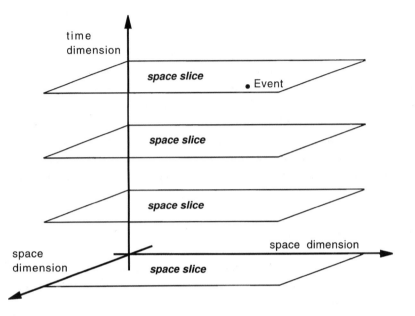

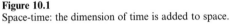

Figure 10.1
Space-time: the dimension of time is added to space.

for a period of time, it does not occupy just a single space-time point, but rather has a life history occupying many events. Let us look at some examples. First consider the small particles in figure 10.2(i). In space such particles are effectively points, so as they move over time they sweep out various curves—"world lines"—which depend on whether they are: (a) stationary; (b) moving constantly (to the left), covering equal distances in equal times; or (c) accelerating (to the right), so that as time goes on they move an increasing distance per unit time. In a space-time diagram the slope of a world line determines the speed of an object, because the slope equals the distance traveled divided by the time taken. Thus, the faster an object moves, the closer to horizontal is its world line.

   We can also picture objects that are (effectively) one-dimensional in space, such as ropes, or two-dimensional in space, such as cookies (and in three-dimensional space, solid objects such as bananas). An object that has one dimension in space will have a "world sheet" in space-time because it sweeps out a two-dimensional surface as it moves over time. For instance, in figure 10.2(ii) the ends of a rope join to form a loop; the world sheet looks like an open tent. In figure 10.2(iii) a two-dimensional chocolate chip cookie is snapped into two pieces, sweeping out a three-dimensional

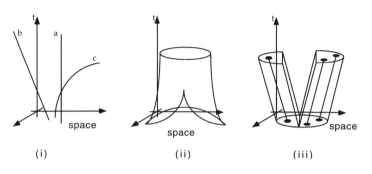

Figure 10.2
Space-time diagrams: (i) particles' world lines, (ii) a rope's world tube, and (iii) a chocolate chip cookie's world tube.

"world tube" in space-time. For simplicity, we will usually talk about the world lines of objects of all dimensions, meaning the world line of the center of mass.

10.3   Newtonian Space-Time

Now that we are somewhat familiar with space-time in general, we can inquire what further specific properties it might have. As we shall see, space-time can take many forms, but the first that we will consider is the form that Newton might have expected it to take. The idea of space-time was not developed until three hundred years after Newton, so our game is to determine from his (and Clarke's) writings concerning absolute space what he might have said had he been aware of the concept. (What might Leibniz have said?—see the problem section for this chap.)

First of all, we can expect that Newton would have taken space-time, like absolute space, to be a substance-like object, independent of matter: he would have been a substantivalist about space-time. Further evidence for this reading is that if space-time is a separate entity from matter, then static shifts in space-time lead to distinct situations, as Newton thought. For instance, if the world tube of the entire material universe were shifted, without deformation, in space or time (or both) then it would be located differently in a substantial space-time. (And if space-time is as featureless as absolute space, then such a shift would be undetectable.)

Newton also took absolute space to allow for a definition of absolute motion, and this is also possible in space-time. The natural thing to assume is that any two events—space-time points—are a definite distance and a definite time apart. In this case, any object travels a definite distance in a definite time between two points on its

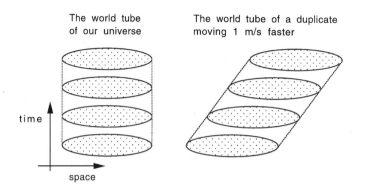

Figure 10.3
The kinematic shift in space time: all trajectories are identically skewed.

world line, and so has a definite (average) speed during the trip: the distance traveled divided by the time taken. As we saw in figure 10.2(i), this speed is the slope of the world line: for instance, particle (a) travels no distance as time progresses, and so has zero velocity. This motion is absolute in the general sense that it does not require a relative reference frame in order to define it.

Newtonian space-time is defined by the following properties: between any two events p and q, let there be a definite, Euclidean spatial distance, $R(p, q)$ and temporal interval, $T(p, q)$.

Again, evidence that a space-time with these properties is appropriate for Newton's views comes from the fact that they make kinematically shifted systems distinct. Imagine that every object in the universe moved 1m/s faster to the right than it does now; in a space-time diagram, skew the world tube of the universe to the right, to change the slope of every world line by a constant amount. ("Skewing" means sliding each slice a fixed distance over the slice below, and leaves the relations of matter unchanged at each instant.)

This new material universe would differ from ours only in absolute velocity, which is undetectable in Newtonian mechanics, so the two universes cannot be distinguished; equivalently, the world line of every object has a definite slope (i.e., absolute velocity), but it is unmeasurable. Space-time as we have just described it thus inherits both the problems concerning the PII that Leibniz raised for absolute space.

On the other hand, this notion of space-time allows for absolute acceleration: absolute acceleration is acceleration relative to a stationary (or constant) trajectory. Since the points of substantival space-time exist independently of matter, such trajectories exist even if no material objects are actually at rest. And as we have discussed at length, an account of absolute acceleration is exactly what is needed to make sense of the law of inertia and to understand inertial effects. In fact there is a nice way to view the matter. Every world line has a definite slope—an absolute speed—so it also has a definite curve: a world line is straight if the slope/velocity remains constant, but as its slope/velocity changes it curves (see figure 10.2[i.c]).

Thus the principle of inertia can be formulated to state that objects have straight world lines unless acted upon by forces, so that those objects with curved world lines will experience inertial effects. This view of space-time can offer the kind of explanation of the bucket that Newton sought: the internal forces due to the concave surface make the world lines of the water molecules follow curved paths around the center of the bucket (see problem 1 below).

Since this view of space-time fits Newton's views about the static and kinematic shifts and his account of inertia, it has become known as *substantival Newtonian space-time*. It is what the notion of absolute space becomes in the space-time context.

10.4 Galilean Space-Time

It might seem that any two space-time points must be a definite distance apart in time and in space, but they need not. We learned in our discussion of Zeno (especially sec. 3.3) that because all segments contain the same uncountable infinity of points, the length of a line is independent of its point composition. That is, distance relations—"metrical properties"—must be "added" once we have a collection of points, so the same collection of points is compatible with many metrical properties. In the present case, then, the same set of space-time points could have various distance relations, perhaps those like Newton's and perhaps others. (Many different metrical properties are mathematically possible; it is another question which are actually true of space-time.)

An alternative conception to Newtonian space-time is "Galilean space-time" (sometimes called "neo-Newtonian space-time"), which is defined as follows: there is a definite time interval between any two points of space-time, but only if two points are simultaneous is there any spatial distance between them. Further, for any segment of a space-time curve it is a definite fact whether it is straight or not.

Galilean space-time is defined by the following properties: between any two events p and q, (i) let there be a definite temporal interval, $T(p, q)$; (ii) if they are simultaneous ($T(p, q) = 0$), let there be a definite spatial distance, $D(p, q)$; (iii) given any curve c through p, let c have a definite curvature at p, $S(c, p)$ (i.e., a curve c is straight if $S(c, p) = 0$ for all points p on c).

Again, it might seem strange that some points have a spatial distance between them when others do not, but points don't have to have every property we can think of. For instance, we could define some point to be the center of the Euclidean plane, so that every point would be a definite distance from the center; but we don't. Similarly, we can define a space-time in which there is no distance between some points. Indeed, it seems plausible that space-time really is this way: How far in space are you from where you were in space a minute ago? 1m? 1km? 1,000km? It is reasonable to think that such a question has no answer.

Let us take a substantival view of Galilean space-time, postulating that space-time exists independently of matter, so that static shifts lead to distinct but undetectable states of affairs. However, a kinematic shift in Galilean space-time does not change anything. The shift was possible in Newtonian space-time because every object had a definite speed, given by the distance traveled between two points divided by the time taken. But in Galilean space-time there is no definite distance between points at different times on a world line, and hence objects have no definite speed. Thus it is impossible for two Galilean universes to differ just because their material contents have motions that differ by a fixed, constant amount: in Galilean space-time this "difference" is no real distinction at all.

It also follows that space-time diagrams misrepresent Galilean space-time in an important regard: they show world lines to have definite slopes—that is, speeds—when they do not. Looking back at figure 10.2(i), we see that it presents one way of drawing Galilean space-time, but that it would have been equally accurate to have skewed the picture so that trajectory (b) was vertical, and (a) sloped to the right. Skewing leaves all the Galilean properties unchanged: the time between two points remains the same, simultaneous points remain the same distances apart, and all straight lines remain straight. Therefore a skewed diagram represents exactly the same Galilean space-time as an unskewed one: when we draw a space-time diagram we have no choice but to make one direction "up," but in Galilean space-time no world line is sloped up more than any other.

The identity of skewed diagrams gives us another way to understand why a kinematic shift is vacuous in Galilean space-time. Such a shift involves, as we saw in

Newtonian space-time, skewing the world tube of the material universe—and in Galilean space-time skewing leads merely to another representation of the same situation. Therefore a kinematic shift has no real effect whatsoever, as Leibniz claimed.

However, substantival Galilean space-time preserves from Newtonian space-time exactly that feature which allows the space-time formulation of the law of inertia: a definite distinction between straight and curved world lines. Just as in Newtonian space-time, we can again say that objects have straight world lines unless acted upon by forces. Alternatively, since straightness is a definite property of curves in Galilean space-time, not just a frame-relative one, absolute acceleration is a definite property of objects: Absolute acceleration is acceleration relative to any straight trajectory.

Therefore, if one adopts substantival Galilean space-time, he avoids Leibniz's kinematic shift problem and can explain what happens in Newton's bucket experiment. It seems that this position is a major improvement over Newton's, though it incorporates his important metaphysical claim that space exists distinct from matter: the core of his disagreement with the relationists. It is thus disappointing that Newton did not discover Galilean space-time, despite coming within a step of it. In Corollary V of the *Principia*, Newton realized that his laws were equally applicable in any inertial frame, from which he might have concluded that all of them were equivalent. The problem with absolute space and Newtonian space-time is that inertial frames are not entirely equivalent, for one is at rest. The central feature of Galilean space-time is that the equivalence is restored, and every inertial frame is as "right" as any other.

Problems

1. Draw space-time diagrams for each of the three stages of the bucket experiment, indicating the world lines of an atom of the bucket and an atom of the water.

Moving the discussion to the context of space-time reveals that between Newton and Leibniz there is not one issue, "absolute-or-relative?" but two: "substantival-or-relative?" and "which space-time?" The following questions help to bring out this point.

2. First we will define relationism to be both the denial that space-time is an independent, substantial entity, and the claim that it is simply the collection of spatio-temporal relations between material objects. ("An order of space-time coexistences," if you like.) Thus we can understand relational Newtonian space-time. Let any point of space-time at which an object is located be called a *material event*. Then, in relational Newtonian space-time, between any two material points there is a definite

time and distance. Explain why in relational Newtonian space-time (i) the universe cannot be statically shifted, (ii) it can be kinematically shifted, and (iii) a relational account of inertia can be given.

3. In Leibnizian space-time, between any two points there is a definite time, but only between simultaneous points is there a distance (like Galilean space-time without a notion of straightness). Does this description fit with Leibniz's ideas? Considering both substantival and relational views of Leibnizian space-time, determine whether (i) the universe can be statically shifted, (ii) it can be kinematically shifted, and (iii) an account of inertia can be given.

4. It seems that relational Galilean space-time should be the ideal theory, for Galilean space-time avoids an unmeasurable absolute velocity while preserving a notion of absolute acceleration, and relationism avoids the static shift problem. But can such a theory be given? Maudlin (1993) suggests not; can you answer his challenge?

Further Readings and Bibliography

Disalle, R. "On Dynamics, Indiscernibility, and Space-Time Ontology." *British Journal for Philosophy of Science* 45 (1994): 265–287.

Earman, J. 1989. *World Enough and Space-Time* (see esp. chaps. 2–3). Cambridge, MA: MIT Press.

Friedman, M. 1983. *Foundations of Space-Time Theories: Relativistic Physics and Philosophy of Science* (see esp. chaps. I–III). Princeton, NJ: Princeton University Press.

Geroch, R. 1978. *General Relativity from A to B* (see esp. chaps. 1–4). Chicago, IL: University of Chicago Press. √

Maudlin, T. "Buckets of Water and Waves of Space: Why Space-Time Is Probably a Substance." *Philosophy of Science* 60, no. 2 (June 1993): 183–203.

11 Kant and Handedness

READING

Concerning the Ultimate Foundation of the Differentiation of Regions in Space

The illustrious *Leibniz* enriched various departments of knowledge with many genuine insights. But the world waited in vain for him to execute projects far greater still. Whether the reason was that his efforts seemed too incomplete to him,—a reservation peculiar to men of distinction, that has continually deprived learning of many valuable fragments,—or whether it was with *Leibniz*, and *Boerhaave* suspects it was with great chemists: that they often claimed the ability to perform certain undertakings, as if they possessed the ability, whereas, in reality, they possessed only the conviction and trust in their own skill, that once they wished to attempt the performance of an undertaking, they could not but be successful: I do not wish to decide here what the explanation is. At least it looks as if a certain mathematical discipline, which he entitled in advance "Analysis situs," the loss of which *Buffon*, in considering the natural folding together in seeds lamented, was probably never anything more than a thing of the imagination. I do not know how far the object, which I propose to examine here, is related to that which the great man had in mind. To judge from the meaning of words alone, I am engaged in a philosophic search for the ultimate foundation of the possibility of that, of which *Leibniz* intended to determine the magnitudes mathematically. For the positions of the parts of space, in relation to each other, presuppose the region, according to which they are ordered in such a relation. In the most abstract sense, region does not consist of the relation of one thing in space to the next. That would really be the concept of position. Region really consists rather in the relation of the system of these positions to absolute space. The position of the parts of any extended object, with respect to each other, can be sufficiently recognised from the object itself. The region, however, to which this order of the parts is directed, is related to space outside, but not with reference to its localities, for this would be nothing else than the position of just those parts in an external relation; region is related rather to space in general as a unity, of which each extension must be regarded as a part. It is no wonder if the reader finds these concepts still very incomprehensible; but they should become clear in due course. I add, therefore, nothing further, except that my intention in this paper is to see whether, in the intuitive judgements of extension, such as include geometry, a clear proof can

Immanuel Kant, "Concerning the Ultimate Foundation of the Differentiation of Regions in Space," *Kant: Selected Precritical Writings and Correspondence with Beck* (pp. 36–43), edited by G. B. Kerford and D. E. Walford. Reprinted by permission of Peter Gray-Lucas.

be found that *absolute space has its own reality independently of the existence of all matter and that it is itself the ultimate foundation of the possibility of its composition.* Everyone knows how futile the efforts of philosophers have been to place this point once and for all beyond dispute, by means of the most abstract judgements of metaphysics. I know of no attempt to execute this a posteriori (namely, by using other undeniable propositions, themselves lying outside the realm of metaphysics, but able, when applied in particular concrete cases, to offer a touchstone of their correctness), apart from the treatise of the distinguished *Euler* the Elder in the history of the Royal Acadamy of Sciences in Berlin for the year 1748. It did not, however, quite fulfil its purpose, since it only shows the difficulties of giving a definite significance to the most general laws of motion, when the only concept of space that is accepted is that which is derived from the abstraction from the relation of real things. But it leaves untouched the not less significant difficulties which remain, when the supposed laws are applied, when one wishes to represent them according to the concept of absolute space, in a particular concrete case. The proof which I am seeking here is intended to place in the hands, not of engineers, as was the intention of Herr *Euler*, but in the hands of geometers themselves a convincing proof that would enable them to assert, with the clearness customary to them, the reality of their absolute space. For this purpose, I make the following preparation.

Because of its three dimensions, three surfaces can be conceived in physical space. They all intersect each other at right angles. Since we know nothing external to us through the senses, except in so far as it stands in relation to ourselves, it is no wonder that we derive from the relation of these intersecting surfaces to our body the ultimate foundation of generating the concept of regions in space. The surface on which the length of our body stands vertically is called, with respect to ourselves, horizontal; and this horizontal surface gives occasion for the differentiation of objects which we indicate by *above* and *below*. Two other surfaces can stand vertically on this surface and they can, at the same time, intersect each other at right angles, so that the length of the human body is conceived along the line of the intersection. One of these vertical surfaces divides the body into two externally similar halves and gives the foundation of the distinction between the *right* and the *left* half; the other vertical surface which stands perpendicularly to it, enables us to conceive the *front* and *back* side. In a sheet of writing for example, we distinguish the upper from the lower part of the writing; we notice the difference between the front and the back side; and then we notice the position of the written characters from left to right, or vice versa. Turn the sheet how one will, the parts which are ordered on the surface always have the same position here with respect to each other, and the figure is, in all parts, one and the same. But by this representation, the distinction of regions comes so much into consideration and is so closely connected with the impression made by the visible object that the very same piece of writing becomes unrecognisable, when it is seen with everything turned from the right to the left, which before had the opposite position.

Even our judgements on terrestrial regions are subordinated to the concept we have of regions in general, in so far as they are determined, in relation to the sides of our bodies. Whatsoever relations we otherwise recognise in the heavens and on the earth, independently of this fundamental concept, are merely the positions of objects in relation to each other. No matter how well I know the order of the parts of the horizon, I can only determine the regions, in accordance with this knowledge, if I am aware of the direction in which the order runs. The most accurate of heavenly charts, no matter how accurately I have it in mind, would not in the end enable me to know from the known region, for example from the north, on which side of the horizon I should seek the rising sun, if, apart from the position of the stars to each other, the regions were not determined by the position of the sketch in relation to my hands. The same holds true of geographical, indeed of our most ordinary knowledge of the position of places; such knowledge is of no help to us, so long as we are unable to place the so ordered things and the whole system of reciprocally related positions, according to regions, through the relation to the sides of our bodies. There even exists a very noted characteristic of the products of nature, which can itself now and then give occasion to the distinction of kinds, in the definite region where the order of their parts is reversed, and whereby two creatures can be distinguished, even though, in respect both of size and proportion and even of the situation of the parts relative to each other, they may be in perfect agreement. The hair on the crown of the head of all human beings is directed from the left to the right hand side. All hops wind round their poles from left to right; beans, however, twist in the opposite direction. Almost all snails, with the exception of perhaps three species, coil from the left side to the right, looking down from above, that is from the point of the shell to the mouth. This definite quality is immutably present in exactly the same species, without any relation to the hemisphere where they are to be found, or to the direction of the daily movement of the sun and moon which, with us runs from left to right, but which for those living in the Antipodes runs from right to left. This is because, in the natural generations mentioned, the cause of the convolutions lies in the seeds themselves. On the other hand, where a certain turning can be attributed to the course of the heavenly bodies, as for example the law *Mariotte* claims to have observed in the case of the winds, which readily run through the whole compass from left to right from new moon to full moon, then these circular movements must run in the opposite direction in the other hemisphere, as indeed *Don Ulloa* really thinks he has found confirmed by his observations in the southern ocean.

Since the distinct feeling of the right and the left side is of such great necessity to the judgement of the regions, nature has at the same time attached it to the mechanical structure of the human body. By its means one side, namely the right hand one, has an undoubted superiority in skill, and, perhaps, also in strength, over the left. Hence all the peoples of the earth are right handed (leaving aside individual exceptions which, like that of being cross-eyed, cannot upset the universality of the rule, according to the natural order). One moves one's body more easily from the right to the left than in the opposite direction when one mounts a horse or steps over a pit. Everywhere one writes with the right hand and one does everything with it, for which skill or strength is required. However, just as the right side seems to have the advantage in mobile power, so the left side has the advantage over the right side in respect of sensitivity, if certain scientists are to be believed—for example *Borelli* and *Bonnet*. The former asserts of the left eye and the latter of the left ear that the sense in them is stronger than that in the identically named organ on the right side. And thus it is that both sides of the human body, irrespective of their great external similarity, are sufficiently distinguished, by means of clear sensation, leaving aside the differing situation of the internal parts and the perceptible beating of the heart, since this muscle in its continual contraction touches, in oblique motion, the left side of the breast with its tip.

We wish, therefore, to show that the complete principle of determining a physical form does not rest merely on the relation and the situation of the parts, with respect to each other, but also on its relation to general absolute space, as conceived by geometers; indeed, in such a way that this relation cannot be immediately perceived, though, perhaps, the physical differences that rest uniquely and alone on this ground can be. When two figures, drawn on a flat surface, are like and similar, they cover each other. But it is often different with physical extension or even with lines and surfaces not lying on a flat surface. They can be perfectly like and similar and yet be in themselves so different that the limits of the one cannot at the same time be the limits of the other. The thread of a screw which goes round its pin from left to right will never fit into a nut where the thread runs from right to left, even though the size of the pin and the number of the screw-turns are the same. A spherical triangle can be perfectly like and similar to another without however covering it. But the most common and the clearest example is to be found in the members of the human body, which are ordered symmetrically with respect to the vertical surface. The right hand is similar to and like the left hand, and merely looking at one of them, at the proportion and the situation of the parts to each other, and at the size of the whole, a complete description of the one must apply, in all respects, to the other.

An object which is completely like and similar to another, although it cannot be included exactly within the same limits, I call its *incongruent counterpart*. In order to demonstrate the possibility of an incongruent counterpart a body is taken which does not consist of two halves arranged symmetrically with reference to a single intersecting surface but rather, for example, a *human hand*. From all points of its surface one extends perpendicular lines to a board placed opposite the object. One extends these lines exactly so far behind the board as the points lie before it. When the end points of these so extended lines are connected, they constitute the surface of a bodily figure, which is the incongruent counterpart of the original object. That is, when the given hand is a right hand, its counterpart is a left hand. The reflection of an object in a mirror rests on exactly the same principles. For the object appears always exactly so far behind the mirror as it stands before its surface. Thus the image of a right hand is always a left hand in the mirror. should the object itself consist of two incongruent counterparts as, for example, does the human body when it is divided from back to front by means of a vertical intersection, then its image is congruent to it. This can be easily seen when one imagines it turned a half circle. For the counterpart of an object's counterpart is, of necessity, congruent to that object.

So much may be sufficient to understand the possibility of completely like and similar and yet incongruent spaces. We turn now to the philosophical application of these concepts. It is already clear from the everyday example of the two hands that the figure of a body can be completely similar to that of another, and that the size of the extension can be, in both, exactly the same; and that yet, however, an internal difference remains: namely, that the surface that includes the one could not possibly include the other. As the surface limiting the bodily space of the one cannot serve as a limit for the other, twist and turn it how one will, this difference must, therefore, be such as rests on an inner principle. This inner principle of difference cannot, however, be connected with the different way in which the parts of the body are connected with each other. For, as one sees from the given example, everything can be perfectly identical in this respect. Let it be imagined that the first created thing were a human hand, then it must necessarily be either a right hand or a left hand. In order to produce the one a different action of the creative cause is necessary from that, by means of which its counterpart could be produced.

If one accepts the concept of modern, in particular, German philosophers, that space only consists of the external relations of parts of matter, which exist alongside one another, then all real space would be, in the example used, simply that *which this hand takes up*. However, since there is no difference in the relations of the parts to each other, whether right hand or left, the hand would be completely indeterminate with respect to such a quality, that is, it would fit on either side of the human body. But that is impossible.

From this it is clear that the determinations of space are not consequences of the situations of the parts of matter relative to each other; rather are the latter consequences of the former. It is also clear that in the constitution of bodies, differences, and real differences at that, can be found; and these differences are connected purely with *absolute and original space*, for it is only through it that the relation of physical things is possible. It is also clear that since absolute space is not an object of external sensation, but rather a fundamental concept, which makes all these sensations possible in the first place, we can only perceive through the relation to other bodies that which, in the form of a body, purely concerns its relation to pure space.

A reflective reader will therefore regard the concept of space in the way geometers regard it, and also as perceptive philosophers have taken it up into the theory of natural science, as other than a mere entity of reason. Nonetheless, there is no lack of difficulties surrounding the concept when one tries to grasp with the ideas of reason its reality, evident enough to the inner sense. But this difficulty appears everywhere, if one still wishes to philosophise about the first data of our experience. But this difficulty is never so decisive as that which emerges, when the consequences of an accepted concept contradict the clearest experience.

COMMENTARY

11.1   Introduction

The preceding essay was published in 1768, and the reading of the next chapter, Kant's *Critique of Pure Reason*, in 1781. In the present reading, Kant offers us another argument in favor of the existence of absolute space, this one based on the familiar (but far from simple) phenomena of reflection. We can profitably compare the logic of his argument with those of the previous three chapters.

Recall the absolutists (or substantivalists) assert the existence of an absolute space that does not depend on any material objects for its existence. Relationists deny that this exists. The argument thus takes the following form: the absolutist tries to show that there is some phenomenon—such as inertial effects—that cannot be explained unless absolute space exists. On the other side, the relationists try to show that postulating the existence of absolute space leads to unacceptable consequences—for instance, the existence of undetectable "absolute locations"—and hence try to argue indirectly that space is merely "an order of things that exist at the same time" (*Correspondence*, LIII.4). Kant's argument fits the first of these two patterns: he wants to show that the relationist cannot give an adequate account of "handedness."

11.2   Incongruent Counterparts

Consider one of Kant's own examples (*Concerning*, this vol., p. 199), that of a map. On the face of it, the successful use of maps seems to speak for the relational conception of space. We don't know where we are in absolute space, but we can use maps to describe the arrangement of objects around us. We don't use maps to determine the absolute location of an object, but rather the position of, say, the interstate in relation to downtown. Even so, Kant believes that maps do require the existence of absolute space. Imagine a map publisher making an error in his printing instructions for the new map of the local area, so that half the maps are printed correctly, and the other half are printed as mirror images (as in fig. 11.1). In an important sense the maps are the same, for the distance between any two objects in one will be exactly duplicated in the other. Therefore, according to Leibniz's relationism, they should be the same map. But only one set of maps can be correct: if I stand facing north then on one map the mountains are on the left and the town on the right, and on the other the town is on the left and the mountains on the right. Only one of these descriptions is correct—for the town actually is on the right from that

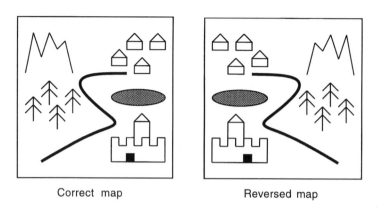

Correct map   Reversed map

Figure 11.1
A map and its mirror image.

perspective—so only one map describes how things actually are, and hence the maps must be representing different situations. Thus we have the typical antirelational argument: the difference is real, but it seems that it cannot be explained in relational terms. Doesn't it follow that absolute space is required to account for the difference?

Rather than pursue the argument with maps (though see the problems at the end of this commentary), we can follow Kant and look at some simpler reflected objects that have similar properties, and hence simplify our analysis. In fact, we will simplify even further by working in two dimensions rather than the three that Kant uses. We shall develop his suggestion (*Concerning*, this vol., pp. 198–199), and consider what happens when we reflect letters of the alphabet, rather than hands. When we are clear about the ideas involved, we will move up to three-dimensions.

Consider the following two sentences.

THE QUICK BROWN FOX JUMPS OVER THE LAZY DOG

and

THE QUICK BROWN ꟻOX JUMPS OVER THE LAZY DOG

These differ in that I have replaced two of the letters by their mirror images in the second line: the letters "E" and "F". It is very striking that you can only tell that I have done this for the "F", and it reveals an important property of certain figures (and, in three dimensions, solids). Consider first reflecting the letter "E". What you notice in figure 11.2 is that the reflection of "E" can be moved back onto the original

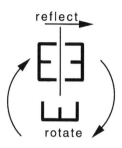

Figure 11.2
Congruent counterparts: the reflection of "E" can be moved back onto "E".

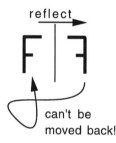

Figure 11.3
Incongruent counterparts: the reflection of "F" cannot be moved back onto "F".

letter simply by sliding it around in the plane of the paper. This is why you can't tell that I replaced "E" with its mirror image: the two can be made to fill just the same place in the sentence. Following Kant, we can say that the mirror image of "E", its "counterpart," is "congruent" to "E". In general (subject to the qualifications made below), any pair of objects that (in principle) can be made to fit in precisely the same place are congruent. For amusement you might like to find all the other letters with congruent counterparts.

Things look quite different for "F," for its mirror image is not congruent to it. Draw an "F" and its counterpart, and try to move them on top of each other: you will find that they cannot be slid in the plane into the exact same place. Hence "F" and its mirror image are "incongruent counterparts," and so you can tell when an "F" has been replaced with its reflection. In general, mirror images are incongruent when they cannot even in principle be made to fit the same space by "rigid motions"—that is, by moving them from place to place without cutting or squashing them in any way.

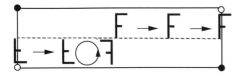

Figure 11.4
The Möbius loop. The loop is shown unrolled—the strip should be twisted around the dotted central line and ends joined so that the two black and two white corners connect. The "F" moving to the right will keep its base on the center line and its top near the white corner as it moves across the join; as a subsequent rotation in the loop shows, the effect of a complete journey around is to reflect the "F."

We need to tidy up what we have just said in a few ways, as it is not an unqualified fact that "F" and its counterpart are incongruent. In the first place, as you might have noticed in sliding the backwards "F" about, if you are allowed to move letters out of the two-dimensional plane then it can be made to fit with "F." To do so, fold the paper over along the line of reflection and the two sit on each other quite happily: effectively you have moved the "F" through three-dimensional space, and back into the plane. These considerations mean that we have to be careful in our definition of congruence. We will say first that two plane figures are incongruent just in case they cannot be made to occupy the same place by rigid motions in two dimensions.

But even this definition is not quite right, for it is not even true that "F" and its counterpart are incongruent in every two-dimensional space. For instance, if you take a strip of paper, put a twist into it and join the ends, you will form a Möbius loop, an object with some remarkable properties. (The following comments will be much clearer if you actually have the loop in front of you.) For instance, if you run your finger around the loop without taking it off, it will traverse both sides of the paper before getting back to the start.

However, if we now think of the loop as a possible model of space, then it doesn't make sense to think of two distinct "sides" in this way. On a piece of paper it is possible to have distinct figures on two sides (or, as in this book, distinct words on two sides), because paper has a finite thickness. Two-dimensional space does not, so there is no distinction between "points on the front" and "points on the back." In other words, if we take a sheet of paper to be our model of space, and hold it flat between the tips of two fingers, then they must be considered to be at the same point of space. Similarly with the Möbius loop, the finger's trip around "both sides" corresponds to a trip twice around Möbius space: a trip once around Möbius space is completed when you reach the place where you started, but on the other side of the paper.

This brings us to an even more remarkable feature of the loop. By the time a figure has traveled once around Möbius space in this sense, it will have turned into its mirror image (see figure 11.3 to see that this is true for the letter "F"). On our paper model we see that this is so because the figure is now on the other side of the paper from which it started—but as we saw, the different "sides of space" aren't really distinct places, so this is only a crude way of picturing the process. In spatial terms, Möbius space has the astonishing property that any object can be turned into its counterpart simply by taking it around some closed path! Such a space is called *nonorientable*. In contrast, the Euclidean plane is orientable.

In this space then, the backwards "F" can be moved onto a regular "F" simply by taking it around the loop (and then rotating it in the plane): according to our proposed definition, they are no longer incongruent. So, the question of whether two objects will fit onto one another depends importantly on the shape of space as a whole: for instance, is it a plane or is it a Möbius loop? We can evade this problem by saying finally that two nearby plane figures are incongruent just in case they cannot be made to occupy the same place by rigid motions in a (sufficiently) closely surrounding region of two-dimensional space.

With these qualifications in the back of our minds, we should have a better grasp of the idea of an incongruent counterpart in two dimensions. Now we must see how the concept applies in three dimensions. Left and right hands (ignoring warts and so on) are indeed exact mirror images of one another, but there is no way to get them to fit identical spaces simply by movements in three dimensions: hence Kant's claim that they are incongruent counterparts. Anyone who has tried to put a left hand glove onto a right hand will appreciate this. Importantly, however, motions through four dimensions would allow them to coincide, as would trips around nonorientable three-dimensional spaces. That is, if the left-handed glove were sent on a trip around a three-dimensional equivalent of Möbius space, it could come back fitting on the right hand, not the left! Thus similar care in the definition is required. (Of course there are also solids that correspond to "E": spheres and cubes, for instance, have congruent counterparts.)

What this shows is that handedness ("chirality" to give it its technical name) is tied to incongruence. When mirror images of some object are congruent (for instance, those of a cube), then there are no left- and right-hand kinds of that object, but when mirror images are incongruent, there are. We have left and right hands and feet, left and right screws, and we can say now, left and right instances of "F" (but only one kind of "E"). To adopt a more useful term here, let us call either kind of "F" an "eff," and let us call the normal, left-handed letter "F" a "leff." The abnormal right-handed mirror image we shall call a "reff," so leffs and reffs are the two incongruent kinds of effs.

11.3   Kant's Argument for Absolute Space

The crucial point in Kant's argument for absolute space is that left- and right-handed mirror images are different, for they are incongruent, but, as in the map example, they do not differ in any intrinsic spatial relations. This is because of the way reflection works. For instance, if I hold my hands so that they are reflections of each other, then the distance between any pair of points on one hand—say, between the tips of my thumb and little finger—exactly equals the distance between the reflected points on the other. So, if you were to catalogue all the relative distances between parts of my left hand, and all the relative distances between parts of my right hand, they would be exactly alike. There is no way to distinguish them by their internal distance relations.

The same holds for the left- and right-handed effs: the leffs and reffs. They have the same height, the same width, and the central crossbar is the same distance up, and the same length on both, and so on. In other words, the two hands or two letters or two maps, or indeed any pair of mirror images are exactly alike in their intrinsic spatial relations. However, if they are incongruent counterparts then they must be different in some way: one is left and the other right. And it seems reasonable to postulate that this difference is purely spatial, for reflections are spatial transformations and hence do not affect nonspatial properties such as weight, color, flavor, electric charge, and so on. (Let us just note that what goes on this list is far from trivial. For instance, if our taste organs have incongruent counterparts, then reflected food could taste differently from its counterpart.)

Kant's challenge to the relationist is to account somehow for handedness, given that the distinction between left and right is a spatial distinction, that the only spatial facts to which the relationist can appeal are the distance relations between material objects, and that the internal distance relations are identical for both left and right. If there is no relational difference between left and right, then the relationist account again seems inadequate. We can draw a parallel between the present case and the bucket argument for absolute space: Newton believed that the bucket experiment revealed an absolute distinction between rotating and nonrotating that could not be understood as a relational difference; Kant believes that there is an absolute distinction between left and right that cannot be understood as a relational difference. In the former case, Newton infers absolute space abductively, but Kant's "geometer's proof" offers a stronger conclusion: that it is impossible for a relationist to account for left and right. (How does absolute space help? Kant doesn't say, but right hands are congruent to right-hand-shaped regions of absolute space and left hands are not, so in that sense at least they are absolutely different.)

But surely there is also a relational difference between leffs and reffs. In our "LAZY DOG" example, the relationist is not really faced with any problem; she can point out that, keeping all the other letters fixed, there is no way to make the reff stand in the same relations to the rest of the sentence as the leff does. One can move the reff so that its vertical bar is the same distance from the "N" and the "O," but then its crossbars will be too near the "N" and too far from the "O." There are relations that the leff can bear to the other letters, but which the reff cannot—the leff "fits" in a way that the reff does not.

Try as you like, there is no way to fit the reff into the sentence in the way that the leff does. But "fitting" is a perfectly respectable relational property, for something fits just in case it can be moved into appropriate relations with other objects. So here the relationist has no difficulty at all. She simply says that the (relational) difference between leffs and reffs is that leffs fit into sentences of Latin letters correctly, and reffs don't. Similarly, the difference between left and right hands rests on such facts as that left hands fit correctly into left-handed gloves, and right hands do not. Once again, whether a hand "fits" a particular glove can be seen as a relational matter: for instance, a left hand can be in contact with—at zero distance from—the inside surface of a left-hand glove, but not of a right-hand glove. So it seems that the relationist can answer Kant's challenge, and the apparently "absolute" distinction between left and right is relational after all.

But doesn't this line of thought merely postpone the problem? The relationist claims that being a left hand, for instance, is a matter of fitting left-handed gloves, but what makes the glove left-handed rather than right-handed? To put the point another way, on the relational view, a right hand could be turned into a left by the simultaneous reflection of everything else in the world: the hand would then fit in all the gloves that it previously couldn't. Or, to use our simplified two-dimensional example, in the mirror image of the whole phrase, what looks like the reff fits correctly, not the leff.

... XOꟻ WO ...   vs.   ... XOF WO ...

The reff fits the mirror image ... and the leff does not.

So according to the relationist fitting theory of handedness, in the reflected sentence the reff has become a leff! Let's think about this issue more carefully. Compare the original sentence with its mirror image:

... BROWN FOX ...   vs.   ... XOℲ WO

If, as our relationist proposes, handedness is just "fitting" the sentence, then we should say that the effs in both original and mirror image have the same handedness for they both fit in their respective sentences. Of course, the actual letters printed above also have to fit with the rest of the words on this page, but what if the plane were the entirety of space, and the sentence the only figure? Then we could consider two distinct "mirror-image universes": one in which we have a plane containing the sentence alone, and one in which the plane contains only the reflection of that sentence. The relationist's "fitting" account holds that the effs in the sentence and its mirror image are both leffs. Similarly, the hands that are left in our three-dimensional universe are also left in its mirror image.

Isn't this false? Reflecting something changes its handedness, independently of whether everything else is reflected. The reflection of a leff is always a reff, and the reflection of a left hand is always a right. If so, then the relationist account of handedness just sketched, which says that effs and hands have the same handedness in mirror-image universes, must be wrong.

But why should the relationist accept that everything has a reversed handedness in a universal mirror image? Not because our universe can somehow be "lined up" next to its reflection for comparison, for our universe is all that there is (similarly for the two planes considered above—in each case the single plane is taken to be "all that there is"). The argument against the relationist claims that all the distance relations could have been just as they are now, and yet hands or effs have a different handedness. But now it is unclear what to say: *Within* a world, the handedness of an object is the opposite of that of its mirror image, but this we can understand in relational terms, as a matter of fitting. However, I, at least, find myself at a loss when asked whether everything in the mirror image of the whole universe would have a reversed handedness. Unless one can answer this question positively, the case against relationism has not yet been made.

Kant brilliantly attempts to complete this case. It's unclear whether he is worrying specifically about the relationist account of handedness that I've proposed, but it's evident that he is concerned to focus the debate by considering a world in which a hand is the only object. To paraphrase in terms of our model and a two-dimensional space: "Let it be imagined that the first created thing were an eff, then it must necessarily be either a reff or a leff. In order to produce the one a different action of the creative cause is necessary from that by means of which its counterpart could be produced" (*Concerning*, this vol., p. 201).

When there is only one thing in the whole universe, there are no external distance relations and no cases of "fitting" with other objects by which to determine handedness. In this case, however, Kant claims there are two possibilities: a lone hand (or eff) is either left or right. If so, then it is most reasonable to say that a left hand would be a right hand in the mirror-image universe. But the fitting relations do not differ between the two universes (for there is nothing at all to fit with), so the relationist account must hold that the handedness of the hands cannot differ either. (Indeed, if handedness just is fitting, then in cases in which there is nothing to fit with, the relationist cannot ascribe handedness to an object at all.)

The pattern of argument is again parallel to what we saw in the *Correspondence*. Recall that Clarke challenged Leibniz on the grounds that if the material universe as a whole were to be *displaced*, then there would be a distinct situation, though no spatial relations would change; Kant claims that if the material universe as a whole were to be *reflected*, then there would be a distinct situation, though no spatial relations would change. In either case, the absolutist claims that there are distinct states of affairs that the relationist must describe as identical, indirectly refuting relationism. But both arguments are ultimately disastrous for the absolutist because—unlike Newton's bucket argument—they are not based on observable phenomena.

Clarke's argument backfired, for Leibniz reanalyzed his "static shift" argument as one that speaks for relationism and speaks against absolutism. Certainly, in *absolute* space a static shift leads to a distinct situation (for things would then be elsewhere in absolute space), but since the difference is entirely unobservable and Clarke provided no other grounds for supposing it a real difference, Leibniz could point to such absolute differences as undesirable consequences of absolutism that are contrary to the PII.

Does Kant's argument similarly backfire for the absolutist? This seems to be a genuine danger; again, certainly in absolute space a reflection generally leads to a distinct state of affairs. In Kant's example, a left hand just won't fit into the same (glove-shaped) region of absolute space that a right hand would. But is the difference between the two universes, one with just a left hand and one with just a right hand, in any way observable? To whom? Kant talks about the "creative cause," so perhaps he has God in mind, but how are we supposed to speculate about God's perception? And if the difference is entirely undetectable, then what other grounds are there for supposing it real? (Perhaps Kant's observation that on the relationist view the lone hand will "fit on either side of the human body" could help.) If no satisfactory grounds are forthcoming, this argument must be added to those misfires aimed back at the absolutist (though given its great similarity to the static shift, perhaps it should not even be considered a wholly new problem). If the two universes are indiscernible, then aren't they identical, contrary to Newtonian absolutism?

Ultimately then, although Kant has introduced some important aspects of the geometry of mirror images, he has not managed to show that there is some phenomenon that the relationist is unable to account for. Indeed, it seems that our notions of handedness can very plausibly be thought of as relational. However, we should not think that we have exhausted all the questions here, for Kant's proposal continues to puzzle and stimulate philosophers, and the questions and suggested readings below give some indication of the scope of this work.

At this point, however, we have finished our discussion of the absolute/relative controversy, and so must move on to a new topic: the question of how we can come to know the geometry of space. The first reading on this topic is also by Kant, but written (as I noted earlier) rather later, at a time in which he had rejected Newton's notion of absolute space—ironically, in part because of his further work on mirror images.

Problems

1. Can you think of other arguments based on the notion of incongruent counterparts that are more successful against the relationist? For instance, what if there are two hands in the world and nothing else; they are different, but is there a relational difference? Can the relationist explain the idea of a nonorientable space, such as the Möbius loop? Can the relationist specify when an object is the kind of thing that has an incongruent counterpart?

2. Kant makes a further suggestion in the essay, one that is not fully developed but which has received a lot of attention: He points out that many natural phenomena (beans growing around poles, hair growing in a spiral) have a certain handedness— clockwise and anticlockwise are incongruent counterparts, and nature seems to pick one. So maybe the laws themselves have a handedness. Could this be given a relationist explanation? Could the absolutist do any better?

3. How might the relationist's "fitting" account of handedness explain the example involving maps? How can maps be the same relationally, and yet so different?

Further Readings and Bibliography

Broad, C. D. C. 1978. *Kant: An Introduction*. Cambridge, UK: Cambridge University Press.
Van Cleve, J., and Frederick, R., eds. 1991. *The Philosophy of Left and Right*. Dordrecht: Kluwer. $\sqrt{}$

12 Kant and Geometry

READING

The Critique of Pure Reason

Introduction

I. The Distinction between Pure and Empirical Knowledge

There can be no doubt that all our knowledge begins with experience. For how should our faculty of knowledge be awakened into action did not objects affecting our senses partly of themselves produce representations, partly arouse the activity of our understanding to compare these representations, and, by combining or separating them, work up the raw material of the sensible impressions into that knowledge of objects which is entitled experience? In the order of time, therefore, we have no knowledge antecedent to experience, and with experience all our knowledge begins.

But though all our knowledge begins with experience, it does not follow that it all arises out of experience. For it may well be that even our empirical knowledge is made up of what we receive through impressions and of what our own faculty of knowledge (sensible impressions serving merely as the occasion) supplies from itself. If our faculty of knowledge makes any such addition, it may be that we are not in a position to distinguish it from the raw material, until with long practice of attention we have become skilled in separating it.

This, then, is a question which at least calls for closer examination, and does not allow of any off-hand answer:—whether there is any knowledge that is thus independent of experience and even of all impressions of the senses. Such knowledge is entitled *a priori*, and distinguished from the *empirical*, which has its sources *a posteriori*, that is, in experience. . . .

II. We Are in Possession of Certain Modes of *A Priori* Knowledge, and Even the Common Understanding Is Never Without Them

What we here require is a criterion by which to distinguish with certainty between pure and empirical knowledge. Experience teaches us that a thing is so and so, but not that it cannot be otherwise. First, then, if we have a proposition which in being thought is thought as *necessary*, it is an *a priori* judgment; and if, besides, it is not derived from any proposition except one which also has the validity of a necessary

Excerpts from Immanuel Kant: *Critique of Pure Reason* (pp. 41–74), translated by N. K. Smith. © 1969 by St. Martin's Press, Inc. Reprinted by permission of St. Martin's Press, Inc. and Macmillan Press Ltd.

judgment, it is an absolutely *a priori* judgment. Secondly, experience never confers on its judgments true or strict, but only assumed and comparative *universality*, through induction. We can properly only say, therefore, that, so far as we have hitherto observed, there is no exception to this or that rule. If, then, a judgment is thought with strict universality, that is, in such manner that no exception is allowed as possible, it is not derived from experience, but is valid absolutely *a priori*. Empirical universality is only an arbitrary extension of a validity holding in most cases to one which holds in all, for instance, in the proposition, "all bodies are heavy." When, on the other hand, strict universality is essential to a judgment, this indicates a special source of knowledge, namely, a faculty of *a priori* knowledge. Necessity and strict universality are thus sure criteria of *a priori* knowledge, and are inseparable from one another. . . .

Now it is easy to show that there actually are in human knowledge judgments which are necessary and in the strictest sense universal, and which are therefore pure *a priori* judgments. If an example from the sciences be desired, we have only to look to any of the propositions of mathematics; if we seek an example from the understanding in its quite ordinary employment, the proposition, "every alteration must have a cause," will serve our purpose. . . .

IV.   The Distinction between Analytic and Synthetic Judgments

In all judgments in which the relation of a subject to the predicate is thought (I take into consideration affirmative judgments only, the subsequent application to negative judgments being easily made), this relation is possible in two different ways. Either the predicate B belongs to the subject A, as something which is (covertly) contained in this concept A; or B lies outside the concept A, although it does indeed stand in connection with it. In the one case I entitle the judgment analytic, in the other synthetic. Analytic judgments (affirmative) are therefore those in which the connection of the predicate with the subject is thought through identity; those in which this connection is thought without identity should be entitled synthetic. The former, as adding nothing through the predicate to the concept of the subject, but merely breaking it up into those constituent concepts that have all along been thought in it, although confusedly, can also be entitled explicative. The latter, on the other hand, add to the concept of the subject a predicate which has not been in any wise thought in it, and which no analysis could possibly extract from it; and they may therefore be entitled ampliative. If I say, for instance, "All bodies are extended," this is an analytic judgment. For I do not require to go beyond the concept which I connect with "body" in order to find extension as bound up with it. To meet with this predicate, I have merely to analyse the concept, that is, to become conscious to myself of the manifold which I always think in that concept. The judgment is therefore analytic. But when I say, "All bodies are heavy," the predicate is something quite different from anything that I think in the mere concept of body in general; and the addition of such a predicate therefore yields a synthetic judgment.

Judgments of experience, as such, are one and all synthetic. For it would be absurd to found an analytic judgment on experience. Since, in framing the judgment, I must not go outside my concept, there is no need to appeal to the testimony of experience in its support. That a body is extended is a proposition that holds *a priori* and is not empirical.... On the other hand, though I do not include in the concept of a body in general the predicate "weight," none the less this concept indicates an object of experience through one of its parts, and I can add to that part other parts of this same experience, as in this way belonging together with the concept. From the start I can apprehend the concept of body analytically through the characters of extension, impenetrability, figure, etc., all of which are thought in the concept. Now, however, looking back on the experience from which I have derived this concept of body, and finding weight to be invariably connected with the above characters, I attach it as a predicate to the concept; and in doing so I attach it synthetically, and am therefore extending my knowledge. The possibility of the synthesis of the predicate "weight" with the concept of "body" thus rests upon experience. While the one concept is not contained in the other, they yet belong to one another, though only contingently, as parts of a whole, namely, of an experience which is itself a synthetic combination of intuitions.

But in *a priori* synthetic judgments this help is entirely lacking. [I do not here have the advantage of looking around in the field of experience.] Upon what, then, am I to rely, when I seek to go beyond the concept A, and to know that another concept B is connected with it? Through what is the synthesis made possible?... Upon such synthetic, that is, ampliative principles, all our *a priori* speculative knowledge must ultimately rest; analytic judgments are very important, and indeed necessary, but only for obtaining that clearness in the concepts which is requisite for such a sure and wide synthesis as will lead to a genuinely new addition to all previous knowledge.

Transcendental Doctrine of Elements

Transcendental Aesthetic

In whatever manner and by whatever means a mode of knowledge may relate to objects, *intuition* is that through which it is in immediate relation to them, and to which all thought as a means is directed. But intuition takes place only in so far as the object is given to us. This again is only possible, to man at least, in so far as the mind is affected in a certain way. The capacity (receptivity) for receiving representations through the mode in which we are affected by objects, is entitled *sensibility*. Objects are *given* to us by means of sensibility, and it alone yields us *intuitions*; they are *thought* through the understanding, and from the understanding arise *concepts*. But all thought must, directly or indirectly, by way of certain characters, relate ultimately to intuitions, and therefore, with us, to sensibility, because in no other way can an object be given to us.

The effect of an object upon the faculty of representation, so far as we are affected by it, is *sensation*. That intuition which is in relation to the object through sensation, is entitled *empirical*. The undetermined object of an empirical intuition is entitled *appearance*.

That in the appearance which corresponds to sensation I term its *matter*; but that which so determines the manifold of appearance that it allows of being ordered in certain relations, I term the *form* of appearance. That in which alone the sensations can be posited and ordered in a certain form, cannot itself be sensation; and therefore, while the matter of all appearance is given to us *a posteriori* only, its form must lie ready for the sensations *a priori* in the mind, and so must allow of being considered apart from all sensation.

I term all representations *pure* (in the transcendental sense) in which there is nothing that belongs to sensation. The pure form of sensible intuitions in general, in which all the manifold of intuition is intuited in certain relations, must be found in the mind *a priori*. This pure form of sensibility may also itself be called *pure intuition*. Thus, if I take away from the representation of a body that which the understanding thinks in regard to it, substance, force, divisibility, etc., and likewise what belongs to sensation, impenetrability, hardness, colour, etc., something still remains over from this empirical intuition, namely, extension and figure. These belong to pure intuition, which, even without any actual object of the senses or of sensation, exists in the mind *a priori* as a mere form of sensibility.

The science of all principles of *a priori* sensibility I call *transcendental aesthetic*. . . .

Space

Metaphysical Exposition of this Concept   By means of outer sense, a property of our mind, we represent to ourselves objects as outside us, and all without exception in space. In space their shape, magnitude, and relation to one another are determined or determinable. Inner sense, by means of which the mind intuits itself or its inner state, yields indeed no intuition of the soul itself as an object; but there is nevertheless a determinate form [namely, time] in which alone the intuition of inner states is possible, and everything which belongs to inner determinations is therefore represented in relations of time. Time cannot be outwardly intuited, any more than space can be intuited as something in us. What, then, are space and time? Are they real existences? Are they only determinations or relations of things, yet such as would belong to things even if they were not intuited? Or are space and time such that they belong only to the form of intuition, and therefore to the subjective constitution of our mind, apart from which they could not be ascribed to anything whatsoever? In order to obtain light upon these questions, let us first give an exposition of the concept of space. By *exposition* (*expositio*) I mean the clear, though not necessarily exhaustive, representation of that which belongs to a concept: the exposition is *metaphysical* when it contains that which exhibits the concept *as given a priori*.

1. Space is not an empirical concept which has been derived from outer experiences. For in order that certain sensations be referred to something outside me (that is, to something in another region of space from that in which I find myself), and similarly in order that I may be able to represent them as outside and alongside one another, and accordingly as not only different but as in different places, the representation of space must be presupposed. The representation of space cannot, therefore, be empirically obtained from the relations of outer appearance. On the contrary, this outer experience is itself possible at all only through that representation.

2. Space is a necessary *a priori* representation, which underlies all outer intuitions. We can never represent to ourselves the absence of space, though we can quite well think it as empty of objects. It must therefore be regarded as the condition of the possibility of appearances, and not as a determination dependent upon them. It is an *a priori* representation, which necessarily underlies outer appearances.

3.* The apodeictic certainty of all geometrical propositions, and the possibility of their *a priori* construction, is grounded in this *a priori* necessity of space. Were this representation of space a concept acquired *a posteriori*, and derived from outer experience in general, the first principles of mathematical determination would be nothing but perceptions. They would therefore all share in the contingent character of perception; that there should be only one straight line between two points would not be necessary, but only what experience always teaches. What is derived from experience has only comparative universality, namely, that which is obtained through induction. We should therefore only be able to say that, so far as hitherto observed, no space has been found which has more than three dimensions.

---

*The following section 3 appears only in the first (1781) edition of the *Critique*; the rest of the selection, including the second section 3, follows the revised second (1787) edition.

3. Space is not a discursive or, as we say, general concept of relations of things in general, but a pure intuition. For, in the first place, we can represent to ourselves only one space; and if we speak of diverse spaces, we mean thereby only parts of one and the same unique space. Secondly, these parts cannot precede the one all-embracing space, as being, as it were, constituents out of which it can be composed; on the contrary, they can be thought only as *in* it. Space is essentially one; the manifold in it, and therefore the general concept of spaces, depends solely on [the introduction of] limitations. Hence it follows that an *a priori*, and not an empirical, intuition underlies all concepts of space. For kindred reasons, geometrical propositions, that, for instance, in a triangle two sides together are greater than the third, can never be derived from the general concepts of line and triangle, but only from intuition, and this indeed *a priori*, with apodeictic certainty.

4. Space is represented as an infinite *given* magnitude. Now every concept must be thought as a representation which is contained in an infinite number of different possible representations (as their common character), and which therefore contains these *under* itself; but no concept, as such, can be thought as containing an infinite number of representations *within* itself. It is in this latter way, however, that space is thought; for all the parts of space coexist *ad infinitum*. Consequently, the original representation of space is an *a priori* intuition, not a concept.

The Transcendental Exposition of the Concept of Space   ... Geometry is a science which determines the properties of space synthetically, and yet *a priori*. What, then, must be our representation of space, in order that such knowledge of it may be possible? It must in its origin be intuition; for from a mere concept no propositions can be obtained which go beyond the concept—as happens in geometry.... Further, this intuition must be *a priori*, that is, it must be found in us prior to any perception of an object, and must therefore be pure, not empirical, intuition. For geometrical propositions are one and all apodeictic, that is, are bound up with the consciousness of their necessity; for instance, that space has only three dimensions. Such propositions cannot be empirical or, in other words, judgments of experience, nor can they be derived from any such judgments (Introduction, II).

  How, then, can there exist in the mind an outer intuition which precedes the objects themselves, and in which the concept of these objects can be determined *a priori*? Manifestly, not otherwise than in so far as the intuition has its seat in the subject only, as the formal character of the subject, in virtue of which, in being affected by objects, it obtains *immediate representation*, that is, *intuition*, of them; and only in so far, therefore, as it is merely the form of outer *sense* in general.

Our explanation is thus the only explanation that makes intelligible the *possibility* of geometry, as a body of *a priori* synthetic knowledge. Any mode of explanation which fails to do this, although it may otherwise seem to be somewhat similar, can by this criterion be distinguished from it with the greatest certainty.

Conclusions from the Above Concepts

(*a*) Space does not represent any property of things in themselves, nor does it represent them in their relation to one another. That is to say, space does not represent any determination that attaches to the objects themselves, and which remains even when abstraction has been made of all the subjective conditions of intuition. For no determinations, whether absolute or relative, can be intuited prior to the existence of the things to which they belong, and none, therefore, can be intuited *a priori*.

(*b*) Space is nothing but the form of all appearances of outer sense. It is the subjective condition of sensibility, under which alone outer intuition is possible for us. Since, then, the receptivity of the subject, its capacity to be affected by objects, must necessarily precede all intuitions of these objects, it can readily be understood how the form of all appearances can be given prior to all actual perceptions, and so exist in the mind *a priori*, and how, as a pure intuition, in which all objects must be determined, it can contain, prior to all experience, principles which determine the relations of these objects.

It is, therefore, solely from the human standpoint that we can speak of space, of extended things, etc. If we depart from the subjective condition under which alone we can have outer intuition, namely, liability to be affected by objects, the representation of space stands for nothing whatsoever. This predicate can be ascribed to things only in so far as they appear to us, that is, only to objects of sensibility. The constant form of this receptivity, which we term sensibility, is a necessary condition of all the relations in which objects can be intuited as outside us; and if we abstract from these objects, it is a pure intuition, and bears the name of space. Since we cannot treat the special conditions of sensibility as conditions of the possibility of things, but only of their appearances, we can indeed say that space comprehends all things that appear to us as external, but not all things in themselves, by whatever subject they are intuited, or whether they be intuited or not. For we cannot judge in regard to the intuitions of other thinking beings, whether they are bound by the same conditions as those which limit our intuition and which for us are universally valid. If we add to the concept of the subject of a judgment the limitation under which the judgment is made, the judgment is then unconditionally valid. The proposition, that all things are side by side in space, is valid under the limitation that these things are viewed as objects of our sensible intuition. If, now, I add the condition to the concept, and say that all things, as outer appearances, are side by side in space, the rule is valid universally and without limitation. Our exposition therefore establishes the *reality*, that is, the objective validity, of space in respect of whatever can be presented to us outwardly as object, but also at the same time the *ideality* of space in respect of things when they are considered in themselves through reason, that is, without regard to the constitution of our sensibility. We assert, then, the *empirical reality* of space, as regards all possible outer experience; and yet at the same time we assert its *transcendental ideality*—in other words, that it is nothing at all, immediately we withdraw the above condition, namely, its limitation to possible experience, and so look upon it as something that underlies things in themselves....

The transcendental concept of appearances in space, on the other hand, is a critical reminder that nothing intuited in space is a thing in itself, that space is not a form inhering in things in themselves as their intrinsic property, that objects in themselves are quite unknown to us, and that what we call outer objects are nothing but mere representations of our sensibility, the form of which is space. The true correlate of sensibility, the thing in itself, is not known, and cannot be known, through these representations; and in experience no question is ever asked in regard to it....

COMMENTARY

12.1 Introduction

Kant, who lived from 1724–1804, proposed many of the most profound and influential ideas in Western philosophy since Aristotle. Unfortunately, his writing can be quite hard to penetrate at first, in part because he presents his arguments methodically, starting with precise definitions then arguing for "theorems of philosophy," so that the work is rather technical. However, as we shall see, it is well worth the effort, and it illustrates the point that in philosophy, as in other disciplines, precise definitions can be important for organizing complex topics. To help us get inside Kant's ideas, we first need a sketch of his general stance on space.

So far, we have seen some ways in which both empiricist and rationalist philosophers contributed to the development of our understanding of space. Sometimes, rationalism—the idea that true knowledge comes from pure reason—has driven the development, and sometimes empiricism—claiming that knowledge is based on direct experience—has dominated, but neither has seemed sufficient. For instance, Descartes's rationalism allowed him to formulate the principle of inertia; but it also led him to a factually incorrect theory of motion. And strict empiricism, though instrumental in the development of relativity, seems to deny the reality of absolute acceleration, contrary to what's shown by the bucket experiment. Kant saw the strengths and weakness of both programs, and he attempted to formulate a third alternative. He saw that rationalism could not succeed because much knowledge can only come from experience; and he believed that empiricism led to an understanding of knowledge that was too narrow—in particular, he believed that our empirical knowledge requires absolutely certain first principles, among them a conception of space.

Kant thus claims that every experience of the physical world can be split into two components: sensations of things, and the framework in which these sensations are organized. In particular, we find that sensations are always organized spatially: things appear to us as located in various places in space, next to each other, or above one another, and so on. That is, space is the framework within which all our experiences of the physical world occur. From this observation, Kant draws two conclusions: First, the framework is required for us to have experiences, and so it cannot come from experience but is provided, in advance, by us. Second, since the framework is provided prior to our experiences, our experiences will always be spatial and we can be certain in our knowledge of space. Thus we can know that every experience we will have will involve objects in Euclidean space. Perhaps an analogy can help illustrate these points: pigeonholes provide a framework within which various letters and documents can be arranged. The letters themselves will often differ from day to day, but something remains the same, namely, the pigeonholes.

So much for a sketch of the territory to be covered. Now we shall look at Kant's thought in more detail, before we consider that in fact the geometry of space might not be Euclidean at all.

12.2   Two Distinctions

To clarify his philosophy of space, Kant emphasized two distinctions. First, he distinguishes two kinds of knowledge: the *a posteriori* and the *a priori*. The first kind of knowledge is empirical and hence obtained from experience: that it is raining today, that low interest rates can cause the economy to overheat, that penicillin is an antibiotic, and so on. Such knowledge can be gathered firsthand, through everyday personal experience or scientific inquiry, or secondhand from books or word-of-mouth, for instance. It includes both specific knowledge—about today's weather perhaps—and general laws—about economics, for example. What all *a posteriori*, or "empirical," knowledge has in common is that if one asks for its ultimate justification, the answer will be an account of experiences that somebody has had. For instance, the grounds for our belief in the laws of economics might be the data collected by researchers from various retailers about their prices, compared against interest rates. When Kant acknowledges the existence of such knowledge he thereby implicitly rejects the Cartesian program of rationalism, according to which all knowledge can be derived by reason from "self-evident" first principles.

All other knowledge is *a priori*, and does not rely on experience at all for its justification. Some examples seem uncontroversial (though some philosophers question whether any knowledge is independent of experience): for instance, that newspapers contain news (for that is what it means for something to be a newspaper). Or again, that $2 + 2 = 4$. Kant argues that we know mathematical propositions to be *a priori*, because they are necessarily and universally true; and it does seem right that such propositions don't depend for their justification on the fact that we tend to get four items whenever we add two and two of them. However, the history of ideas is littered with discarded beliefs that at one time were taken to be *a priori*, such as Descartes's mechanics, and also in particular many ideas concerning morality. Kant will argue that our knowledge of space—that is, that it is correctly described by Euclidean geometry—is *a priori*; in the next section, we will see why such a view is untenable.

The second distinction that Kant draws is between *analytic* and *synthetic* statements (or *judgments*). Analytic statements are those such as "newspapers contain news" that are true in virtue of definitions alone. Kant takes it that statements are in subject-predicate form, so that some property (named by the predicate) is ascribed to something (the subject). Then a statement is analytic just in case the predicate is part of the definition of the subject; "the predicate B belongs to the subject A, as something which is (covertly) contained in this concept A" (*Critique*, this vol., p. 214). For instance, a newspaper is defined to be "A publication ... containing current news, editorials, feature articles, and usually advertising" (*The American Heritage Dictionary*), a definition which includes "containing news," revealing that it is analytic that papers contain news. An analytic statement, then, does not tell you anything new or informative about its subject: it only makes explicit a part of the definition, which you know beforehand if you know what the word means. Kant thus calls analytic statements "explicative," since they involve making a definition clear, or explicating the meaning of a word.

Analyticity also explains why "newspapers contain news" is *a priori*: "in framing the judgment, I must not go outside my concept, there is no need to appeal to the testimony of experience in its support" (*Critique*, this vol., p. 215). If someone asks for the justification for believing that newspapers contain news, the appropriate response is not to point to newspapers that we have read and explain that time and again they present articles on the current state of affairs, but to explain what the word "newspaper" means. If you like, experience cannot be the justification of analytic beliefs, because no experience could undermine such beliefs: no *newspaper* could fail to contain news, on pain of simply not being a newspaper.

On Kant's view, all other statements are synthetic, and involve ascribing some new, nondefinitional property to their subject: the "[predicate] B lies outside the concept A, although it does indeed stand in connection to it" (*Critique*, this vol., p. 214). Thus it is not part of the definition of the *Chicago Tribune* that it costs 50¢, and so when I tell you "the *Tribune* costs 50¢," my statement is synthetic. You can know the meaning of "the *Chicago Tribune*" without knowing the paper's price, and indeed nothing in the phrase's definition precludes the paper costing any amount in principle. Since such statements go beyond an initial definition, "amplifying" it, Kant calls them *ampliative*.

Since according to Kant all analytic statements are *a priori*, it follows on his view that all *a posteriori* (empirical) statements are synthetic. Whatever I learn from experience about the weather, economics, medicine, newspapers, and so on, is not definitional, but involves discovering new properties of things. Thus there is *a priori* analytic knowledge and *a posteriori* synthetic knowledge, but no statements are both *a posteriori* and analytic. The scheme contains one further possibility: *a priori* synthetic knowledge. Such knowledge would be both necessary and universal—since *a priori*—and genuinely new—since synthetic. If we could obtain it then we would learn new facts that could be known with certainty, for they would not require the messy and often misleading business of empirical enquiry. For Kant, empirical knowledge can be left to the scientists, but the discovery of *a priori* synthetic truths requires not experiment, but reason alone. We now turn to Kant's attempt to find and explain this kind of knowledge, in his claim that our knowledge of space is of just this kind.

12.3   Space

Consider Euclidean geometry, the foundations of which are the definitions and axioms (and "common notions") laid out by Euclid at the start of the *Elements*. From these (or rather, from Hilbert's completion of the system) all the geometrical theorems follow as a matter of logical necessity; but what is the status of the axioms themselves, according to Kant's scheme? It seems that they are necessarily true: to use Kant's example, how could it be false that any two points lie on only one straight line, thereby uniquely determining it? And which of the other axioms could be untrue of space? As Kant says, "geometric propositions are one and all apodeictic" (*Critique*, this vol., p. 218), meaning that they are evidently necessary. It follows then, for Kant, that they are *a priori* truths. On the other hand, the axioms apparently add new information: that two points define a circle, for example, adds to the definitions of point and circle. The axioms are thus also synthetic in Kant's scheme. So, Kant claims, Euclidean geometry is a system of synthetic *a priori* truths, and hence of just the kind that interests him. When he acknowledges the existence of such knowledge, Kant thereby implicitly rejects empiricism, according to which all (ampliative) knowledge is obtained from experience. He also rejects our conception of Euclidean geometry as a normal "science" of space, for he thinks he can justify the Euclidean hypothesis nonexperimentally. We shall soon see reasons, however, for thinking we were right to view geometry as a science after all.

   Given the singular character of synthetic *a priori* knowledge—which genuinely adds to our picture of reality but which does not require justification by experience—we naturally want to know what its basis could be. Understanding Kant's answer takes us to the core of his philosophy.

   When we have, say, a visual experience of the world—when we have what Kant calls an "empirical" (or "sensible") "intuition"—an image of the world—an "appearance"—appears to us. Kant analyzes such an appearance into two parts: First, it contains a host of sensations caused by the objects and parts of objects we're looking at; second, there is the manner in which this multitude of appearances is organized into a single, coherent visual field. Look around the room and you will be able to distinguish the many patches of color, brightness and texture from the way they have been put together to form an image. The image could be shattered and the fragments put back together in an incoherent jumble: the patches would still be there, but organized in a new way. Kant calls this—whatever it is that orders the many components of an experience into a whole—the *form* of the experience. If we reflect on our experiences, it seems that this form is space, for whatever we see, it is organized spatially: we perceive things to be next to, or behind, or above one another.

Kant believes that the form itself is not something that we learn from experience, but something that is required in advance in order to have an experience at all, rather than an incoherent jumble of sensations. That is, the "form must lie ready for the sensations *a priori* in the mind" (*Critique*, this vol., p. 216). Then, when objects act on us to produce sensations, the mind is activated to arrange them within the form of experience: in space. Thus the general spatial properties of experience are not themselves learned from experience, but rather both precede all experiences and are necessarily present in all experiences. They are, in other words, known *a priori*: they are "pure intuition." But what are the general properties of space? According to Kant, these are described by Euclid's geometry! Kant believes that, because the form of all experience is Euclidean, all experiences—and indeed any conceptualization of the world—must be of objects or events in Euclidean space. This analysis explains for him the puzzling *a priori* character of geometry. (And since the properties of the form are not a matter of mere definition but rather present genuine information about the world, Euclidean geometry is of course synthetic.)

An immediate consequence of this view that experience involves an essential "subjective" component is that we can never take an entirely "objective" view of the world (though if all human minds are the same, experience does not depend subjectively on each individual, but on the species). Every experience involves the form of appearance as well as the sensations produced by objects, and so we never have direct access to "things in themselves," but only ever to things as they are organized by the mind. The price of the certainty of geometry is that it is only applicable to experience, not to the mind-independent world. On the other hand, the world of experience is what really matters, so this is not such a high price: it matters that we experience certain plants to provide nourishment, that we experience certain chemicals to have medicinal properties, and that we experience clocks to keep track of time. A particularly important aspect of this point is that space is, in a sense, not *real* at all. That is, it is something added into experience by the mind, not something that exists "in itself": "we assert [space's] transcendental ideality ... it is nothing at all, immediately we withdraw ... its limitation to possible experience, and so look upon it as something that underlies things in themselves" (*Critique*, this vol., p. 220).

Unfortunately for Kant's view that space necessarily has a Euclidean geometry, there are other logically consistent possibilities. Early in the nineteenth century, in the years immediately after Kant's death, logically consistent, non-Euclidean geometries were discovered and appreciated. In the next section we will consider an example of such a geometry, before finally discussing the implications for Kant's position. It should be noted, however, that although Kant's ideas regarding space were undermined by later developments, the distinctions that he made, the problems that he posed, and the spirit of his philosophical proposals have deeply influenced most of subsequent philosophy.

12.4   Non-Euclidean Geometry

We will consider two non-Euclidean axiomatic geometries: *elliptical* and *Bolyai-Lobachevskian* (or *BL* for short), the latter named after the early nineteenth-century mathematicians Bolyai and Lobachevski. (The actual axioms that we will use stand in approximately the same relation to rigorous elliptic and BL geometry as Euclid's do to Hilbert's formulation.) Both of these new geometries adopt (with some changes) the first four of Euclid's axioms but revise the fifth axiom, the "parallel postulate": in elliptical geometry no pair of lines is parallel, and in BL geometry many lines through a single point will be parallel to a given line. A few comments are worth bearing in mind here: First, as a matter of pure geometry, there is no question of one of these geometries being the "correct" one, since they simply aim to describe different possible "Platonic paradises" (see sec. 1.3). Second, Euclid's fifth postulate is equivalent to the claim that there is a unique parallel to a line through any point not on the line, and it might seem simply inconceivable that any other situation is possible. If you try to picture a second parallel, it seems that it must cross the original line somewhere. It is of course this inconceivability that lends plausibility to Kant's claim that the axiom is a necessary truth. So, the job of this section is to overcome our intuitions, illustrating the possibility of non-Euclidean geometry by showing that a model of elliptic geometry exists (we will look at BL geometry in the next chapter). (Note: non-Euclidean lines are composed of points and segments in just the same way as in Euclidean geometry, so all of Zeno's objections apply equally well in either case. Indeed, we should really think of Zeno as attacking the idea that space is geometrical at all.)

The axioms of elliptic geometry are (we take "line" to mean "straight line") again,

1. Any two points lie on a line.

2. Any segment can be continued indefinitely.

3. Any two points (the center and a point on the circumference) define a circle.

4. All right angles are equal.

5. Whatever interior angles are made by a line falling on two lines, the two lines will intersect if continued indefinitely. (Equivalently, every pair of lines will intersect: *there are no parallel lines in elliptic geometry.*)

As I noted above, with some small but significant qualifications the first four axioms agree with Euclid's, so the crucial difference lies in the two systems' parallel postulates. The fifth postulate here has been given in a similar form to that in the *Elements*, and in an equivalent way that brings out its meaning most clearly.

To demonstrate that this system of axioms is consistent, we will show that it correctly describes geometry on a sphere (the two-dimensional *surface* of a ball). We will thus prove consistency, because consistency just means that there is a model in which all the axioms are true. (The proof also requires that the sphere be a possible geometric object, which follows if Euclidean geometry is consistent.) Note that the

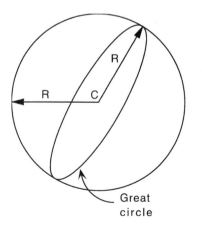

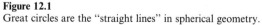

Figure 12.1
Great circles are the "straight lines" in spherical geometry.

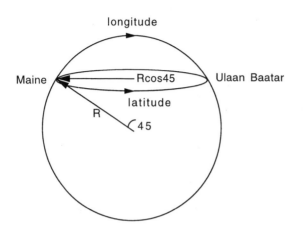

Figure 12.2
The great circle route over the pole is shorter than the route due east.

sphere, though we may imagine it "embedded" in three-dimensional Euclidean space, is two-dimensional, like the plane. A creature in the plane can move only in two orthogonal directions, and the same is true if it is restricted to the sphere; roughly speaking, we are restricted in a similar way to the two-dimensional surface of the Earth and normally move only on the surface, not above or below it. In considering two dimensions we make the usual simplification: non-Euclidean geometries can be extended to three (or more) dimensions, but as the essential properties remain the same we stick to the simpler case.

We shall look at each of the axioms in turn and verify intuitively that they hold on the sphere.

1. In our discussion of Euclidean geometry, to clarify our intuitive notion of a straight line we defined it to be the shortest curve between two points. Our first job, then, in understanding elliptic geometry, is to find out which curves are shortest on the sphere; they turn out to be segments of "great circles." On a sphere of radius R and center C, any circle of radius R and center C is a great circle. Great circles, with circumference $2\pi R$, are in fact the longest circles that can be drawn on the sphere, but they fit our definition, and so they are (straight) lines in spherical geometry. The fact that such lines close in on themselves is only one of the important changes from Euclidean geometry.

It is perhaps surprising that great circles provide the shortest paths between points. Lines of latitude—which run east to west around the globe—are not great circles (except the equator), but to travel to a point that lies due east it seems natural to walk due east, along a line of latitude. However, since this path does not lie on a great circle, it is not the shortest route (though if the points are close, compared to the size of the Earth, it will not be noticeably longer). Perhaps the following example will help. Imagine traveling from a point halfway between the equator and the North Pole to another point similarly located, but directly on the other side of the Earth: roughly speaking, a trip from central Maine to somewhere a couple of hundred miles south of Ulaan Baatar in Mongolia would be an example. Compare two paths between the points: the great circle route over the North Pole, along a line of longitude, and the route directly east, around the line of latitude.

Since both points are halfway between the equator and pole, the length of the polar route is one quarter of the whole way around the great circle, that is, $1/4 \cdot 2\pi R$. The latitudinal route follows a circle, which by basic trigonometry has radius $R\cos45°$, and since the trip follows half this circle, from one side of the sphere to the other, the total length is $1/2 \cdot 2\pi R\cos45°$. Putting in the values (the radius of the Earth is approximately 6300km) we find that the great circle route is 10,000km and the route due east 14,100km long. This is part of the reason long air flights fly high toward the north to reach a point to the east or west; they are going the shortest way.

We can see that axiom (1) is correct in spherical geometry, for between any pair of points it is always possible to draw a great circle—that is, a straight line. Just take any great circle and slide it around the surface until it passes through both points. Note, however, that an infinite number of great circles lie between any two "antipodal" points. For instance, every line of longitude passes through both the North and South Pole. This is, of course, quite unlike the situation in Euclidean geometry, where any two points lie on exactly one line.

2. To extend a line segment in spherical geometry, you continue it further along the great circle. For instance, one can extend the segment between Paris and Lagos on down to the South Pole, along a line of longitude. Of course, since lines are great circles, if a segment is continued far enough it will close back in on itself. But this just means that the start of the segment has been reached—not the end of the line—so it is quite possible to continue the line, running around the complete length indefinitely many times. Indeed, circles don't have ends of any sort, which are the only things that would prevent indefinite continuation. So the second axiom holds of spheres.

3. It should also be clear that any two points define a circle, in the same way that they do in a plane. One point is the center, and the second point lies on the circum-

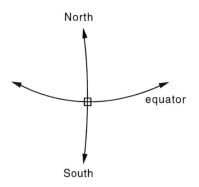

North

equator

South

Figure 12.3
The equator and any line of longitude are at right angles.

ference, determining the radius; the circle is the set of all points the same distance from the center along a straight line on the sphere. Thus the third axiom is true in spherical geometry.

4. An example of two lines on the sphere that are at right angles is the intersection of the equator and a line of longitude. (By inspection, the angles between the lines are 90°, but the lines are also at right angles according to Euclid's more fundamental definition.)

We can see intuitively in figure 12.3 that any other pair of lines that cross at right angles on the sphere will be identical, by imagining sliding these "crosshairs" around until they rest on top of the second pair. The two pairs will line up perfectly, and so right angles are always congruent, and the fourth axiom holds true.

5. Finally then, we come to the new parallel postulate. It is easy to see that all pairs of lines on the sphere intersect. Just pick any two great circles, G, and H. Now pick any point P on H; since it is a great circle H, will also pass through the antipodal point P' (the point directly on the other side of the sphere from P). And since P and P' are antipodal, they must lie in the two different hemispheres defined by G: hence H must cross G in passing between P and P'. Indeed, if you think about it, every pair of great circles intersects exactly twice, and so, since great circles are (straight) lines in spherical geometry, there are no parallels according to Euclid's definition of "parallel." Thus the new fifth postulate, holds for the geometry of the sphere, instead of Euclid's.

Of course, there are many curves through P that don't intersect the line, but these are not straight lines. For instance, no line of latitude will intersect the equator but, as we've seen, lines of latitude other than the equator are not straight.

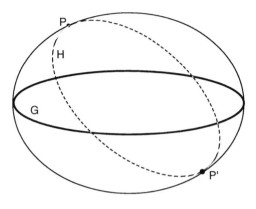

Figure 12.4
Any two great circles intersect.

Thus all the axioms of elliptic geometry hold of spheres, and moreover we now see how it is possible for there to be no parallel lines. The block to our understanding was that we were imagining all geometry to be carried out on a plane, and hence we implicitly assumed Euclid's postulates, when in fact it is perfectly proper to discuss the geometries of other surfaces. The point is an extension of our earlier discussion of metric properties (sec. 3.3): We saw that a set of points have no intrinsic length, so that the notion of distance had to be added onto the set. At the time we were just thinking that points in the plane might turn out to be any distance apart. But metrical properties also determine the geometry of a set of points, so the consistency of elliptic geometry shows that any set of points comes with no intrinsic geometry. In other words, when the notion of distance is added to the set, so is the particular geometry.

One point often causes confusion: we have been imagining the sphere as embedded in three-dimensional Euclidean space, in which case the shortest line between two points is, it seems, not a great circle, but the line through the inside of the sphere. But if this line is allowed, then we are no longer talking about two dimensions, but three, and are considering a different geometry. The point is that it is convenient to imagine the sphere embedded in three-dimensional space, but logically, the sphere can exist without being embedded in anything. So when we do spherical geometry, strictly speaking there is no "inside" to the sphere, just the surface itself. Indeed, there is no reason not to seriously entertain the possibility that the space we inhabit has a (three-dimensional) non-Euclidean geometry. But we don't need to imagine physical space embedded in an even larger-dimensioned Euclidean space to make

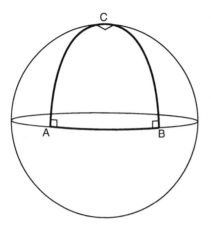

Figure 12.5
A triangle with a pole and two equatorial points one quarter of a circumference apart as corners: all three
angles are right angles.

sense of this idea: Physical space has the usual three dimensions of up-down, left-
right, and backward-forward, just put together to satisfy non-Euclidean axioms.
Thus, in spherical geometry, great circles literally are the shortest paths between two
points.

To get a better feel for elliptic geometry, it is helpful to see some of the logical
consequences of the new axioms and compare them with Euclid's theorems. In particular, we will reconsider the internal angles theorem and show that it does not hold
on a sphere, because it depends on Euclid's parallel postulate.

Consider a triangle, ABC, whose base, AB, is one quarter of the equator, and
whose third vertex, C, is a pole of the sphere; its other two sides, AC and BC, are
quarter segments of lines of longitude. Such a figure of course fits the definition of
a triangle, for it is a closed figure with three straight sides in spherical geometry. All
three internal angles of this triangle, shown in figure 12.5, are 90°, so the sum of the
internal angles is 270°. ∠CAB and ∠CBA are 90° because both are formed by lines
of longitude (due north to south) crossing the equator (which runs due east to
west). ∠ACB is 90° because AB is a quarter of the equator, and so the angle it
makes at the pole is one quarter of 360°. In elliptical space, whether two- or three-
dimensional, the internal angles of a triangle always add up to more than two right
angles. In the present example the variation is strikingly large; in much smaller triangles, however, the sum of the angles becomes increasingly close to 180°.

In general, figures have different properties depending on the geometry (see the questions for further examples), and so we can understand the differences between geometries by studying such properties. These differences make it possible to carry out empirical tests of the geometry of space. When we discussed Euclid, we considered Gauss's experimental test of the internal angles theorem. At the time it seemed unmotivated, but now we see its purpose: if the internal angles had equalled more than 180° he would have concluded that space had an elliptic, not Euclidean, geometry.

Kant thought that Euclidean geometry was synthetic *a priori* knowledge: that it was both genuinely informative and necessarily true. We've seen that the existence of consistent non-Euclidean geometries demonstrates that the truth of Euclidean geometry is not a logical necessity. The only logical necessity involved in pure geometry lies in the deduction of theorems from axioms. This is an *a priori* matter, for it requires logical reasoning, not experience, to test for validity.

But this is not the sense of *a priori* that Kant intended, for he believed that we could know *a priori* that Euclidean geometry correctly described space: the "form of experience." One possible way of understanding such a position in the light of non-Euclidean geometry is as the claim that all our experiences and concepts of space must always be Euclidean. Perhaps this is plausible, for it is rather hard to imagine what it would be like to inhabit a three-dimensional non-Euclidean space. However, even this claim does not appear to be correct, for there are experimental tests of geometry—such as Gauss's—which seem to rely on the possibility of experiencing non-Euclidean geometry. In the next chapter we will consider in more detail what kind of experiences one might have in a non-Euclidean space, and hence what kind of experiments could be undertaken to determine the geometry of space. Given that there are such experiments, it seems that Kant was indeed wrong to think that the geometry of space is anything other than an *a posteriori* matter, to be settled empirically.

Problems

1. What are examples of *a priori* knowledge? *A posteriori*? What are examples of analytic statements? Synthetic? Are these categories unequivocal?

2. Assuming spherical geometry, compute the ratio of the circumference to the radius of a circle, drawn halfway between equator and pole. How does it compare to the Euclidean ratio of 2π? (The radius should be measured along the straight lines of spherical geometry, the great circles.)

3. Show that the largest triangle in spherical geometry has internal angles that sum to 540°. (Remember, a triangle is any figure bounded by three straight line segments.)

4. Aristotle (*On the Heavens*, Bk. I, chap. 8–9), Descartes (*Principles*, sec. 22), and now Kant (*Critique*, Transcendental Aesthetic, sec. 2.3) have all defended the doctrine that there is only one world or space. How do their arguments compare, and what does this comparison reveal about the differences between their philosophies? (Consider especially the differences between empiricist and rationalist approaches.)

Further Readings and Bibliography

Glymour, C. 1992. *Thinking Things Through: An Introduction to Philosophical Issues and Achievements* (see esp. chap. 3). Cambridge, MA: MIT Press. √

Greenberg, M. J. 1980. *Euclidean and Non-Euclidean Geometries: Development and History*, second edition (see esp. chaps. 5–8). San Francisco, CA: W. H. Freeman and Co.

Salmon, W. C. 1980. *Space, Time, and Motion: A Philosophical Introduction*, second edition (see chap. 1). Minneapolis, MN: University of Minnesota Press. √

Sklar, L. 1976. *Space, Time, and Spacetime* (see chap. II, A–B, D–E). Berkeley, CA: University of California Press. √

Torretti, R. 1978. *Philosophy of Geometry from Riemann to Poincaré*. Dordrecht: D. Reidel Publishing Co.

13 Poincaré

READING

Space and Geometry

Let us begin with a little paradox. Beings whose minds were made as ours, and with senses like ours, but without any preliminary education, might receive from a suitably-chosen external world impressions which would lead them to construct a geometry other than that of Euclid, and to localise the phenomena of this external world in a non-Euclidean space, or even in space of four dimensions. As for us, whose education has been made by our actual world, if we were suddenly transported into this new world, we should have no difficulty in referring phenomena to our Euclidean space. Perhaps somebody may appear on the scene some day who will devote his life to it, and be able to represent to himself the fourth dimension....

Solid Bodies and Geometry. Among surrounding objects there are some which frequently experience displacements that may be thus corrected by a *correlative* movement of our own body—namely, *solid bodies*. The other objects, whose form is variable, only in exceptional circumstances undergo similar displacement (change of position without change of form). When the displacement of a body takes place with deformation, we can no longer by appropriate movements place the organs of our body in the same *relative* situation with respect to this body; we can no longer, therefore, reconstruct the primitive aggregate of impressions.

It is only later, and after a series of new experiments, that we learn how to decompose a body of variable form into smaller elements such that each is displaced approximately according to the same laws as solid bodies. We thus distinguish "deformations" from other changes of state. In these deformations each element undergoes a simple change of position which may be corrected; but the modification of the aggregate is more profound, and can no longer be corrected by a correlative movement. Such a concept is very complex even at this stage, and has been relatively slow in its appearance. It would not have been conceived at all had not the observation of solid bodies shown us beforehand how to distinguish changes of position.

If, then, there were no solid bodies in nature there would be no geometry.

Another remark deserves a moment's attention. Suppose a solid body to occupy successively the positions α and β; in the first position it will give us an aggregate of impressions A, and in the second position the aggregate of impressions B. Now let there be a second solid body, of qualities entirely different from the first—of different colour, for instance. Assume it to pass from the position α, where it gives us the aggregate of impressions A' to the position β, where it gives the aggregate of impressions B'. In general, the aggregate A will have nothing in common with the aggregate A', nor will the aggregate B have anything in common with the aggregate B'. The transition from the aggregate A to the aggregate B, and that of the aggregate A' to the aggregate B', are therefore two changes which *in themselves* have in general nothing in common. Yet we consider both these changes as displacements; and, further, we consider them the *same* displacement. How can this be? It is simply because they may be both corrected by the *same* correlative movement of our body. "Correlative movement," therefore, constitutes the *sole connection* between two phenomena which otherwise we should never have dreamed of connecting.

On the other hand, our body, thanks to the number of its articulations and muscles, may have a multitude of different movements, but all are not capable of "correcting" a modification of external objects; those alone are capable of it in which our whole body, or at least all those in which the organs of our senses enter into play are displaced *en bloc*—*i.e.*, without any variation of their relative positions, as in the case of a solid body.

To sum up:

1. In the first place, we distinguish two categories of phenomena:—The first involuntary, unaccompanied by muscular sensations, and attributed to external objects—they are external changes; the second, of opposite character and attributed to the movements of our own body, are internal changes.

2. We notice that certain changes of each in these categories may be corrected by a correlative change of the other category.

3. We distinguish among external changes those that have a correlative in the other category—which we call displacements; and in the same way we distinguish among the internal changes those which have a correlative in the first category.

Thus by means of this reciprocity is defined a particular class of phenomena called displacements. *The laws of these phenomena are the object of geometry.*

Law of Homogeneity. The first of these laws is the law of homogeneity. Suppose that by an external change we pass from the aggregate of impressions A to the aggregate B, and that then this change α is corrected by a correlative voluntary movement β, so that we are brought back to the aggregate A. Suppose now that another external change α' brings us again from the aggregate A to the aggregate B.

Experiment then shows us that this change α', like the change α, may be corrected by a voluntary correlative movement β', and that this movement β' corresponds to the same muscular sensations as the movement β which corrected α.

This fact is usually enunciated as follows:—*Space is homogeneous and isotropic.* We may also say that a movement which is once produced may be repeated a second and a third time, and so on, without any variation of its properties. In the first chapter, in which we discussed the nature of mathematical reasoning, we saw the importance that should be attached to the possibility of repeating the same operation indefinitely. The virtue of mathematical reasoning is due to this repetition; by means of the law of homogeneity geometrical facts are apprehended. To be complete, to the law of homogeneity must be added a multitude of other laws, into the details of which I do not propose to enter, but which mathematicians sum up by saying that these displacements form a "group."

The Non-Euclidean World.   If geometrical space were a framework imposed on *each* of our representations considered individually, it would be impossible to represent to ourselves an image without this framework, and we should be quite unable to change our geometry. But this is not the case; geometry is only the summary of the laws by which these images succeed each other. There is nothing, therefore, to prevent us from imagining a series of representations, similar in every way to our ordinary representations, but succeeding one another according to laws which differ from those to which we are accustomed. We may thus conceive that beings whose education has taken place in a medium in which those laws would be so different, might have a very different geometry from ours.

Suppose, for example, a world enclosed in a large sphere and subject to the following laws:—The temperature is not uniform; it is greatest at the centre, and gradually decreases as we move towards the circumference of the sphere, where it is absolute zero. The law of this temperature is as follows:—If R be the radius of the sphere, and r the distance of the point considered from the centre, the absolute temperature will be proportional to $R^2 - r^2$. Further, I shall suppose that in this world all bodies have the same co-efficient of dilatation, so that the linear dilatation of any body is proportional to its absolute temperature. Finally, I shall assume that a body transported from one point to another of different temperature is instantaneously in thermal equilibrium with its new environment. There is nothing in these hypotheses either contradictory or unimaginable. A moving object will become smaller and smaller as it approaches the circumference of the sphere. Let us observe, in the first place, that although from the point of view of our ordinary geometry this world is finite, to its inhabitants it will appear infinite. As they approach the surface of the sphere they become colder, and at the same time smaller and smaller. The steps they take are therefore also smaller and smaller, so that they can never reach the boundary of the sphere. If to us geometry is only the study of the laws according to which invariable solids move, to these imaginary beings it will be the study of the laws of motion of solids *deformed by the differences of temperature* alluded to.

No doubt, in our world, natural solids also experience variations of form and volume due to differences of temperature. But in laying the foundations of geometry we neglect these variations; for besides being but small they are irregular, and consequently appear to us to be accidental. In our hypothetical world this will no longer be the case, the variations will obey very simple and regular laws. On the other hand, the different solid parts of which the bodies of these inhabitants are composed will undergo the same variations of form and volume.

Let me make another hypothesis: suppose that light passes through media of different refractive indices, such that the index of refraction is inversely proportional to R^2-r^2. Under these conditions it is clear that the rays of light will no longer be rectilinear but circular. To justify what has been said, we have to prove that certain changes in the position of external objects may be corrected by correlative movements of the beings which inhabit this imaginary world; and in such a way as to restore the primitive aggregate of the impressions experienced by these sentient beings. Suppose, for example, that an object is displaced and deformed, not like an invariable solid, but like a solid subjected to unequal dilatations in exact conformity with the law of temperature assumed above. To use an abbreviation, we shall call such a movement a non-Euclidean displacement.

If a sentient being be in the neighbourhood of such a displacement of the object, his impressions will be modified; but by moving in a suitable manner, he may reconstruct them. For this purpose, all that is required is that the aggregate of the sentient being and the object, considered as forming a single body, shall experience one of those special displacements which I have just called non-Euclidean. This is possible if we suppose that the limbs of these beings dilate according to the same laws as the other bodies of the world they inhabit.

Although from the point of view of our ordinary geometry there is a deformation of the bodies in this displacement, and although their different parts are no longer in the same relative position, nevertheless we shall see that the impressions of the sentient being remain the same as before; in fact, though the mutual distances of the different parts have varied, yet the parts which at first were in contact are still in contact. It follows that tactile impressions will be unchanged. On the other hand, from the hypothesis as to refraction and the curvature of the rays of light, visual impressions will also be unchanged. These imaginary beings will therefore be led to classify the phenomena they observe, and to distinguish among them the "changes of position," which may be corrected by a voluntary correlative movement, just as we do.

If they construct a geometry, it will not be like ours, which is the study of the movements of our invariable solids; it will be the study of the changes of position which they will have thus distinguished, and will be "non-Euclidean displacements," and *this will be non-Euclidean geometry*. So that beings like ourselves, educated in such a world, will not have the same geometry as ours.

The World of Four Dimensions.   Just as we have pictured to ourselves a non-Euclidean world, so we may picture a world of four dimensions.

The sense of light, even with one eye, together with the muscular sensations relative to the movements of the eyeball, will suffice to enable us to conceive of space of three dimensions. The images of external objects are painted on the retina, which is a plane of two dimensions; these are *perspectives*. But as eye and objects are movable, we see in succession different perspectives of the same body taken from different points of view. We find at the same time that the transition from one perspective to another is often accompanied by muscular sensations. If the transition from the perspective A to the perspective B, and that of the perspective A′ to the perspective B′ are accompanied by the same muscular sensations, we connect them as we do other operations of the same nature. Then when we study the laws according to which these operations are combined, we see that they form a group, which has the same structure as that of the movements of invariable solids. Now, we have seen that it is from the properties of this group that we derive the idea of geometrical space and that of three dimensions. We thus understand how these perspectives gave rise to the conception of three dimensions, although each perspective is of only two dimensions,—because *they succeed each other according to certain laws*. Well, in the same way that we draw the perspective of a three-dimensional figure on a plane, so we can draw that of a four-dimensional figure on a canvas of three (or two) dimensions. To a geometer this is but child's play. We can even draw several perspectives of the same figure from several different points of view. We can easily represent to ourselves these perspectives, since they are of only three dimensions. Imagine that the different perspectives of one and the same object occur in succession, and that the transition from one to the other is accompanied by muscular sensations. It is understood that we shall consider two of these transitions as two operations of the same nature when they are associated with the same muscular sensations. There is nothing, then, to prevent us from imagining that these operations are combined according to any law we choose—for instance, by forming a group with the same structure as that of the movements of an invariable four-dimensional solid. In this there is nothing that we cannot represent to ourselves, and, moreover, these sensations are those which a being would experience who has a retina of two dimensions, and who may be displaced in space of four dimensions. In this sense we may say that we can represent to ourselves the fourth dimension.

Conclusions. It is seen that experiment plays a considerable rôle in the genesis of geometry; but it would be a mistake to conclude from that that geometry is, even in part, an experimental science. If it were experimental, it would only be approximative and provisory. And what a rough approximation it would be! Geometry would be only the study of the movements of solid bodies; but, in reality, it is not concerned with natural solids: its object is certain ideal solids, absolutely invariable, which are but a greatly simplified and very remote image of them. The concept of these ideal bodies is entirely mental, and experiment is but the opportunity which enables us to reach the idea. The object of geometry is the study of a particular "group"; but the general concept of group pre-exists in our minds, at least potentially. It is imposed on us not as a form of our sensitiveness, but as a form of our understanding; only, from among all possible groups, we must choose one that will be the *standard*, so to speak, to which we shall refer natural phenomena.

Experiment guides us in this choice, which it does not impose on us. It tells us not what is the truest, but what is the most convenient geometry. It will be noticed that my description of these fantastic worlds has required no language other than that of ordinary geometry. Then, were we transported to those worlds, there would be no need to change that language. Beings educated there would no doubt find it more convenient to create a geometry different from ours, and better adapted to their impressions; but as for us, in the presence of the same impressions, it is certain that we should not find it more convenient to make a change.

READING

Experiment and Geometry

1. I have on several occasions in the preceding pages tried to show how the principles of geometry are not experimental facts, and that in particular Euclid's postulate cannot be proved by experiment. However convincing the reasons already given may appear to me, I feel I must dwell upon them, because there is a profoundly false conception deeply rooted in many minds.

2. Think of a material circle, measure its radius and circumference, and see if the ratio of the two lengths is equal to π. What have we done? We have made an experiment on the properties of the matter with which this *roundness* has been realised, and of which the measure we used is made.

3. *Geometry and Astronomy*. The same question may also be asked in another way. If Lobatschewsky's geometry is true, the parallax of a very distant star will be finite. If Riemann's is true, it will be negative. These are the results which seem within the reach of experiment, and it is hoped that astronomical observations may enable us to decide between the two geometries. But what we call a straight line in astronomy is simply the path of a ray of light. If, therefore, we were to discover negative parallaxes, or to prove that all parallaxes are higher than a certain limit, we should have a choice between two conclusions: we could give up Euclidean geometry, or modify the laws of optics, and suppose that light is not rigorously propagated in a straight line. It is needless to add that every one would look upon this solution as the more advantageous. Euclidean geometry, therefore, has nothing to fear from fresh experiments.

4. Can we maintain that certain phenomena which are possible in Euclidean space would be impossible in non-Euclidean space, so that experiment in establishing these phenomena would directly contradict the non-Euclidean hypothesis? I think that such a question cannot be seriously asked. To me it is exactly equivalent to the following, the absurdity of which is obvious:—There are lengths which can be expressed in metres and centimetres, but cannot be measured in toises, feet, and inches; so that experiment, by ascertaining the existence of these lengths, would directly contradict this hypothesis, that there are toises divided into six feet. Let us look at the question a little more closely. I assume that the straight line in Euclidean space possesses any two properties, which I shall call A and B; that in non-Euclidean space it still possesses the property A, but no longer possesses the property B; and,

finally, I assume that in both Euclidean and non-Euclidean space the straight line is the only line that possesses the property A. If this were so, experiment would be able to decide between the hypotheses of Euclid and Lobatschewsky. It would be found that some concrete object, upon which we can experiment—for example, a pencil of rays of light—possesses the property A. We should conclude that it is rectilinear, and we should then endeavour to find out if it does, or does not, possess the property B. But *it is not so*. There exists no property which can, like this property A, be an absolute criterion enabling us to recognise the straight line, and to distinguish it from every other line. Shall we say, for instance, "This property will be the following: the straight line is a line such that a figure of which this line is a part can move without the mutual distances of its points varying, and in such a way that all the points in this straight line remain fixed"? Now, this is a property which in either Euclidean or non-Euclidean space belongs to the straight line, and belongs to it alone. But how can we ascertain by experiment if it belongs to any particular concrete object? Distances must be measured, and how shall we know that any concrete magnitude which I have measured with my material instrument really represents the abstract distance? We have only removed the difficulty a little farther off. In reality, the property that I have just enunciated is not a property of the straight line alone; it is a property of the straight line and of distance. For it to serve as an absolute criterion, we must be able to show, not only that it does not also belong to any other line than the straight line and to distance, but also that it does not belong to any other line than the straight line, and to any other magnitude than distance. Now, that is not true, and if we are not convinced by these considerations, I challenge any one to give me a concrete experiment which can be interpreted in the Euclidean system, and which cannot be interpreted in the system of Lobatschewsky. As I am well aware that this challenge will never be accepted, I may conclude that no experiment will ever be in contradiction with Euclid's postulate; but, on the other hand, no experiment will ever be in contradiction with Lobatschewsky's postulate. . . .

COMMENTARY

13.1   Bolyai-Lobachevskian Geometry

In this chapter we will further consider what experimenters might observe if space were non-Euclidean, and the question of how they could interpret the data that they would gather. To explore these issues, we will consider the analogous world described by Poincaré. In this case, the non-Euclidean geometry observed is not the elliptic geometry of the sphere, which we discussed in the previous chapter. Instead, the geometry is that of Bolyai and Lobachevski (BL geometry), which is defined by the following axioms:

1. Any two points lie on a (unique) line.

2. Any segment can be continued indefinitely.

3. Any two points (the center and a point on the circumference) define a circle.

4. All right angles are equal.

5. Even if the interior angles made by a line falling on two lines are less than two right angles on the same side, the two lines may fail to intersect if extended indefinitely: indeed, *for any line and any point, there are many lines through the point parallel to the given line.*

Thus BL geometry is a third possibility relative to the fifth axiom: elliptic geometry has no parallels, Euclidean geometry a unique parallel defined by any line and point, and BL geometry has many such parallels. We have already seen the consistency of alternatives to the Euclidean parallel postulate, so we will not prove explicitly that the axioms hold of a particular surface (as we did for the elliptic axioms and the sphere), but rather simply accept them. (Note however that geometric constructions in the world described by Poincaré follow the axioms of BL geometry, so the example is a model for that geometry, showing its consistency.)

Euclid's internal angles theorem requires the fifth postulate for its proof, so we should expect it to fail in non-Euclidean geometries. In elliptic geometry, every triangle has internal angles whose sum is greater than 180°, and correspondingly, in BL geometry, every triangle has internal angles whose sum is less than that of two rights. In other words, an experiment such as Gauss's in principle could be used to determine which of the three geometries gives a correct description of space: from the measurement of the actual internal angles of a triangle we can infer the geometry of space. However, the internal angles theorem is not the only consequence of geomet-

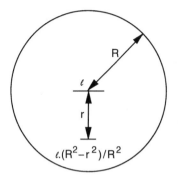

Figure 13.1
Poincaré's disk: all objects contract as they move away from the center.

ric systems that can be tested, and we will consider a further difference between the three geometries that could be detected experimentally.

In Euclidean geometry, it is a theorem that the ratio of the circumference, c, of any circle to its diameter, d, is a constant, π: in elementary geometry we learned that $c = \pi d$. This theorem depends on the parallel postulate, so we should expect it not to hold in non-Euclidean geometries, which is indeed what we find. In elliptic geometry the ratio of circumference to diameter is always less than $\pi(c < \pi d)$, and in BL geometry it is always greater than $\pi(c > \pi d)$. As we turn to the analogy given by Poincaré, these "predictions" are what we will try to test: one should be able to determine the geometry of space by measuring the circumferences and diameters of various circles and calculating their ratios. A result other than π would seem to show that the Euclidean hypothesis is false, and that the geometry of space is non-Euclidean.

13.2   Poincaré's Non-Euclidean World

As before, we will simplify the discussion to two dimensions. Poincaré describes a world in which creatures live on a two-dimensional disk, radius R, in the Euclidean plane. The crucial feature of this world is that the length of any material object decreases as it moves further from the center. Specifically, if an object is l meters long at the center, then at a distance r from the center it will be $l \cdot (R^2 - r^2)/R^2$ meters long.

Poincaré explains this variation in length as due to a change in temperature as one moves away from the center: he stipulates that everything contracts equally as temperature decreases. However, realistically, temperature affects different materials differently, so we shall just imagine that the contraction is due to a new, all-pervading, unavoidable "universal force." We shall thus capture the most important aspect of the contraction: that it affects absolutely everything in exactly the same way. This crucially distinguishes it from the usual effects of heat: we can see the different effects of heat on different objects, say, steel and wooden rods—or, in a thermometer, the varying effects on mercury and glass. In Poincaré's world, however, since the effect of contraction is entirely regular or universal, there is no immediate way of noticing it: objects made of steel, wood, mercury, glass, or indeed anything at all are affected identically. Thus the inhabitants of the disk will not be aware of this phenomenon: they believe and experience objects to remain the same length as they move about their space, just as we do in ours.

The thought experiment now calls on us to consider the attempts of the two-dimensional beings living in the disk to experimentally determine the geometry of their world. (Of course, the whole point of the analogy is that we are ultimately to compare these beings and their geometric experiments to ourselves.) Their scientists—let us call them "surveyors"—have the usual pieces of equipment available: pieces of string, rulers, protractors, light sources and sighting equipment, and so on. Of course, such equipment will change size at it is moved around space, but as we emphasized, the surveyors have no way of knowing that this is the case, since all the equipment will change in the same ways. The first measurement that they try to make is to determine the radius of their world. Will they find that it is R meters, the correct answer?

Suppose that the surveyors perform the measurement by walking outward from the center along a straight line, recording the distance traveled with a cyclometer. That is, they roll along the line a wheel (of circumference w meters) that clicks after every complete revolution: n clicks along a curve means the curve is measured to be $n \cdot w$m long. For convenience, let us assume that the wheel has a circumference of 1m at the center of the disk, or a diameter of $1/\pi$m. By the time the surveyors are D meters from the center, the diameter of the cyclometer wheel will be $1/\pi \cdot (R^2 - D^2)/R^2$m, and its circumference $1 \cdot (R^2 - D^2)/R^2$m, which is less than 1m. The further the cyclometer is from the center, the smaller the wheel is, so the less distance along the line it has to go to complete a revolution and click. Thus the surveyors will register more than D clicks from their "1m" cyclometer along a line Dm long from the center, and so they will measure it to be more than Dm long; remember that they do not realize that their cyclometer has shrunk. Indeed, since objects would shrink to $(R^2 - R^2)/R^2 = 0$ at the very perimeter, the cyclometer wheel shrinks so fast that a finite number of revolutions along the line will never add

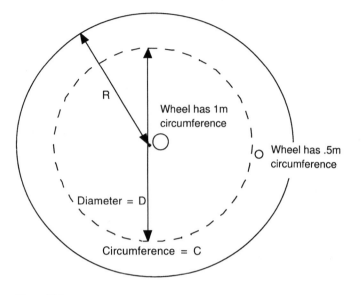

Figure 13.2
Measuring the ratio of circumference to diameter on Poincaré's disk.

up to Rm. The surveyors will never reach the boundary, and so they will conclude that their space is infinite!

It is crucial to remember that because everything changes size in the same way as it moves about the disk, there is no way for the surveyors to realize that their cyclometer is shrinking, and that they are hence "mis-measuring" the radius of space. If they used a ruler as well, for instance, it would shrink at the same rate, and so would always measure the diameter of the wheel to be $1/\pi$m. And of course the surveyors themselves shrink correspondingly, so they have no sensation of the apparatus changing: proportionally, it remains the same size. And since Poincaré specifies that the refractive index of space changes around the plate, there is also no optical way to determine that the cyclometer, ruler, and surveyor have all shrunk. Their experiences of their apparatuses are identical to those of surveyors in a world in which objects remain the same size—except, as we shall soon see, in the geometry of space that they observe with that equipment. Thus they will have no reason to doubt their conclusion that space is infinite: they will see a cyclometer rolling ever outward without reaching the edge, and have not the least suspicion of what is happening. We might say that "for them," the disk *is* infinite, for their error is completely inaccessible to them.

What now will the surveyors find when they attempt to determine the geometry of space, say by measuring the circumference-to-diameter ratio for some circle? Suppose that they measure a circle whose center is the center of the plate, and whose actual diameter, Dm, is such that objects have shrunk to one half their maximum length at the circumference (of actual length Cm). What will the surveyors find for the measured circumference, c, and diameter, d, of the circle? Since everything, including the cyclometer wheel, is half its true size at the perimeter, they will measure the circumference to be twice its actual length, $C : c = 2Cm$. They use a .5m wheel but count every revolution to be 1m. However, the surveyors will not measure the diameter to be twice the actual diameter. As they walk across the circle, the wheel of their cyclometer will grow from a smallest size of .5m in circumference at the perimeter of the circle, to 1m at the center, and then shrink back to .5m. But it is almost everywhere longer than .5m, and so there must be fewer than $2D$ revolutions along the path, and so a diameter of less than twice the actual diameter will be measured: $d < 2D$.

What ratio has thus been found? $c/d > 2C/2D = C/D = \pi$, since C and D are the actual Euclidean circumference and diameter. But $c/d > \pi$ means that the surveyors have found their space to have BL geometry, even though it is actually a disk in the Euclidean plane!

Let the surveyors survey a circle, centered on the center of the disk, of diameter $D = \sqrt{2} \cdot Rm$, and circumference $C = \pi D = \sqrt{2} \cdot \pi Rm$.

The circumference is $r = D/2 = R/\sqrt{2}\,$m from the center, and so on the circle a 1m measuring device is

1. $\{R^2 - (R/\sqrt{2})^2\}/R^2 = 1 \cdot (R^2 - R^2/2)/R^2 = 1 \cdot R^2/2R^2 = .5$m long.

The measured circumference is thus $c = 2Cm$.

Within the circle, a 1m measuring device is $>.5$m long, so the measured diameter is thus $d < 2Dm$.

The ratio of circumference to diameter is thus $c/d > 2C/2D = \pi$.

The first point that Poincaré wishes to make—in the first essay, *Space and Geometry*—is that the spatial experiences of the native inhabitants of such a world would be non-Euclidean. Since all objects are identically affected by the universal force, it is overwhelmingly likely that the inhabitants, at least before science reaches an advanced stage, will be utterly unaware of it, and will in no way see or infer the contractions. As they move around their space, their measuring apparatuses will look as rigid to them as ours do to us. And yet, when they survey their space, they will observe it to have non-Euclidean properties. In other words, their experiences will be non-Euclidean, contrary to Kant's claim that it is *a priori* necessary that our spatial experiences will be Euclidean. Consequently, we can expect that their "Euclid" will construct the BL geometry of experience, and only later will "non-BL" geometries be discovered: "Beings [like us] ... might receive from a suitably-chosen external world impressions which would lead them to construct a geometry other than that of Euclid, and to localise the phenomena of this external world in a non-Euclidean world...." (*Science and Hypothesis*, this vol., p. 235). Of course, experience might determine which geometry is first constructed, and indeed which geometry is adopted in the study of nature, but this does not make mathematical geometry an empirical science: as Poincaré notes at the end of the first essay, pure geometry is an *a priori* matter of logical construction.

13.3 Conventionalism

But suppose that non-BL geometries (both Euclidean and elliptic) have been discovered: must the surveyors conclude from their experiments that space has a BL geometry? The second essay by Poincaré—*Experiment and Geometry*—argues for a negative answer: "... no experiment will ever be in contradiction with Euclid's postulate; [and] no experiment will ever be in contradiction with Lobachevsky's postulate" (*Science and Hypothesis*, this vol., p. 242).

Suppose that the surveyors publish their results, with the conclusion that space has a BL geometry. Other scientists could accept their measurements but dispute their conclusions, arguing that they had found, not that space is non-Euclidean, but that material objects change size as they move around space. We know that this second conclusion is also compatible with the data, for in our story that is exactly what does happen. Is there any way in which this dispute could be settled experimentally? It seems not, for there is no way to directly inspect space to discover its geometry: we can only observe the results of measurements involving material objects. But by construction of the example, everything that could be observed using rigid apparatuses in BL space would also be observed using Poincaré's "shrinking" apparatuses in the Euclidean-disk space. And remember that "everything" means *everything*: other than the measurements of space, there is no reason for the surveyors to suspect that their equipment changes length.

We can sum up the situation with a schematic "Poincaré equation":

Geometry of space + Behavior of apparatus = Survey measurements.

Like any such equation, many different pairs of terms on the left "add up" to the same "quantity" on the right. As we have seen, BL geometry plus apparatuses of fixed length adds up to the same set of measurements as do Euclidean geometry plus apparatuses whose length depends on the distance to the center. But the situation is even more extreme: A given set of measurements can be fitted to an infinite variety of geometries by assuming the appropriate behavior for the apparatus. That is, if the surveyors were to make every measurement that they possibly could, it would still be compatible with an infinite number of geometries, given suitable assumptions about the variations in their equipment. (There are an infinite number of elliptic geometries corresponding to spheres of different radii, and similarly for BL geometry; and regions of different geometries can be "pasted together.")

So, are the inhabitants of the disk (and analogously, are we) to live in a state of uncertainty, never drawing a conclusion about space? Not quite, according to Poincaré; "[Experiment] tells us not what is the truest, but what is the most convenient geometry" (*Science and Hypothesis*, this vol., p. 240). That is, we cannot determine by experiment which geometry is the correct one, but we can stipulate it, by "convention": the surveyors can pick a geometry that is true "for them." It is, for instance, a convention (in many societies) that shaking hands is an appropriate greeting; but there is nothing absolute about that fact, since there could be a society whose convention was that any public physical contact was disgusting and insulting. Similarly, the surveyors cannot determine the absolute geometry of their space, but they could pick one of them to be correct by convention, a kind of agreement between scientists about which to accept. Which convention is adopted is, according to Poincaré, a matter of scientific convenience: the geometry that most simplifies theoretical and experimental science will be chosen as true.

What is the status of "truth by convention"? From what we have said so far it seems that it is a secondary type of truth, which is used only when the "actual truth" cannot be found. But that is not the only way to conceive it, for it could also be the case that there *is* no "actual truth" about this issue. Poincaré determined the real geometry of the disk by stipulating it in his story, but we could retell the story without specifying a particular geometry, only the results of survey measurements. We could do this by saying that all measurements are "as if" space were a Euclidean disk in which objects change length as they move around. We might mean that there is a particular but unmentioned geometry, but it could also be that we mean that the space somehow has no specific geometry at all—it is indeterminate between various geometries. In the latter case there is no truth for the surveyors to find, beyond the results of their experiments. If so, "true by convention" does not mean "the most convenient choice, but perhaps actually false, though we can never tell." Instead, if

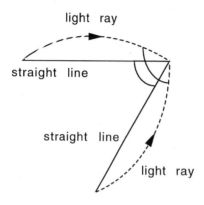

Figure 13.3
Gauss's experiment: if light does not travel in straight lines then in Euclidean space the measured angles will be too large.

there is no actual truth, there is no way for the convention to be wrong: truth literally is descriptive convenience. If geometry is conventional is this sense, then it fails to be "absolute" in a new way. One might think that space must have a definite or "absolute" geometry, but what is suggested here is that perhaps space has no particular intrinsic geometry at all. (Note: Leibniz did not deny that space was absolute in this sense: he believed that between any two objects was a definite, not conventional, distance—but in his time the only geometry was Euclidean.)

If we now reflect that the surveyors in the disk are a metaphor for us and for our attempts to determine the geometry of space, then we see that we are in an analogous position. Suppose, for example, that Gauss (see sec. 2.3) had found that the internal angles of his triangle added up to more than two right angles; would he have *had* to conclude that space was elliptic? No, for he constructed his triangle by sighting the tops of the mountains, so that its sides were rays of light. He could only conclude that space itself was non-Euclidean on the *further* assumption that light rays travel along straight lines, but perhaps they don't (*Science and Hypothesis*, this vol., p. 238). An experimental violation of the Euclidean internal angles theorem can be explained in at least two ways: if we assume that light travels in straight lines, then space must be non-Euclidean; but if we assume that space is Euclidean, we can explain the violation if the light rays travel between the mountain tops along paths that bend out, arriving at the surveying equipment at too great an angle. When we add up three such angles they total more than the two right angles made by the three straight sides.

Gauss's experiment thus cannot unequivocally determine the geometry of space, for any result is compatible with an infinite variety of geometries, as long as an appropriate assumption about the behavior of light is made. Hence we are in exactly the same position as the surveyors on the disk. It is possible that all the material objects in our world change as they move across space in a way that is absolutely undetectable, because all objects are affected in the same way. To all appearances, our equipment would be exactly the same as in a world in which it was rigid, except when we measured the geometry of space. Thus when we survey space, the Poincaré equation applies to us: An infinite range of geometries and appropriate hypotheses about the behavior of our equipment will "add up" to whatever we find. Nothing we can do will determine whether space is curved, or our apparatus is expanding and contracting, or both. It seems that we too must adopt a geometry by convention, for our own convenience. And as a matter of fact, science has adopted the convention that light does travel in straight lines, and that rulers don't change size under a mysterious, all-pervading, unavoidable force. The result of such an assumption is that space is indeed curved.

We have thus adopted a convention about geometry, but what kind of convention is it? Does space have a true geometry which we cannot discover, making us settle for a convention as the next best thing? Or do we face the second kind of situation, in which space has no absolute true geometry, and so a convention is all that there is? It is impossible to decide this issue easily, and these questions are still hotly debated.

Problems

1. Write up the surveyors' experiment as you would a piece of lab work, with a description of the apparatus, the method, the results, and the conclusion. Show how it is that many conclusions about the geometry of space are possible.

2. One reply to Poincaré's conventionalism argues that he presents us with a false alternative: that in fact, Euclidean space + changing apparatus, and BL space + rigid apparatus, are one and the same situation. Consider the "two theories" you get when you write Newtonian mechanics in metric and imperial units: they aren't two distinct possibilities, but really the same theory with different definitions of length, weight, and so on. Similarly, perhaps the two geometries are the same theory but with separate definitions of what it is to be 1m: either 1m can be defined everywhere as the length of a unit rod, or as equal to an increasing number of rods away from the center. In this case, the convention is the quite ordinary, uncontroversial one of picking definitions. Would this be a good response to Poincaré?

3. At the start of the book, we saw an (inconclusive) argument from Aristotle (*On the Heavens*, Bk. I, chap. 1) to the effect that space must have three dimensions. Kant also believed that three-dimensionality was certain, as an aspect of the form of experience (*Critique*, this vol., p. 218). Poincaré, however, claims that we can conceptualize a four-dimensional world; what examples does Abbot's *Flatland* provide to support Poincaré's claim?

Further Readings and Bibliography

Abbott, E. A. 1992. *Flatland: A Romance in Many Dimensions.* New York: Dover. √

Glymour, C. "The Epistemology of Geometry." *Noûs* 11 (1977): 227–251.

Nerlich, G. 1994. *The Shape of Space,* second edition (see chaps. 3–9). Cambridge, UK: Cambridge University Press.

Ray, C. 1991. *Time, Space, and Philosophy* (see chap. 4). London and New York: Routledge, 1991. √

Reichenbach, H. 1958. *The Philosophy of Space and Time* (see chap. 1), translated by M. Reichenbach and J. Freund. New York: Dover.

Sklar, L. 1976. *Space, Time, and Spacetime* (see chap. II, F–H). Berkeley, CA: University of California Press.

Sklar, L. 1992. *Philosophy of Physics* (see esp. pp. 53–69). Boulder, CO and San Francisco, CA: Westview Press. √

14 Einstein

READING

The Problem of Space, Ether, and the Field in Physics

Scientific thought is a development of pre-scientific thought. As the concept of space was already fundamental in the latter, we must begin with the concept of space in pre-scientific thought. There are two ways of regarding concepts, both of which are indispensable to understanding. The first is that of logical analysis. It answers the question, How do concepts and judgments depend on each other? In answering it we are on comparatively safe ground. It is the certainty by which we are so much impressed in mathematics. But this certainty is purchased at the price of emptiness of content. Concepts can only acquire content when they are connected, however indirectly, with sensible experience. But no logical investigation can reveal this connection; it can only be experienced. And yet it is this connection that determines the cognitive value of systems of concepts.

Take an example. Suppose an archaeologist belonging to a later culture finds a textbook of Euclidean geometry without diagrams. He will discover how the words "point," "straight-line," "plane" are used in the propositions. He will also recognize how the latter are deduced from each other. He will even be able to frame new propositions according to the rules he recognized. But the framing of these propositions will remain an empty play with words for him as long as "point," "straight-line," "plane," etc., convey nothing to him. Only when they do convey something will geometry possess any real content for him. The same will be true of analytical mechanics, and indeed of any exposition of a logically deductive science.

What does it mean that "straight-line," "point," "intersection," etc., convey something? It means that one can point to the sensible experiences to which those words refer. This extra-logical problem is the problem of the nature of geometry, which the archaeologist will only be able to solve intuitively by examining his experience for anything he can discover which corresponds to those primary terms of the theory and the axioms laid down for them. Only in this sense can the question of the nature of a conceptually presented entity be reasonably raised.

With our pre-scientific concepts we are very much in the position of our archaeologist in regard to the ontological problem. We have, so to speak, forgotten what features in the world of experience caused us to frame those concepts, and we have

Albert Einstein, "The Problem of Space, Ether, and the Field in Physics," translated by S. Bargmann, in *Ideas and Opinions.* © 1954, renewed 1982 by Crown Publishers, Inc. Reprinted by permission of Crown Publishers, Inc.

great difficulty in calling to mind the world of experience without the spectacles of the old-established conceptual interpretation. There is the further difficulty that our language is compelled to work with words which are inseparably connected with those primitive concepts. These are the obstacles which confront us when we try to describe the essential nature of the pre-scientific concept of space.

One remark about concepts in general, before we turn to the problem of space: concepts have reference to sensible experience, but they are never, in a logical sense, deducible from them. For this reason I have never been able to understand the quest of the *a priori* in the Kantian sense. In any ontological question, our concern can only be to seek out those characteristics in the complex of sense experiences to which the concepts refer.

Now as regards the concept of space: this seems to presuppose the concept of the solid body. The nature of the complexes and sense-impressions which are probably responsible for that concept has often been described. The correspondence between certain visual and tactile impressions, the fact that they can be continuously followed through time, and that the impressions can be repeated at any moment (touch, sight), are some of those characteristics. Once the concept of the solid body is formed in connection with the experiences just mentioned—which concept by no means presupposes that of space or spatial relation—the desire to get an intellectual grasp of the relations of such solid bodies is bound to give rise to concepts which correspond to their spatial relations. Two solid bodies may touch one another or be distant from one another. In the latter case, a third body can be inserted between them without altering them in any way; in the former, not. These spatial relations are obviously real in the same sense as the bodies themselves. If two bodies are equivalent with respect to filling out *one* such interval, they will also prove equivalent for other intervals. The interval is thus shown to be independent of the selection of any special body to fill it; the same is universally true of spatial relations. It is evident that this independence, which is a principal condition of the usefulness of framing purely geometrical concepts, is not necessary *a priori*. In my opinion, this concept of the interval, detached as it is from the selection of any special body to occupy it, is the starting point of the whole concept of space.

Considered, then, from the point of view of sense experience, the development of the concept of space seems, after these brief indications, to conform to the following schema—solid body; spatial relations of solid bodies; interval; space. Looked at in this way, space appears as something real in the same sense as solid bodies.

It is clear that the concept of space as a real thing already existed in the extra-scientific conceptual world. Euclid's mathematics, however, knew nothing of this concept as such; it confined itself to the concepts of the object, and the spatial relations between objects. The point, the plane, the straight line, the segment are solid objects idealized. All spatial relations are reduced to those of contact (the intersection of straight lines and planes, points lying on straight lines, etc.). Space as a continuum does not figure in the conceptual system at all. This concept was first introduced by Descartes, when he described the point-in-space by its coordinates. Here for the first time geometrical figures appear, in a way, as parts of infinite space, which is conceived as a three-dimensional continuum.

The great superiority of the Cartesian treatment of space is by no means confined to the fact that it applies analysis to the purposes of geometry. The main point seems rather to be this: the Greeks favor in their geometrical descriptions particular objects (the straight line, the plane); other objects (e.g., the ellipse) are only accessible to this description by a construction or definition with the help of the point, the straight line, and the plane. In the Cartesian treatment, on the other hand, all surfaces, for example, appear, in principle, on equal footing, without any arbitrary preference for linear structures in building up geometry.

In so far as geometry is conceived as the science of laws governing the mutual spatial relations of practically rigid bodies, it is to be regarded as the oldest branch of physics. This science was able, as I have already observed, to get along without the concept of space as such, the ideal corporeal forms—point, straight line, plane, segment—being sufficient for its needs. On the other hand, space as a whole, as conceived by Descartes, was absolutely necessary to Newtonian physics. For dynamics cannot manage with the concepts of the mass point and the (temporally variable) distance between mass points alone. In Newton's equations of motion, the concept of acceleration plays a fundamental part, which cannot be defined by the temporally variable intervals between points alone. Newton's acceleration is only conceivable or definable in relation to space as a whole. Thus to the geometrical reality of the concept of space a new inertia-determining function of space was added. When Newton described space as absolute, he no doubt meant this real significance of space, which made it necessary for him to attribute to it a quite definite state of motion, which yet did not appear to be fully determined by the phenomena of mechanics. This space was conceived as absolute in another sense also; its inertia-determining effect was conceived as autonomous, i.e., not to be influenced by any physical circumstance whatever; it affected masses, but nothing affected it.

And yet in the minds of physicists space remained until the most recent time simply the passive container of all events, without taking any part in physical occurrences. Thought only began to take a new turn with the wave-theory of light and the theory of the electromagnetic field of Faraday and Maxwell. It became clear that there existed in free space states which propagated themselves in waves, as well as localized fields which were able to exert forces on electrical masses or magnetic poles brought to the spot. Since it would have seemed utterly absurd to the physicists of the nineteenth century to attribute physical functions or states to space itself, they invented a medium pervading the whole of space, on the model of ponderable matter—the ether, which was supposed to act as a vehicle for electromagnetic phenomena, and hence for those of light also. The states of this medium, imagined as constituting the electromagnetic fields, were at first thought of mechanically, on the model of the elastic deformations of solid bodies. But this mechanical theory of the ether was never quite successful so that gradually a more detailed interpretation of the nature of etheric fields was given up. The ether thus became a kind of matter whose only function was to act as a substratum for electrical fields which were by their very nature not further analyzable. The picture was, then, as follows: space is filled by the ether, in which the material corpuscles or atoms of ponderable matter swim around; the atomic structure of the latter had been securely established by the turn of the century.

Since the interaction of bodies was supposed to be accomplished through fields, there had also to be a gravitational field in the ether, whose field-law had, however, assumed no clear form at that time. The ether was only supposed to be the seat of all forces acting across space. Since it had been realized that electrical masses in motion produce a magnetic field, whose energy provided a model for inertia, inertia also appeared as a field-action localized in the ether.

The mechanical properties of the ether were at first a mystery. Then came H. A. Lorentz's great discovery. All the phenomena of electromagnetism then known could be explained on the basis of two assumptions: that the ether is firmly fixed in space— that is to say, unable to move at all, and that electricity is firmly lodged in the mobile elementary particles. Today his discovery may be expressed as follows: physical space and the ether are only different terms for the same thing; fields are physical states of space. For if no particular state of motion can be ascribed to the ether, there does not seem to be any ground for introducing it as an entity of a special sort alongside of space. But the physicists were still far removed from such a way of thinking; space was still, for them, a rigid, homogeneous something, incapable of changing or assuming various states. Only the genius of Riemann, solitary and uncomprehended, had already won its way by the middle of the last century to a new conception of space, in which space was deprived of its rigidity, and the possibility of its partaking in physical events was recognized. This intellectual achievement commands our admiration all the more for having preceded Faraday's and Maxwell's field theory of electricity. Then came the special theory of relativity with its recognition of the physical equivalence of all inertial systems. The inseparability of time and space emerged in connection with electrodynamics, or the law of the propagation of light. Hitherto it had been silently assumed that the four-dimensional continuum of events could be split up into time and space in an objective manner—i.e., that an absolute significance attached to the "now" in the world of events. With the discovery of the relativity of simultaneity, space and time were merged in a single continuum in a way similar to that in which the three dimensions of space had previously been merged into a single continuum. Physical space was thus extended to a four-dimensional space which also included the dimension of time. The four-dimensional space of the special theory of relativity is just as rigid and absolute as Newton's space.

The theory of relativity is a fine example of the fundamental character of the modern development of theoretical science. The initial hypotheses become steadily more abstract and remote from experience. On the other hand, it gets nearer to the grand aim of all science, which is to cover the greatest possible number of empirical facts by logical deduction from the smallest possible number of hypotheses or axioms. Meanwhile, the train of thought leading from the axioms to the empirical facts or verifiable consequences gets steadily longer and more subtle. The theoretical scientist is compelled in an increasing degree to be guided by purely mathematical, formal considerations in his search for a theory, because the physical experience of the experimenter cannot lead him up to the regions of highest abstraction. The predominantly inductive methods appropriate to the youth of science are giving place to tentative deduction. Such a theoretical structure needs to be very thoroughly elaborated before it can lead to conclusions which can be compared with experience. Here, too, the observed fact is undoubtedly the supreme arbiter; but it cannot pronounce sentence until the wide chasm separating the axioms from their verifiable consequences has been bridged by much intense, hard thinking. The theorist has to set about this Herculean task fully aware that his efforts may only be destined to prepare the death blow to his theory. The theorist who undertakes such a labor should not be carped at as "fanciful"; on the contrary, he should be granted the right to give free reign to his fancy, for there is no other way to the goal. His is no idle daydreaming, but a search for the logically simplest possibilities and their consequences. This plea was needed in order to make the listener or reader more inclined to follow the ensuing train of ideas with attention; it is the line of thought which has led from the special to the general theory of relativity and thence to its latest offshoot, the unified field theory. In this exposition the use of mathematical symbols cannot be completely avoided.

We start with the special theory of relativity. This theory is still based directly on an empirical law, that of the constancy of the velocity of light. Let P be a point in empty space, P' an infinitely close point at a distance $d\sigma$. Let a flash of light be emitted from P at a time t and reach P' at a time $t + dt$. Then

$$d\sigma^2 = c^2\,dt^2$$

If dx_1, dx_2, dx_3 are the orthogonal projections of $d\sigma$, and the imaginary time coordinate $\sqrt{-1}\,ct = x_4$ is introduced, then the above-mentioned law of the constancy of the velocity of light propagation takes the form

$$ds^2 = dx_1^2 + dx_2^2 + dx_3^2 + dx_4^2 = 0$$

Since this formula expresses a real situation, we may attribute a real meaning to the quantity ds, even if the neighboring points of the four-dimensional continuum are so chosen that the corresponding ds does not vanish. This may be expressed by saying that the four-dimensional space (with an imaginary time-coordinate) of the special theory of relativity possesses a Euclidean metric.

The fact that such a metric is called Euclidean is connected with the following. The postulation of such a metric in a three-dimensional continuum is fully equivalent to the postulation of the axioms of Euclidean geometry. The defining equation of the metric is then nothing but the Pythagorean theorem applied to the differentials of the coordinates.

In the special theory of relativity those coordinate changes (by transformation) are permitted for which also in the new coordinate system the quantity ds^2 (fundamental invariant) equals the sum of the squares of the coordinate differentials. Such transformations are called Lorentz transformations.

The heuristic method of the special theory of relativity is characterized by the following principle: only those equations are admissible as an expression of natural laws which do not change their form when the coordinates are changed by means of a Lorentz transformation (covariance of equations with respect to Lorentz transformations).

This method led to the discovery of the necessary connection between momentum and energy, between electric and magnetic field strength, electrostatic and electrodynamic forces, inert mass and energy; and the number of independent concepts and fundamental equations in physics was thereby reduced.

This method pointed beyond itself. Is it true that the equations which express natural laws are covariant with respect to Lorentz transformations only and not with respect to other transformations? Well, formulated in that way the question really has no meaning, since every system of equations can be expressed in general coordinates. We must ask: Are not the laws of nature so constituted that they are not materially simplified through the choice of any one *particular* set of coordinates?

We will only mention in passing that our empirical law of the equality of inert and gravitational masses prompts us to answer this question in the affirmative. If we elevate the equivalence of all coordinate systems for the formulation of natural laws into a principle, we arrive at the general theory of relativity, provided we retain the law of the constancy of the velocity of light or, in other words, the hypothesis of the objective significance of the Euclidean metric at least for infinitely small portions of four-dimensional space.

This means that for finite regions of space the (physically meaningful) existence of a general Riemannian metric is postulated according to the formula

$$ds^2 = \sum_{\mu\nu} g_{\mu\nu} dx_\mu \, dx_\nu,$$

where the summation is to be extended to all index combinations from $1, 1$ to $4, 4$.

The structure of such a space differs quite basically in *one* respect from that of a Euclidean space. The coefficients $g_{\mu\nu}$ are for the time being any functions whatever of the coordinates x_1 to x_4, and the structure of the space is not really determined until these functions $g_{\mu\nu}$ are really known. One can also say: the structure of such a space is as such completely undetermined. It is only determined more closely by specifying laws which the metrical field of the $g_{\mu\nu}$ satisfy. On physical grounds it was assumed that the metrical field was at the same time the gravitational field.

Since the gravitational field is determined by the configuration of masses and changes with it, the geometric structure of this space is also dependent on physical factors. Thus, according to this theory space is—exactly as Riemann guessed—no longer absolute; its structure depends on physical influences. (Physical) geometry is no longer an isolated self-contained science like the geometry of Euclid.

The problem of gravitation was thus reduced to a mathematical problem: it was required to find the simplest fundamental equations which are covariant with respect to arbitrary coordinate transformation. This was a well-defined problem that could at least be solved.

I will not speak here of the experimental confirmation of this theory, but explain at once why the theory could not rest permanently satisfied with this success. Gravitation had indeed been deduced from the structure of space, but besides the gravitational field there is also the electromagnetic field. This had, to begin with, to be introduced into the theory as an entity independent of gravitation. Terms which took account of the existence of the electromagnetic field had to be added to the fundamental field equations. But the idea that there exist two structures of space independent of each other, the metric-gravitational and the electromagnetic, was intolerable to the theoretical spirit. We are prompted to the belief that both sorts of field must correspond to a unified structure of space.

COMMENTARY

14.1 Introduction

Einstein is one of the icons of our time, requiring no introduction (though see the bibliography nevertheless). His essay takes us beyond the scope of this book and into modern relativistic physics, but it also presents relativity as the latest stage in the development of our conception of space, which is an idea that has shaped our discussion. We have adopted this picture in order to highlight, in their historical context, certain ideas that are important to the modern view of space. The reader should, however, be aware that it is not usually accurate to think of the history of science as a straightforward progression toward new and better ideas. For instance, we remarked that falling down was considered a natural motion by both Aristotle and Einstein, but not by Newton: this idea disappeared and then reappeared.

Given the path we've taken throughout this book, this piece makes a perfect conclusion to our history, reminding us of many of the central lessons that have been learned and demonstrating how the classic texts point toward Einstein's general theory of relativity. To draw out these points we can do no better then follow the history as Einstein lays it out, step by step.

14.2 Ancient Views of Space

How did we come by our conception of space? According to Einstein, it originated in our experiences of solid bodies, and in particular from our experiences of their spatial relations. For example, when humans realized that two different solid objects could fit in the same "interval" between bodies one after the other, they came to think of that place as something separate from any particular object. From such an idea it would have been natural then to conceive of space as we did earlier, as the collection of all such places. If Einstein is correct in this "psychological archeology," then we can understand Plato's *Parmenides* as an early recognition that our experiences of matter imply the existence of a "home" for all things. And Plato's claim that space and matter are in fact one and the same is a reaction that many have had to the idea that such a space is something separate. Or again, Aristotle's notion of place seems very close to Einstein's interval (in three dimensions), for an Aristotelian place is the inner surface of whatever bodies surround it.

Our readings, however, reveal three shortcomings in Einstein's history at this point. First, it is true that Aristotle rejected the idea of space as a real entity separate from matter (an "extension between the extremities," *Physics*, 211b7), he did acknowledge the idea within the "scientific conceptual world." Second, although the ancients did not think, as Descartes did, of basing geometry on a system of coordinates in space, our reading of Zeno shows that they wrestled with the idea of the continuum. Finally, Einstein does not emphasize, as Aristotle did, that the demand for a theory of mechanics also pushes one to recognize the concept of space: the notion of place played a privileged role in Aristotelian mechanics, as determining the natural motions of bodies.

14.3 Space in Newtonian Mechanics

The next big step in geometry came with the development, by Descartes (and Leibniz), of the three-dimensional continuum. Descartes gave us a new way of understanding geometry, in which axes laid out in space are imagined, determining the coordinates of every point. Almost the entire geometry of Euclid is captured in the following idea: take a point with coordinates (x, y, z), and consider a second point displaced from it by distances, dx, dy, and dz, along each axis, with coordinates $(x + dx, y + dy, z + dz)$. The distance, ds, between the two points is given by $ds^2 = dx^2 + dy^2 + dz^2$. This assumption is the three-dimensional form of the Pythagorean theorem (*Elements*, Proposition I.47).

From this property, and the properties of the numbers along the axes, all the results of Euclidean geometry follow. Since the numbers are the real (or decimal) numbers, the mathematics of which is called "analysis," Descartes's geometry is "analytic." We should also note that defining a geometry in this way, by stipulating

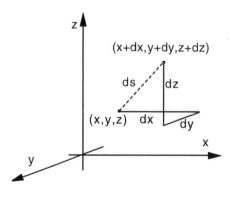

Figure 14.1
The distance between two points.

the distance between points, is to explicitly specify "metrical" properties for a collection of points. By specifying a metric in this way, Descartes exactly followed the logic that we found in our discussion of Zeno: metrical properties must be added to a bare collection of points.

Having conceived of space in this formal way, Descartes was naturally led, like Plato and Aristotle before him, to consider its nature. He decided that space and matter, both in essence being "extension," are one and the same. That is, the universe is a continuous field of matter in motion, a field which is space. In this case, the only sense of position, and hence motion, is relative to some reference body or other.

Newton did not see Descartes's relationism as offering a tenable understanding of space. If all motions are motions relative to some material reference frame or other, then there can be no absolute sense of constant motion or acceleration, and thus the all-important law of inertia is unintelligible. If, however, one postulates the existence of an underlying absolute space, then absolute acceleration is acceleration relative to space itself, and the principle of inertia states that objects will remain in constant motion relative to absolute space unless acted upon by a force. It seems that Newton's theory of motion, and the privileged status that it grants to acceleration, requires the existence of a space separate from matter: a space that determines the inertial movements of matter, but is itself unaffected by matter.

Unfortunately, as Leibniz, Berkeley, and Mach made clear, the postulation of absolute space means that objects not only have absolute accelerations, but also undetectable absolute velocities and locations. In particular, there is absolutely no way of distinguishing, using mechanical experiments, between frames moving at constant relative velocities, when, according to Newton, such motions are absolutely different. Determined empiricists (or rationalists believing in the identity of indiscernibles) find such undetectable properties too much to swallow, and so seek to reject absolute space. To do so, of course, they must answer Newton's challenge, and give a relational account of inertia: a challenge that, it seems, has not been met.

14.4   Relativity and Non-Euclidean Geometry

As Einstein points out, if space really were as Newton conceived, then there could, after all, be a way of distinguishing between frames moving with constant velocities relative to one another: electromagnetic experiments would depend on an "absolute" velocity of the system in question. Prior to Einstein, physicists believed that electric forces moved through an "ether," a kind of Cartesian matter field in space. They supposed, for instance, that light—an electromagnetic phenomenon—would move at a fixed speed relative to the ether, regardless of the speed of its source. Thus by measuring the relative speed of light in different frames, one could determine the "absolute" velocity of frames through the ether: an observer moving in the same direction as a pulse of light would see it moving more slowly than would an observer at rest in the ether.

However, such differences were never detected, despite diligent efforts. These failures led, through the work of Lorentz and Einstein, to the special theory of relativity, which is founded on the principle that even the phenomena of electromagnetism will not differentiate frames with constant relative motions. This theory requires that space and time be welded together into a space-time that differs from any that we have considered: a space-time in which different frames disagree not only on relative positions and motions, but also on elapsed intervals and lengths. (As Descartes described Euclidean space with a spatial metric, so Einstein describes the "Minkowski" space-time of special relativity with a space-time metric. See the references for full treatments of special relativity.)

The second crucial post-Newtonian advance was the discovery of non-Euclidean geometries, which we saw in the readings from Kant and Poincaré. Einstein mentions Riemann's (1854) construction of a general theory which covers all the geometries that we have studied. His idea is that one first attaches coordinates to every point in space and then specifies a particular geometry by specifying a metric function, *ds*. If one picks the Cartesian metric then one picks Euclidean space, but spaces with different metrics may be either elliptic or Bolyai-Lobachevskian. In this sense Riemann revealed the underlying similarity of all our geometries: they are special cases of a general analytic geometry.

We saw, as Einstein suggests, that we cannot obtain *a priori* knowledge of the geometry of the actual space that we inhabit; instead we must rely on observations of material objects. When we read Poincaré we discovered that such experiments involving "rigid" bodies can never be conclusive, and that many different conventions concerning the geometry of space are possible, given suitable hypotheses about the behavior of measuring devices.

Now, if one were to think of actually assigning coordinates to the points of space (space-time, really) one would of course have to use such devices as rulers, light beams, and cyclometers (and clocks) to mark out axes and measure locations. If we subscribe to Poincaré's conventionalism then we are led to think that the rigidity of such apparatuses, and hence the coordinate system itself, is only conventional. But if coordinates are a matter of convention, then intuitively, we should not expect the laws of nature to depend on how axes—arbitrary labelings of points—are chosen. This sort of reasoning led Einstein to extend the special principle of relativity to the principle of *general covariance*: "Are not the laws of nature so constituted that they are not materially simplified through the choice of any one *particular* set of coordinates?" (*The Problem*, this vol., p. 259). From this principle Einstein developed the general theory of relativity; how he did it is the subject of much research. In essence, the theory is an equation for the metric of space-time, in terms of the distribution of matter. In other words, the metric, and hence the geometry of space-time, depends on the way in which matter is distributed. Since space-time determines which motions are inertial, in general relativity we reach a situation in which there is a symmetry in the actions and reactions of space and matter.

Finally, let us consider what answers we have obtained in this book to our three initial questions: the metaphysical question, "What kind of thing is space?"; the epistemological question, "How we can learn about space?"; and the physical question, of the role of space in science. Working backward, we have learned, heuristically at least, a lot about the role of space in the phenomenon of inertia, and that matter has an effect on space, determining how it curves.

Next, we have seen that we can learn about the nature of space by studying its effects on matter, though it is unsettled just what such experiments show. We have discovered that there are, in principle, problems with conclusively determining the geometry of space, which might reveal a lack of intrinsic geometry. We have seen the significance of inertial effects hotly debated. And we have considered whether the phenomenon of handedness can lead to interesting conclusions about space.

Our metaphysical question seems in a sense even less resolved, as we have discovered two competing conceptions of space, the relational and the absolute (or substantival, when we are discussing space-time). We have seen how one might construct arguments based on our experiences of space for either camp, but ultimately the debates have not been conclusive. Indeed, the basic question remains in the context of contemporary science: does general relativity support relationism or substantivalism? This question, whose ancestor faced Plato, troubles philosophers and scientists even today, as the suggested readings will testify.

Further Readings and Bibliography

Geroch, R. 1978. *General Relativity from A to B* (see chaps. 5–8). Chicago, IL: University of Chicago Press. √

Friedman, M. 1983. *Foundations of Space-Time Theories: Relativistic Physics and Philosophy of Science* (see chaps. IV–V). Princeton, NJ: Princeton University Press.

Pais, A. 1982. *Subtle Is the Lord: The Science and Life of Albert Einstein*. Oxford: Basil Blackwell.

Ray, C. 1991. *Time, Space, and Philosophy* (see chaps. 2–3, 7–10). London and New York: Routledge. √

Schwartz, J. 1979. *Einstein for Beginners*. New York: Pantheon Books. √

Stein, H. 1977. "Some Philosophical Prehistory of General Relativity." In *Minnesota Studies in the Philosophy of Science* VIII: "Foundations of Space-Time Theories," edited by J. Earman, C. Glymour, and J. Stachel. Minneapolis, MN: University of Minnesota Press.

Taylor, E. F., and Wheeler, J. A. 1966. *Space-Time Physics*. San Francisco, CA: W. H. Freeman and Co.

Index

Abductive inference, 11–12
Absolute acceleration, 130n, 133
 and bucket experiment, 185, 221
 and empiricism, 221
 and inertial effects, 136–137
 and Leibniz, 161, 166–167
 and Mach, 183–186
 and Newton, 133, 139, 165–166, 183, 187, 263
 and Newtonian space-time, 193
Absolute location, 181, 263
Absolute motion, 130n
 and Newton, 108, 119, 121–122, 128, 130, 154, 191
Absolute space. *See also* Container view of space; Substantivalism
 Berkeley on, 169–171, 181–182, 263
 and bucket experiment, 182
 and circular motion, 172
 Kant on, 197–202, 203, 208–212
 and Leibniz, 140, 160, 263
 and Mach, 179, 182, 183, 185, 263
 and Newton, 118, 127, 128, 129–130, 137, 263
  and absolute acceleration, 133
  and absolute motion, 130, 191
  and Berkeley, 174
  and inertia, 139, 166–167, 182–183
  and Kant, 212
  and Mach, 177
  and relationism, 132
 and Newton's modern-day followers, 186
 points alike in, 161
 and space-time, 193
Absolute velocity, 104, 161–162, 181, 192, 263
Acceleration, 127. *See also* Absolute acceleration
 and inertial effects, 135–137
 Newton on, 134, 165–166
 relative, 131
Achilles and the tortoise (Zeno), 34–35
Actual/potential distinction, 40
Allegory of the Cave (Plato), 4
Analytic and synthetic judgments, Kant on, 214–215, 223
Angles, Euclid's definitions of, 15
A priori knowledge, 222
 Kant on, 213–214, 222
A priori synthetic knowledge, Kant on, 215, 218, 224
Aquinas, Saint, 89
Archimedes, 145
Aristotelian tradition, 85–88, 89
Aristotle, 72–73
 Clarke on, 145
 on Democritus, 170
 on the earth, 68–71
 as empiricist, 99

Galileo's objections to, 88
 on infinity, 32, 39–40, 41, 43
 and knowledge of space, 6
 on motion (locomotion),7, 53, 56–57, 62–66, 69–70, 77–80, 80–81, 82
 circular (rotation), 62–63, 85, 134
 and falling as natural, 80, 261
 and flying arrow paradox, 35
 of heavens, 68
 and study of space, 127–128
 as teleological, 74
 vs. Newton, 80
 On the Heavens, 61–71, 74, 77, 80–81, 88
 Physics, 53–60, 73, 74, 75, 87
 on place, 53–60, 73, 74, 75–77, 78–79, 100–101
 as centered, 140
 on space, 77, 78, 80, 82, 100–101, 261–262
 as centered, 7, 78
 considered as cause, 54
 and study of motion, 127–128
 and space-matter relation, 5, 82
 on Zeno's paradoxes, 31, 32–33, 34, 35–36, 37, 39
Arithmetic, finite, 41–43
Arrow, in critiques of Aristotle, 87, 88
Arrow paradox (Zeno), 35, 48–50
Atlantis, myth of, 3
Augustine, Saint, 89
Axiomatic geometry, 21–23, 226
 chain proofs in, 23
Axioms, in Euclid's geometry, 22

Bacon, Francis, 146
Barbour and Bertotti, 186
Berkeley, George, 169–173, 181
 on absolute motion, 183
 and absolute space, 169–171, 181–182, 263
 as empiricist, 99
 and knowledge of space, 6
 as relationist, 186–187
 and space-matter relation, 5, 7
Boerhaave, Hermann, 197
Bolyai-Lobachevskian (BL) geometry, 226, 243–244
Bucket experiment of Newton, 122, 137–140, 182–183, 186
 and absolute acceleration, 185, 221
 Berkeley on, 171, 172, 186–187
 Copernican vs. Ptolemaic interpretation of, 184–185
 and Galilean space-time, 195
 and Kant's arguments, 208
 and Leibniz, 167
 Mach on, 174, 175, 176–177, 183–184, 185, 186
 and space-time, 193